French Furniture of the Eighteenth Century

PIERRE VERLET

French Furniture of the Eighteenth Century

TRANSLATED BY

Penelope Hunter-Stiebel

University Press of Virginia

Charlottesville and London

Translation copyright © 1991
by the Rector and Visitors
of the University of Virginia

First published 1991

Originally published in 1955 as
Les Meubles Français du XVIIIe Siècle by Pierre Verlet

1re édition en 2 volumes: 4e trimestre 1955
2e édition entièrement refondue: 1982, mars
© Presses Universitaires de France, 1956
108, boulevard Saint-Germain, 75006 Paris

Library of Congress Cataloging-in-Publication Data

Verlet, Pierre.
   [Meubles français du XVIIIe siècle. English]
   French furniture of the eighteenth century / Pierre Verlet : translated by Penelope Hunter-Stiebel.
      p. cm.
   Translation of: Les meubles français du XVIIIe siècle.
   Includes bibliographical references and index.
   ISBN 0-8139-1290-3
   1. Furniture—France—History—18th century. I. Title.
NK2548.V4313 1991
749.24'09'033—dc20   90-45672
                                                                  CIP

Printed in the United States of America

Contents

CONTENTS

CONTENTS

Preface

Everything exists. It is up to you to find it.
—Pierre Verlet (1909–1988)

THE CREDO that motivated Pierre Verlet's career was incomprehensible to me when I first heard it in 1968, seated with a small group of museum professionals and selected graduate students of the Institute of Fine Arts of New York University in an improvised classroom in the curatorial offices of the Metropolitan Museum of Art. Universally acknowledged as the foremost authority on eighteenth-century French furniture, Monsieur Verlet had been brought to the United States by the great American collectors of French eighteenth-century decorative arts Jayne and Charles Wrightsman to instill the rudiments of a field that had previously languished beyond the ken of art history.

To our bewilderment Monsieur Verlet offered no academic introduction composed of generalities that could be copied down and committed to memory. Instead, our classes were devoted to four or five works of art, each accompanied by a detective story. Like a Gallic Sherlock Holmes he presented us with relevant clues he had gleaned from contemporary documents. It was difficult for the uninitiated to follow the trail, but for our Holmes it was, of course, elementary. Rigorous training in archival research in France's famed Ecole de Chartes had prepared Pierre Verlet for his mission of illuminating the mysteries of the specialized art of French furniture. Inspired by the belief that all the greatest examples survive, waiting only to be discovered, he identified masterpieces, their makers and patrons, the specifics of their commission, the circumstances in which they were used, and the history of their passage through the hands of successive owners.

His main purpose was far from academic. Pierre Verlet was first and foremost a museum curator. In his youth he put his detective skills to the vast and idealistic task of restoring the châteaus of France with their original furnishings. When experience taught him this goal was unrealistic, he turned with the same passion to the enrichment of his country's most important museums. As curator of the Louvre, where he entered the Département des Objets d'Art in 1945 and retired as Conservator en Chef in 1972, and additionally of the Museums of Cluny (1945–1972), Sèvres, and Adrien-

Dubouché at Limoges (1945–1965), he made full use of his scholarly acumen to effect key acquisitions of previously unidentified works.

Unlike other European art historians of his generation, Pierre Verlet was generous with his information. That generosity, too, benefited the Louvre, as he earned the gratitude of major collectors who in turn became benefactors of the museum.

Yet it is as a pioneer scholar that Pierre Verlet will be best remembered. The first volume of his *Mobilier Royal Français,* published in 1945, is credited by British authority Sir Francis Watson with revolutionizing the study of French furniture. It explained for the first time the extensive record-keeping system of the royal administration by which the furniture made for the crown could be identified, and by extension offered benchmarks by which other works could be assessed. Additional volumes followed in 1955 and 1963. The fourth and final volume, published posthumously in 1990, was edited by his widow, Nicole Verlet, mother of their ten children, archivist and authority on French hallmarks, and lifelong collaborator in her husband's research.

My own personal favorite among Monsieur Verlet's many books is his 1966 *La Maison du XVIIIe Siècle en France* (translated by George Savage as *The Eighteenth Century in France,* Charles E. Tuttle, 1967). Here he dealt with the broad topic of the context in which the special types of French furniture developed and functioned, amplifying his information with the visual documentation of paintings and graphics of the time. There is no better introduction to *l'art de vivre* of the ancien régime.

French Furniture of the Eighteenth Century first appeared in 1956 (as *Les Meubles Français du XVIIIe Siècle*) presenting Monsieur Verlet's startling revelation of the strict division between two branches of furniture, *menuiserie* and *ébénisterie,* unique to its time and place. Marshaled under these two rubrics (two separate volumes in the first edition) is a wealth of information assembled over a career of direct examination of documents and works of art.

The 1982 edition, which I have translated here, has an additional discussion of collectors and collections, and new illustrations, including many previously unpublished pieces that Monsieur Verlet discovered in remote corners of the world. It does not make easy reading. It could be compared to a mine from whose labyrinthine passages gold ore of the highest grade can be extracted. (An index is provided in this translation to assist the reader in finding his way to the main lode.) The literary style is pure Verlet. From the start, he instructed me, "Do not clarify"; and the master painstakingly corrected every page of typed translation sent off at intervals over the years his former student labored at the task.

Monsieur Verlet felt I was better qualified than a professional translator because of my years of experience in French eighteenth-century art at the Metropolitan Museum and subsequently at the Rosenberg and Stiebel gallery. For my part the difficulties of translation were recompensed by the chance to relive my studies with him. Two decades after my unpromising initiation, I can fully understand the master's words, but I remain awed at the unique breadth of the scholarship expressed in this single volume which stands as the résumé of Pierre Verlet's findings on the art of furniture.

New York City   PENELOPE HUNTER-STIEBEL

Introduction

THE FIRST EDITION of this work goes back to 1955. That edition has sold out, and copies have become almost unobtainable. I set myself the tasks of improving it, and writing a study of decorative bronzes. This last will be forthcoming, God willing. Other work has occupied my time, principally that connected with museums. Today I have the honor to present the first stage in token of a promise fulfilled.

The original publication was two volumes in the series *L'Oeil du Connaisseur.* That became a single volume, but without my giving up the separation between *menuiserie* and *ébénisterie.* That division appears to me to be essential; it has its source in the very techniques themselves; since I first proposed the idea, it has been the accepted as obvious. It has, so to speak, brooked no exception. I maintain it in full here, even to listing the names and marks of the *menuisiers* separately from those of the *ébénistes.*

The chapters covering general subjects, history, styles, the market, and the evolution of taste have been combined and recast. The illustrations have been entirely redone; most of the furniture previously reproduced seemed too familiar, some pieces having even been acquired by the Louvre. There has been an effort to keep an equitable balance between works in public collections and those in private hands, or, if you prefer, between those that anyone can study at will and those that remain little known or unpublished. In the same way, a balance has been maintained between full-page reproductions, which permit appreciation of the beauty of the furniture and the noting of interesting details, and small-scale illustrations that multiply documentation. The range has been made as broad as possible to allow for the juxtaposition of luxury and simple furniture and to include a variety of types, forms, and decorations. It would be foolhardy to claim to fully encompass the power of invention that was the glory of eighteenth-century France; the picture presented here is an attempt at an overview.

I hope that, in spite of the brevity necessary for this book, I have driven home two points that in my opinion more historians and collectors should keep in mind: the distinction to be underscored and stressed between architectural and informal furniture; and the position of Paris, which must be distinguished from the provinces, not to mention colonies, in the overall subject of French furniture of the eighteenth century.

In differentiating the furniture that I term architectural from what, for want of a more elegant expression, I provisionally designate as furniture created for comfort and amenity, I insist on denoting two different conceptions, two distinct avenues of intent and composition in Parisian furniture of the eighteenth century.

By widening the field to cover the influence of Paris, I hope to attract young scholars to the study of a diffusion that was prodigious. Parisian furniture was sent to the provinces and exported to all of Europe. It is necessary to become better acquainted with the character, the authors, and even the marks of furniture copied in France and beyond its borders by local *menuisiers* and *ébénistes,* of *provincial* furniture, and of *European* furniture in the Parisian taste, as well as often inept *imitations* that give pause for thought. There is the tendency in France to dismiss all too quickly as regional a category I would identify as *rustic Parisian*. Finally there is furniture made as far away as the French colonies in the eighteenth century, which is designated either as *French colonial* or *provincial*. The subject is so vast that one must compress it to present even the roughest outline.

We have learned a great deal over the past twenty-five years. A good many new things have turned up; unknown pieces of furniture have emerged from the shadows; documents and studies have come to light. Since it was necessary to take all those into account, the chapter on public collections and the bibliography have been augmented.

The activity of collectors, dealers, auctioneers, curators, researchers, and interested amateurs has led to the discovery of innumerable pieces of furniture of which all trace had been lost or which were previously unknown. Adding to its aesthetic and scientific interest has been the steady increase in monetary value of this furniture, about which record prices are constantly being quoted to us. Long gone are the days when André Malraux, forseeing this phenomenon, was astonished at the low prices of antique French furniture. As a consequence of the revival of enthusiasm, museum collections have been enriched, patronage being a law of nature. In view of the considerable quantity of furniture that it has become possible for the *amateur* or historian to study today, the attempt has been made to outline its geographic distribution.

Publications have followed a parallel progression. Even limiting oneself to those that seem most original and useful, the titles that any *amateur* worthy of the name can and must bring together in his library have multiplied, ranging from a short article, which is sometimes important, to the volumes that illustrate unpublished pieces or groupings. Hence the broad scope of even a summary bibliography.

This book has been augmented by new material given to us in the form of texts, images, and furniture. It has kept, however, its character of a handbook: develop, delete, that is the rule the author must obey. To keep it a practical volume, useful to students as well as collectors, to dealers as well as historians, that is my aim. If I have attained that goal, I must acknowledge what I owe to all who have contributed to my progress. I cannot name all the people in France and across the world who have encouraged and helped me. I hope they will all accept my thanks.

PART ONE

Structures

Chapter I

THE FRENCH WORLD

OF THE EIGHTEENTH CENTURY

The time has come to say, the French world.
—Translated from Rivarol, after Baldensperger, *Le mouvement
des idées dans l'émigration*

THE FRENCH WORLD, the century of Louis XV, the *siècle des lumières,* the world of sciences, arts, and crafts—the terms are of little consequence. A unity of spirit, culture, and taste spread through part of the Western world. French was the language spoken. Furnishing was done in the Paris style. This phenomenon must be explained at the start.

SOCIETY

With the exception of its very start and close, the eighteenth century was an era of prosperity produced by peace and progress rare in the history of

France. A single sovereign dominated the period, with his nonchalant air, love of life, intelligence, and artistic flair, as well as the restraint and sensitivity of a member of the highest aristocracy. Less combative and proud than his predecessor, with clearer thinking and more will power than his successor, he was, like it or not, the king who led what is called "the golden age of French furniture" (fig. 2).

More than the wars, the products of peace were the source of profit for the society of the time. France still occupied the position of primary importance in Europe. A bureaucracy that was old-fashioned but often efficient extended to the provinces and colonies. An extraordinary diffusion propagated the arts of France in the multiple Latin, Germanic, Scandinavian, and Slavic spheres; it penetrated England; and it even insinuated itself into the Orient. The effort of the entire nation made it possible for luxury industries to flourish.

French society was sustained by the strength and security of established positions in secular institutions: the nobility, especially, together with those who joined or approached it; and the workers, once they were incorporated in communities. It was a time of immense fortunes that seemed unshakeable and were at the disposal of people who were often unaware of the extent of their debts. At the other extreme was the mob, who endured economic misery but felt an almost superstitious devotion to their king. There was an immorality that is still famous and a piety that has remained hidden. There were frivolity, sensitivity, and grace, which concealed strength of character. It was a diverse society, unified by the search for beauty and an appreciation of work well done.

One should try to become acquainted with the French society of the eighteenth century through its furniture: study the classes and hierarchies with the aid of the furniture and decorations that are indicated in old inventories and bills; then the illustrations provided by so many surviving pieces of furniture, scattered evidence insufficiently explained. I began with the furniture of Versailles and the royal châteaus. Ranking immediately after is the furniture made for the princes. I have already gathered information on the slightly crazed opulence of the comte d'Artois (fig. 25) at the time of Louis XVI, as well as the more classic luxury of the Condé princes at the Palais-Bourbon and at Chantilly (fig. 5) and the duc de Penthièvre in his numerous residences (figs. 40, 41). The study of the furniture of the dukes would take much more time; that of the nobility would be immense and would furnish diverse examples according to whether courtiers, magistrates, or provincial nobles were in question.

Setting aside all political or moral judgment, I love the *fermiers généraux* (tax collectors) whose lavish spending benefited Parisian decorative arts. Several examples of their furniture will be encountered in the illustrations of this book. Nouveaux riches? Not necessarily. The major study of this ostentatious caste published by Yves Durand in 1971 reveals many gradations in the origins and connections of its members. Their passion for imitating the court tempered their excesses (figs. 98, 125, 156). A Perrinet created vicomte, a Roslin sieur d'Ivry, a Randon de Boisset, a Grimod de La Reynière were assimilated into the nobility, but had greater facility in spending money. They knew how to furnish.

Useful comparisons can be made between the beginning and the end of the century by perusing the inventories of people of the same social class. Let us begin with those of certain prominent artists and artisans published in the *Archives de l'Art français.* That of Alexis Loir, goldsmith to Louis XIV, who died in comfortable circumstances in 1713, shows us a vestibule decorated with paintings and faience, a bedroom in which we find two armchairs and six side chairs covered in needlepoint, a footstool covered in an inexpensive velveteen, a dressing table mirror, some pieces of faience, a mirror, and a verdure tapestry on the walls. Finally there is a small room furnished with six chairs of ebonized wood with green serge cushions, an oak workbench with turned legs, and a small marquetry checkerboard. The 1727 inventory of the estate of the enamel miniaturist Charles Boit listed three chairs with straw seats, three oak tables, a walnut desk, an ebonized wood backgammon table, and a harpsichord mounted on an ebonized wood base in the room that served as his studio. The painter Noël-Nicolas Coypel died in 1734 in the cloister of Saint-Germain-l'Auxerrois, with somewhat more furniture in his possession: in his waiting room, there were two benches covered in linen brocade and, on the walls, a verdure tapestry; in his bedroom, a bed of red serge with white silk braid, a stool, a small "antique" desk of tortoiseshell marquetry, a dressing table, and a small bookshelf displaying six coffee cups. In the next room, there were a bed, two walnut armchairs covered in green damask, two stools, one covered in red pile and the other in tapestry, a small marble table on a console base, and a small ebonized wood table with a garniture of coffee cups; in the last room, an old sofa, a tapestry-covered armchair, an ebonized wood table and a table for playing quadrille. On his death in 1737, François Lemoine had been first painter to the king for a year. His anteroom was hung with tapestries and furnished with a table with a marble top on a gilded wood base, a large buffet with four doors, and a red copper fountain with its basin; his bedroom was decorated with an Auvergne verdure tapestry, a bed of crimson serge with silk braid, eight polished walnut chairs *à la capucine* with gros point embroideries, a *demi-bergère* armchair with straw upholstery and colorful linen cushions, a beechwood night table, and a small bookshelf. The inventory drawn up on the death of Soufflot in 1780 shows not only the importance of the architect but also the evolution of manners in the matter of furniture. The most important room was the salon, decorated with numerous paintings; four bronze or marble sculptures on marbleized wood pedestals; and furnished with a tapestry-covered settee; twelve armchairs covered with crimson Utrecht velvet; four small voyeuse chairs (straddled while watching games) also covered in velvet, two in crimson, two in green; three game tables, two round and one square, covered with green cloth; an ebonized wood desk, with "mains et entrées de cuivre dore" (handles and escutcheons of gilded copper); a rosewood commode with pulls and escutcheons also of gilded copper; and an Antin marble top. The home of the engraver Jacques-Philippe Le Bas (d. 1783) was an apartment in which every other room was supplied with a faience stove. The bedroom was hung with verdure tapestries, and one notes among its ornaments a barometer and a thermometer. The large study was decorated with a mirror above the mantelpiece and was furnished with a desk covered with a green cloth, an oak drafting table, a table for playing piquet provided with a green cloth, a lathe-turned walnut *guéridon* (a small round table) with copper candle-arms, a gilded copper clock, two chimneypiece lights of varnished copper, and a green fabric portiere. The next study, hung with goffered green serge, contained a daybed and a buffet with four shutters. The dining room had a dining table and a red-copper fountain and its basin; the last small room contained some dishes in an old cupboard with wire mesh doors. These bourgeois interiors are similar to those painted by Boucher, Chardin (fig. 7), or Boilly.

The petite bourgeoisie and the least poor of the peasantry must be considered separately. One need go no farther than what can be perceived in Paris and the Ile-de-France. It is not easy to penetrate the homes of people of modest means, without history, and of reduced needs and resources. Yet studies have been undertaken that are interesting, notably the one published by Roger Dauvergne on the winegrowers of Ivry-sur-Seine. His comparison of the peasants of 1701 with others of the early years of the reign of Louis XVI on the basis of their inventories is relevant to the history of furniture: almost nothing relieved the destitution of the former, who still lived as they had in the Middle Ages; the latter began to breathe the air of the eighteenth century, and one finds the beginnings of comfort in their homes, a tendency toward the beautiful. Around 1775–80, the advances achieved during the Louis XV era are clear, with new types of furniture and minor refinements, intermixed as they still were with the remains of the former austerity. The lower part of a "two-door buffet in beechwood with a dresser," a "beechwood commode with 2 large and 2 small drawers, pulls and escutcheons of varnished copper," "a dining table on its folding base," was next to "an old oak table with 4 legs, an old coffer and a breadbox of different woods," and one notes the "chairs stuffed with straw, a very old chair covered with tapestry, stuffed with hair, two copper candlesticks, a large board serving as a bench." There is the dawning of aspirations to frivolity or pure decoration. Beside the pewter dishes and the "plaster figure of Christ," one notices a "small fountain of red copper with its lid of the same and triangular oak base," a "warming pan of red copper," and a "wood clock with ropes and weights," and better yet, a "small mirror in its frame and crest of gilded wood," five "engravings under glass with ebonized or gilded wood frames." Place settings of iron do not prevent the presence of a dishcover; "12 pieces in faience and plaster serving as a garniture on top of an armoire," a "printed cotton quilt," hangings and cover for a bed in "green serge trimmed with green and yellow ribbons" bear witness to new concerns. Luxury is ready to develop in these surroundings with deliberate speed. Furnishings that may appear "rustic" do aspire to a certain elegance, and they reflect in their tasteful simplicity the evolution of a social class.

The following chapters will devote a few pages to provincial furniture, to the colonial world, and the expansion of French furniture. Now we must examine how the society of the eighteenth century, primarily that of Paris, allowed itself to be carried away by the tide of its own success.

THE FURNISHING SPIRIT OF THE EIGHTEENTH CENTURY

A passion, known today only to certain great collectors of antiques, then animated a segment of society and made rivals of a number of enthusiasts in their search for the most extraordinary and the most novel pieces of furniture (figs. 22, 23, 36, 37). This competition was fortunate for French furniture.

In the eighteenth century everyone, from the princes to the middle classes, appreciated beautiful furniture; it occupied an enormously important place in their lives and their expenditures. Painters and engravers did not consider it beneath them to give furniture full value when they depicted it faithfully in portraits or genre scenes. It was the period when the most important figures, the dauphin, son of Louis XV, Mme de Pompadour, Marie-Antoinette, Paris de Monmartel, and many others had their portraits painted surrounded by pieces that one can still recognize easily today. The beauty of a piece of furniture, even the simplest, the familiar pleasure, and the comfort that it gave, can be read from many a canvas. Mme Crozat, painted by Aved, appears to us solidly encamped in a large armchair, of which the frame, still Régence, is upholstered with Aubusson tapestry attached with large gilded nails; she leans heavily with both hands on a small cherrywood table that holds her coffee and whose drawer is shown to us partly open. Jean-François de Troy, who in several elegant compositions seems to have derived particular satisfaction from reproducing in specific detail the beautiful chairs newborn to the Régence, does not allow us to remain unaware, in his *Lecture de Molière,* of what pleasure the elegant took in feeling well ensconced in attractive and comfortable easychairs. At the end of the century the engravings of Janinet or Debucourt, the gouaches of Mallet or Lavreince, give almost as much importance and personality, so to speak, to the furniture as to the subjects themselves. People gave pieces of furniture as gifts and entered them specifically in their wills, like Mme d'Epinay, who bequeathed to Mme Sedaine "a round table and a mahogany folding table" (1782). They were interested enough in furniture to want to embroider it themselves; hence the considerable number of chairs still covered with old petit or gros point that ladies took pleasure and pride in embroidering on a pretty needleworking frame (fig. 34); an embroiderer of the rue Saint-Honore, Mlle Dubucquoy, even specialized in these works: she sold the patterns and the silk for needlework, and she often added the finishing touches.

The incessant renewal evidenced in the art of furniture in the eighteenth century could be illustrated with examples taken from the attitude of two of the most celebrated women of their time, Mme de Pompadour (fig. 14) and Marie-Antoinette (fig. 162), united for a moment in the same concern. Louis XV's mistress ordered from Duvaux and Hébert lacquered or japanned furniture, secretaries, commodes, and innumerable little tables, both charming and practical. She was one of the first people in France to own furniture made of mahogany. Initially in favor of the rococo style, shortly before her death she sought rectilinear furniture and gave commissions in this vein, notably to the *ébéniste* Oeben. As for Marie-Antoinette, to follow the evolution of her taste over some twenty years one merely has to compare the first pieces delivered to her by Joubert, when she was the young dauphine, to those she commissioned from Jacob or Riesener when she became queen: extraordinary pieces of furniture, constantly renewed in decoration, color, or material, serve, in a way, as milestones of her reign. The queen had her own *garde-meuble* (furniture warehouse and administration); the most precious pieces were created for her private apartments and often guided fashion.

The level of interest is shown in the care with which innovations were surrounded. A wealthy client had a drawing (fig. 12) presented to him, a wax model, and sometimes a full-scale model. Before buying, he wanted to judge the effect, like the treasurer de Boullongne whom Duvaux billed 9 livres in July 1758 for "transport and return of commodes, firedogs, and wall-lights to be tried out in place." Of necessity he visited the studio, and was no snob in his dealings with the artisan, but he threatened suit if the specifications he had given were not followed, like the former musketeer shown in 1783 in the *Rapports d'experts* published by Georges Wildenstein demanding the examination of the base of a table: it "was not at all of the shape he wanted and the console was not at all what he had ordered." Motives of chicanery and reluctance to make good on debts, but proof also of real attention. The same source gives details of a dispute that erupted in 1767 between the *ébéniste* Macret and his clients the Beaumanoirs; the latter had modified in the course of execution the secretary they had ordered; they had the fall-front cut down in order to add three drawers in the top, but their instructions remained verbal; the *ébéniste* had prudently kept the pieces, but this did not prevent a painstaking review of the piece where the experts picked out several imperfections.

Svend Eriksen has performed a great service by publishing a dozen letters, earlier pointed out by Vial, which were addressed by the marquis de Marigny to his *ébéniste,* Pierre Garnier, in 1778–79. The brother of the late Mme de Pompadour was then living at his property of Menars, where he enlarged the château. For more than twenty years he had directed the construction projects and manufactories of Louis XV; he did not feel it beneath him to be concerned with the minute details of his own furniture. On the banks of the Loire he dreamed of his town house on the Place des Victoires in Paris. He asked for the measurements, the plans, and a precise detail if memory failed him: "From the study I am making here of the plans of my house and the furniture that I will put in each room, I find that I have three more pieces of furniture to request from you." He sketched solutions, made suggestions, requested drawings, discussed what was proposed to him, and once everything seemed to him just right, he showed his gratitude for a felicitous idea: "I thank you for having given me the idea." There is still something of the self-made man in him: "I was to have a superb secretary . . . in the same room there is my superb commode." One notes at the same time the concern with harmony: "Furniture of ebony and bronze is much more noble than furniture of mahogany especially in a library which is white and gold." He gave orders but he remained open-minded. He would have liked to cling to familiar things: "I already have one of the old pieces in that taste . . . the two ebony cabinets that you made me for my Place du Louvre study." He finally adopted what was proposed to him adroitly by his *ébéniste,* in whom he showed great confidence: "Since the mahogany desk that will be in this room has no bronze, I do not want any on my cabinets; all that I ask of you is not to economize with my budget in the choice and the beauty of the mahogany." Happy era, whose animated correspondence perhaps conveys to us one of its secrets.

The craze for new furniture in principle should signify the rejection of the old. There is room here, however, to observe some nuances and to distinguish between the words *ancien* (old in the sense of "antique") and *vieilli* (old in the sense of "used").

The attraction of the new does not necessarily give a pejorative sense to the old. Commodes veneered with *ancien laque* (antique lacquer) from China were sought in preference to contemporary Parisian japanning. Throughout the eighteenth century the furniture "by the celebrated Boulle" or Boulle *le père* (fig. 15), were brought to the attention of those interested in the sales of the most famous collectors, Fonspertuis, Gaignat, the painter Boucher, Blondel de Gagny, the duc d'Aumont, etc. But one must also admit that, in the same catalogs, one comes across mention of the furniture of *ébénistes* who had died only recently: Cressent, Bernard (Van Risen Burgh or B.V.R.B.), or the "celebrated Oeben" (fig. 154).

The appeal of what was new, bright, and clean worked against things that had aged, were worn, threadbare, or tarnished. No matter how beautiful, a set of furniture covered in silk was replaced after twenty or thirty years, naturally because the upholstery was worn out, but perhaps also because the frames were no longer in style. Thus a sort of hierarchy was established: the old furniture passed on to secondary apartments or residences of lesser importance; it was also sold to dealers who would know how to reuse it, or to people who could only afford secondhand furnishings. Let us recognize that a current of archaism existed among furniture craftsmen who restored or copied pieces of another era (figs. 13, 138): Sené reproduced an armchair by Foliot, Benneman a commode by Joubert, pieces that were ten or fifteen years old, if not more, following tradition with exemplary discipline.

We should admire French society of the eighteenth century, not for its collecting of antiques, but for its own creations. Later we will consider the evolution of styles and the principal types of furniture. We should focus for a moment on the general spirit that laid out the programs. The novel, the beautiful, the comfortable were the felicitous concerns of the furniture of the time.

The distinction that was then clearly drawn between formal apartments and intimate rooms favored in large measure the rejuvenation of furniture. The former, which could retain traditional, even somewhat old-fashioned, furnishings were few in number. Galleries and certain waiting rooms or state rooms were barely decorated, having only large *guéridons* (tall stands for lights), console tables, and stools or benches, whose models could be updated (figs. 11, 38, 153), as Louis XV did at Versailles or the duc d'Orleans at Palais-Royal, and Louis XVI for the bedroom of Louis XIV at Versailles, which had remained almost intact up to that date. The newly created intimate apartments were comprised of furniture that was smaller, more comfortable, and modern. Here furniture had the tendency to multiply and diversify the further one advanced in the century (figs. 9, 18–21, 24, 31–33), and to follow more closely the fluctuations of fashion.

The arrangement of apartments facilitated the demarcation between types of furniture. A simple apartment consisted of a single room, the bedroom, but in more affluent circumstances there would also be an anteroom and a study or salon, a closet, and, in some cases, a bathroom. As the century progressed the dining room, library, and boudoir were added, and the rooms became smaller, better heated, and the spaces more agreeable. The new furniture created in the course of the eighteenth century was going to be inserted quite naturally in fresher and more cheerful settings.

An almost parallel division is reflected in the general classification of pieces of furniture. There were some which were shown off with pride, whose position was fixed, and which had been designed or ordered at the same time as the wall paneling, the chimneypiece, and its mirror. There were others that were moved about at will, lived with on a familiar daily basis, and loved more for their elegance than for their solemnity. The first type was *architectural furniture, meublants* (serving to furnish), more or less majestic and difficult to move because of its weight or because it was screwed or nailed to the wall, or simply because it was customary to keep it in the same place (figs. 5, 27). The second type was furniture for *comfort and amenity,* mobile, light, more responsive to the caprices of fashion and generally less ornate (figs. 10, 35, 44, 67).

One sees the *menuisiers* and *ébénistes* following this dual line in their fabrication, their models, and even their style. While one line remained branded with Louis XIV amplitude, its quantity and placement dictated by tradition, the other constituted the real triumph of the century. For the latter, the *ébéniste* resorted, not to the designs of an architect, but rather to the innovative imagination that was the purview of the *marchand-mercier* (dealer in the decorative arts), and, at the same time, to the pursuit of comfort that was the specialty of the upholsterer.

Two further remarks concern this furniture effort. Harmonies of greater and greater refinement were sought: accord between the furniture and the paneling and between the pieces of furniture themselves. The daybook of the dealer Duvaux provides more than one example. Thus we see one of the Rohan princesses affirm her preferences, or at least those of the moment, purchasing, between 26 May and 8 August 1750, three commodes and one *encoignure* that were painted with flowers and "in the Indian style" on white japanning, with gilded bronzes and white marble tops.

There was much construction in the eighteenth century. New buildings stimulated the revitalization of interior decoration, which went hand in hand with a more or less complete change in furniture: modern paneling prompted a modern console table under a wall mirror and pleasing chairs; a new mantelpiece led to a commode matching the mantel's marble, its style, and often even its bronzes.

Having become accustomed to all the rules of comfort and beauty, the very rich wanted to see them applied everywhere around them, even when they traveled. Hence the great number and variety of furniture *de campagne* (for use in the field) or *de voyage* (for travel) on which great pains were expended. These pieces were made by specialized artisans and could be treated as *ébénisterie,* notably with solid mahogany. They ranged from beds, tables, and chairs that folded and slid into leather cases to chests, caskets and dressing cases, portable secretaries, small bookcases for traveling, and folding game tables (figs. 25, 28–30). In a way they provided a summary of the art of furniture in the eighteenth century: clients making unreasonable demands, artisans displaying technical mastery, and all craving perfection.

Chapter 2

CLIENTS AND ARTISANS

V ERSAILLES EXERTED its influence over rich and poor alike, spread models, diffused royal styles, and fascinated a clientele that was as much French as foreign. But Versailles was not the home of artisanry. To investigate the question of those who originated—as distinct from those who executed—concepts, to examine the relationships between clients and artisans, is to examine the very source of the strength of French furniture in the eighteenth century.

VERSAILLES AND PARIS

By invoking Versailles, one considers the inspiration, the first impulse (figs. 3, 157). For the execution it is necessary to look to Paris. Versailles could be imitated, and occasionally mimicked, only through the intermediary of Paris—Paris, where even the furniture of Versailles was made, thanks to the comings and goings of a community of outstanding craftsmen. Versailles and Paris, the two capitals of the kingdom were twin cities in the success and expansion of the art of French furniture.

At Versailles the ambassadors, the high nobility, and the anonymous masses marveled at Parisian furniture in the royal context for which it was designed. In Paris everyone could contemplate at leisure other furniture that was sometimes just as beautiful and ranged from the simplest to the most ostentatious by going to the establishments of the artisans and merchants who produced and sold it. Sometimes an announcement would appear in the press, like that placed by the gilder Ménage in 1782, which attracted visitors to the establishment of Jacob on the rue Meslay for the exhibition of a great bed commissioned by the elector of the Palatinate (now in the Munich Residenzmuseum). Baroness d'Oberkirch noted in her *Mémoires* the visits she made to the *ébéniste* Hericourt. On one occasion in 1782 she stayed "more than two hours" with this author of "marvelous pieces of furniture." In 1784 she paid a visit to the dealer Daguerre, who was exhibiting to the public a superb buffet commissioned by the duke of Northumberland. Moreover, Mme d'Oberkirch wrote of accompanying Grand Duchess Maria Feodorovna to the establishment of another Paris dealer, Granchez, and touring with her all the Paris houses that were noted for "beauty and richness of furnishing." What a lesson! Pavlovsk was going to profit from it when Maria Feodorovna became czarina (fig. 119). An extraordinary assembly of furniture and bronzes, both Parisian and Russian imitations of Paris, which date precisely from that period, can still be admired today in this northern palace.

A solid class of artisans, composed of two principal groups, the *menuisiers* and the *ébénistes,* plus numerous related trades, assured the renown of Paris. An impatient clientele formed the support of this class of craftsmen. The clients clamored for new models and availed themselves of drawings and prints that were proposed by decorators and ornament designers. They flocked to dealers, the *marchands-merciers,* who comprised a special group in the world of Paris commerce, composing for them and popularizing what was the last word in fashion.

THE PROFESSION OF FURNITURE CRAFTSMEN

Although *menuisiers* and *ébénistes* were united in a single guild in Paris, they functioned as two separate groups. The major lines of their organization will be summarized here.

The furniture *menuisiers* specialized in chairs, tables, armoires, etc., of solid wood, that is to say, any furniture that was not veneered. They differed from *menuisiers en batiments* (carpenters), *en voitures* (carriage makers), and *en billards* (billiard equipment makers), although all of them belonged to the guild of *menuisiers-ébénistes*. It is important to remember that the furniture *menuisiers* were all of French, indeed Parisian, origin; most often the profession was passed from father to son, creating veritable dynasties, where it is not always possible to sort out successive generations (figs. 11, 45, 160). Very few worked on the Faubourg; almost all of them were located in the parish of Notre-Dame de Bonne-Nouvelle, mainly on the rue Cléry.

The *ébénistes* were newcomers to this guild, which was several times a hundred years old. Many of them were isolated, lacking local ties within their profession. About one-third of them were foreign by birth, principally from the Netherlands during the reign of Louis XV (fig. 18) and from Germany during the reign of Louis XVI (figs. 32, 33). The majority were not the sons of master craftsmen: they began their careers as apprentices or journeymen to masters, or as free workmen installed in privileged enclaves, notably that of the Saint-Antoine suburb, which was a dependency of the convent of the same name. Some of them were awarded grants of lodging on royal properties where they could avoid some of the general regulations of the guild: the Boulles were housed at the Louvre, the Oebens at the Gobelins, and J. F. Oeben and Riesener at the Arsenal.

There were technical and historic reasons for the division of crafts within a single profession. The guild of Parisian *menuisiers* had emerged from the powerful guild of carpenters in the Middle Ages and did not accept the intrusion of *menuisiers en ébène* (*menuisiers* working with ebony) as they called the *ébénistes,* without misgivings. The *ébénistes* offended the *menuisiers* with the unprecedented nature of their techniques, their lack of a Paris tradition, and their constant recruitment of artisans of foreign origin, as well as their seduction of the clientele by providing novelty and originality. They belonged to the same guild only because both *menuisiers* and *ébénistes* worked in wood and made pieces of furniture.

Techniques and practices maintained the division between the groups.

Detailed evidence is given in the bills of the artisans themselves and the documentation of royal furniture. Louis XV ordered an armchair *à pupitre* (with a reading stand attached): the *menuisier* Tilliard made the chair frame, the *ébéniste* Gaudreaux made the reading stand, which was mahogany, and a mechanic, Barge, made the iron support for the stand. By the time Louis XVI in turn ordered a "mechanical" armchair for the same purpose, luxury was further developed, and so was the specialization of the crafts: the armchair was richly carved, the reading stand was still mahogany, but it was framed in gilded bronze, and the support was also of gilded bronze in the form of a palm tree. One can calculate that, between the sculptor who produced the model, the *menuisier,* woodcarver, gilder, and upholsterer who made the armchair, the *ébéniste* who made the reading stand, the mechanic, metalworker, and gilder responsible for the iron, and the founder, chaser, and gilder responsible for the bronze, it required the participation of eleven or twelve different artisans belonging to seven guilds.

The distinction between the two great crafts of Parisian furniture in the eighteenth century was not imposed by any regulation; tacit and logical, it entrenched each craft in its specialty. The separation ran so deep that one can establish independent lists, one for the *menuisiers,* and one for the *ébénistes,* and avoid confusing the two, exactly as in the eighteenth century. The exceptions are extremely rare, and deserve comment.

When one tackles the problem of two different stamps on a piece of furniture, one seeks an explanation in the possibility of a carcass made by an *ébéniste* or even a *menuisier* other than the *ébéniste* who was responsible for the veneer or marquetry of the piece. When one deals with Paris furniture of "rustic" character, one should remember that *menuiserie* was most often produced by specialists in this genre: a *menuisier,* and not an *ébéniste,* made a solid wood piece, even if it was not a chair but a type of furniture such as a commode or cabinet that was increasingly being treated as *ébénisterie.*

Beyond these special cases, only three eighteenth-century Parisian artisans of secondary importance, J. Caumont, B.-A. Chaumont, and P. Plée, would give me cause for hesitation, were it proved that they worked indiscriminately in *menuiserie* and *ébénisterie* before the Revolution. I thought it better to repeat them in both lists published in this book. Every distortion of this basic division presupposes a motive, even if it still escapes us. A desk chair, formerly in the Dutasta collection (today in the Rijksmuseum), is veneered in purple wood and ornamented with gilded bronze, but it is caned like many other desk chairs that are solid wood: it bears only the stamp of the *menuisier* Etienne Meunier, but one can be sure that he was not the author of

1. Medal cabinet of the duc d'Orleans, son of the regent (detail of the upper part). Certainly a unique piece, opulent and well adapted to its function (shallow drawers behind massive doors, a sliding shelf at elbow height), novel in its decoration (lively bronze mounts, superbly chased and gilded, violet wood and tulip-wood marquetry in lozenges), a precursor of the age of Louis XV. By Cressent, circa 1730. (Cabinet de Médailles, Bibliothèque Nationale, Paris)

2. Corner of the base of a table treated in the most sumptuous rococo style made to support a stucco top depicting the royal hunt. Carved and gilded wood. Made for the apartment of Louis XV at the château of Compiègne. By the Slodtz brothers. 1739. (Château of Versailles)

3. Corner of a double slant-top desk made for use by two people. Generous forms, delicate tulipwood and violet wood marquetry, chased and gilded bronze mounts. Formerly belonging to the dukes of Argyll. Stamped B.V.R.B., circa 1750. (J. Paul Getty Museum, Malibu, California)

4. Corner of a commode delivered for the bedroom of Madame Louise at Versailles. Transitional Louis XV–Louis XVI style. Régence shape. "Violet wood and tulipwood in latticework veneer," with metal rosettes. Beautifully chased gilt bronze mounts in classical motifs. A high price: 4,810 livres. Formerly in the collection of Chester Beatty. By Joubert, 1769. (J. Paul Getty Museum, Malibu, California)

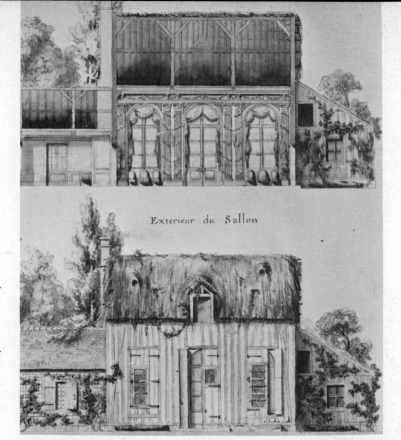

Exterieur du Sallon

5. Watercolor design for one of the houses of the *Hameau* at Chantilly. A palatial room in what pretends to be a hovel. Rigorous symmetry even to the placement of the chairs. The importance of the art of the upholsterer can be seen in the curtain and valance design as much as in the seat upholstery. Circa 1780. (The so-called album of the comte du Nord, Musée Condé, Chantilly)

6. The infante Ferdinand of Parma, grandson of Louis XV, painted by Pietro Ferrari. The desk, file, and clock certainly came from Paris. Circa 1770. (Galleria Nazionale, Parma)

7. *Le Benedicité* (Grace), painted by Chardin and presented by him to Louis XV. A simple interior with sturdy furniture, more traditional than up-to-date. Before 1744. (Musée du Louvre)

8. A "Louis XV" table made in Louisiana of Cyprus and walnut. Rather crude with elegant goat feet of Parisian inspiration. From the Ursuline convent of New Orleans. Second half eighteenth century. (Dr. and Mrs. Robert C. Judice collection, New Orleans)

10. Mirror with a carved and gilded wood frame. While large pier glasses decorated wealthy residences, in the bourgeois interior around 1700 a mirror was presented as a luxury object. Smaller, less ornate mirrors were to be found everywhere in the second half of the century. Circa 1715. (Musée des Arts Décoratifs, Paris)

9. Tobacco box carved from marble, a material favored for this purpose as it kept a constant cool temperature. Said to have belonged to Stanislas Leczinski. Mid-eighteenth century. (Musée Lorrain, Nancy)

11. Stool. Carved and gilded wood. The finest Louis XV shape and decoration. This type of seat, like the folding stool, went out of fashion but remained in use at court. Stamped M. Cresson. Circa 1750. (Versailles cathedral)

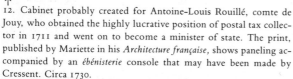

12. Cabinet probably created for Antoine-Louis Rouillé, comte de Jouy, who obtained the highly lucrative position of postal tax collector in 1711 and went on to become a minister of state. The print, published by Mariette in his *Architecture française,* shows paneling accompanied by an *ébénisterie* console that may have been made by Cressent. Circa 1730.

13. Clock on a bracket. Whether wall, mantel, or long-case, clocks were fashionable in every class of society. The movement could be made in the provinces or abroad, but the clock case, whether *ébénisterie,* bronze, marble, or porcelain, was usually made in Paris for export throughout Europe. Boulle and his sons were famous for clock cases, and other *ébénistes* as well made them their specialty. Stamped Saint-Germain, movement by Zeller of Basle. Circa 1760. (Musée Historique, Basle)

14. Vaugondy's terrestrial globe with its base of carved and polychrome varnished wood. There is a matching celestial globe. Belonged to Mme de Pompadour, then to the duc de Penthièvre. Possibly by Verberckt. Circa 1751. (Musée, Chartres)

15. Verso of the toilet mirror delivered to the duchesse de Berry by the dealer Delaroue. Probably the work of A.-C. Boulle, the marquetry inspired by the engravings of Berain. Soon after, a few minor embellishments were added by the goldsmith Ladoireau, and after 1719 the armorial on top was removed and replaced by that of the princesse de Chimay, daughter of the duchesse de Saint-Simon, lady-in-waiting to the duchesse de Berry. 1713. (Wallace Collection, London)

16. Brush with the arms of the notorious François de Beauvilliers de Saint-Aignan, bishop of Beauvais from 1713 to 1728. Made of wood from the Sainte-Lucie forest in Lorraine. Misleadingly termed *bois de Bagard,* this type of work has been attributed by P. Marot to the Foullon family and other sculptors working in Nancy and occasionally in Paris. Circa 1715. (Musée Lorrain, Nancy)

17. Toiletry box. Boullework marquetry with Louis XV bronze mounts. On the lid, in two different colors of copper, the initials LPR for the infamous cardinal Louis, prince de Rohan, 1734–1803. Mid-eighteenth century. (Wallace Collection, London) ➤

18a-b. Cabaret eating table with "a small table on top for use as a bed table" as described by Lazare Duvaux, who sold four such tables between 1750 and 1751 to a Spaniard, the duchesse de Bejar, at a price of 276 livres each. Stamped by A.-M. Criaerd. Mid-eighteenth century. (Oesterreichisches Museum, Vienna)

19a-b. Cabaret eating table with removable bed table. Lacquer top on lower section as on the preceding table; of a model resembling the preceding but incorporating more advanced refinements. Lattice and rosette marquetry. Stamped by Leleu. Circa 1770. (Stavros Niarchos Collection)

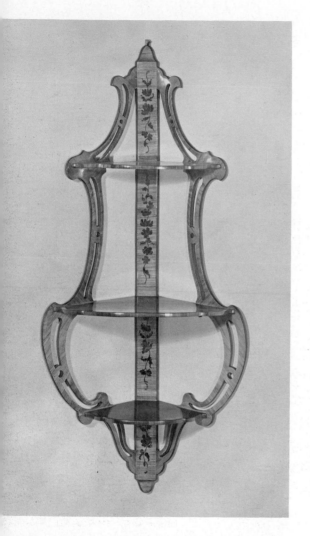

20. Corner shelves (one of a pair), termed *tablette* or *gradin*, of curvilinear openwork form with pendant termination. Descriptions of this type of object, with some variations, can be found in the daybook of the dealer Lazare Duvaux. The dealer who sold this one wrote the price in ink on the back, which seems to have been 120 livres for a pair. Stamped B.V.R.B. Circa 1750. (Wrightsman Collection, Metropolitan Museum of Art, New York)

21. Cabaret eating table. The Sèvres porcelain top would have had a matching Sèvres tea or luncheon service. The border pattern of triangles in the porcelain is echoed in the marquetry of the shelf. Formerly belonging to the Counts Potocki, Lanshut Castle, Poland (Sydney Lamon sale, Christie's, London, Nov. 29, 1973, no. 106). With the signature of the dealer Poirier on the drawer. Certainly by Bernard Van Risen Burgh (B.V.R.B.). Circa 1760. (Private collection)

22. Commode with two doors. Amboyna veneer and Sèvres plaques in a gilt bronze lattice. Belonged in 1770 to the prince de Condé and decorated the music room of the duchesse de Bourbon at the Palais-Bourbon. A highly unusual composition. The records of the Sèvres factory show the purchase of the plaques by the dealer Poirier. Stamped B.V.R.B. 1760. (Private collection)

23. Coffee or tea table with a marble top. Light colored-
mahogany veneer and chased gilt bronze mounts complementing
the neoclassical vigor of the design. Sold for 600 livres by Poirier
and described in his surviving bill as being "in classical antique
form with a single drawer on the side." Unsigned but possibly
by Leleu. 1771. (Private collection)

the veneering. Apropos of the stamp J.-P. Letellier, which appears on a Louis XV *menuiserie* chair in the Dijon Museum and a Louis XVI mahogany worktable in the Victoria and Albert Museum (fig. 35), the following explanation seems reasonable: Jacques-Pierre Letellier was a *menuisier* and author of the Louis XV chair; his son, who had the same name, was an *ébéniste* and responsible for the Louis XVI worktable; they used the same, or similar, marks.

An *ébéniste* could be at the same time a furniture dealer, and, as such, could sell chairs; one knows this to be the case with the Migeons; Salverte noted it of J.-B. Fromageau; I would give the example of L. Boudin. As an *ébéniste* who also sold furniture, he put his stamp, and did not allow the name of the *menuisier* to appear, on a set of chairs that have been in a great Portuguese family since the eighteenth century.

The fashion for mahogany chairs contributed to some hybrids in the Louis XVI period: chairs of solid wood, therefore the work of the *menuisier,* but in mahogany, a wood associated with *ébénistes.* There are armchairs of this type bearing the stamp of the *ébéniste* P. Garnier (fig. 36) and other armchairs or side chairs with the stamps of the *menuisiers* G. Jacob or J.-B. Sené.

Turgot's suppression of the guilds in 1776 only lasted a few months. Their reestablishment, which led to certain regroupings, affected the guild of *menuisiers-ébénistes* very little, and it remained strong until its final dissolution in October 1789. After that, confusion spread rapidly; one notes, for example, the Jacobs, who were formerly *menuisiers,* making a specialty of *ébénisterie* (fig. 124). Strict demarcation between *menuisiers* and *ébénistes* can, however, be considered the rule until the Revolution.

The division within the profession had many consequences: the artisans lived in different neighborhoods, held different attitudes. The guild was directed by a *jurande* (wardenship), elected by the senior members and composed of an equal number of *ébénistes* and *menuisiers.* This wardenship, or office, remained true to the spirit of the *menuisiers* by force of tradition, and mistrusted novelty as well as newcomers to the profession. Within its jurisdiction was the quality control of furniture. The wardens made visits to the workshops, and on the pieces that they approved they placed the stamp of the *jurande des menuisiers-ébénistes* composed of the letters JME. If one draws up a balance sheet of the frequency of the occurrence of this stamp on the Parisian furniture that has come down to us, one realizes that it is the exception rather than the rule to find it on pieces of *menuiserie.*

Finally, the guilds who kept to their own narrow specialty and jealously guarded their rights distributed any supplementary work to various other groups. Things that would be done today by different hands within the same

17

workshop were then executed in different workshops, which were generally grouped in the same street or neighborhood. Even more than the *ébénistes,* the *menuisiers,* who were so attached to their traditions and slow in their evolution, engaged in rivalry and competition with related professions, on whom they nevertheless often relied.

The lathe turners did not appear to be a major force. The seats and other small pieces that they made were inexpensive. Nonetheless, their assistance became invaluable to the *menuisiers* as well as the *ébénistes* when the developing Louis XVI style of furniture included lathe-turned legs and colonettes (figs. 26, 37). In 1776 the lathe turners of Paris were accepted into the guild of *menuisiers-ébénistes.*

The caners gave the *menuisiers* a moment of concern when caned seats became fashionable at the beginning of the century. Their challenge was rapidly quashed; caning would be done on the *menuisier's* premises (fig. 42).

The woodcarvers were of importance, and not only in Paris (fig. 16). They were in constant conflict with the *menuisiers.* The latter, in principle, had only the right to fashion the parts, to carve the moldings, and to assemble their furniture, but they claimed the right to decorate it as well. The woodcarvers protests were frequent and violent: in 1756, the caners of Valenciennes prosecuted a *menuisier* guilty of not having kept to the *gros bois* (unfinished frame), and those of Dijon obtained from the Parlement of Bourgogne an essentially ridiculous judgment obliging the *menuisiers* to go to the woodcarvers for certain separately made ornaments, which they then had to glue onto their furniture. It seems that a compromise was arrived at in Paris: when pieces were carved with minor ornament of an unexceptional nature, the *menuisiers* executed them in their own workshops, but when the decoration was more significant, they addressed themselves, of their own accord, to a woodcarver (figs. 43, 142, 148). This practice led to a remarkable result: two *menuisiers* sometimes used the same woodcarver, and one can therefore find absolutely similar carving on chairs bearing the stamps of two different *menuisiers.*

The *menuisiers* had to go to the guild of painters and gilders to have their chair frames enhanced beyond polishing (figs. 137, 140) and to an upholsterer to have them upholstered. The bitter conflict that had raged between the upholsterers and *menuisiers* in the seventeenth century abated: the upholsterer became, in most cases, the seller of the products of the *menuisier,* who delivered the bare chairs to him. The *menuisier,* on his part, because of the greater importance the frames had assumed in relation to the fabrics that covered them, and thanks to the stamp he put on his work after 1743, came to have a more open and equitable relationship with his principal client, the upholsterer.

Since the reign of Louis XIV, *ébénistes* had been decorating their furniture with gilded bronze mounts. They could not make these bronzes themselves and were obliged to turn to not one but two different and rival guilds if they wanted the mounts properly finished and gilded (fig. 3)—the guild of founders and chasers and that of chasers and gilders, which merged only in 1776. The *ébéniste* was allowed to affix to his furniture in his own workshop the bronze mounts that had been cast or gilded elsewhere (fig. 4). Certain *ébénistes* tried to circumvent the common rule and to execute bronzes of their own design in their own establishments (fig. 1).

The *tabletiers* (makers of small intricate objects), at least in Paris until 1776, belonged to a different guild from that of the *menuisiers* and *ébénistes* and competed with them to some extent. Caskets, game sets, dressing cases, which were the primary wares sold by the *tabletier,* could be made by the *ébéniste* and the fittings then added by the *tabletier;* conversely, the *tabletier* could sell the pieces for backgammon and other games to the *ébéniste,* who would add them to fit out his gaming tables (figs. 117, 126).

The French provinces certainly did not have such powerful organizations for the furniture trades as one encounters in Paris. The statutes could be inspired by those of Paris, or made to conform with them, like that drawn up by the *menuisiers* and *ébénistes* of Orleans in 1768–69. There was a guild system, but it did not constitute such a complex network of artisans competing in the making of a single piece of furniture. The local *menuisier* was often the woodcarver (fig. 72). *Ebénistes* were few: commodes, secretaries, and wall clocks, if they were in marquetry, came from Paris in most cases (fig. 155). Under Louis XV and Louis XVI, large centers attracted Parisian and even German *ébénistes* (figs. 130, 131), whose establishments were granted special exemptions but who still came up against the hostility of the city's *menuisiers.* Surely the *tour de France* of *ébéniste* journeymen, which developed in the second half of the century, contributed substantially to the spread of Parisian techniques and styles through the provinces.

It is hardly necessary to say that the organizations were still more rudimentary in the colonies. Only Canada (fig. 75) seems to have followed very closely the statutes of the Parisian *menuisiers,* without, however, having been forced to do so. There was even a confraternity of Sainte-Anne, which was modeled on that of the Paris *menuisiers.* Trade schools were opened at Cape

Tourmente and at the Quebec seminary during the reign of Louis XIV, but it was primarily by apprenticeship that the master *menuisiers* and woodcarvers of Quebec, Montreal, and Trois-Rivières were educated and recruited.

In Louisiana and the French Antilles the absence of an artisan cadre can be conjectured from such documents as an eighteenth-century inventory published in the *Louisiana Art Quarterly:* in the estate of an agent of the *Compagnie des Indes* named Prévost, they valued at 2,000 livres "a blackman named Joyau, Joseph, *menuisier,* aged 45," and further, at 30 livres, "a set of gilded copper for a commode with goat's feet, 2 escutcheons and 2 button drawer pulls." This information, however summary it may be, reveals that craftsmanship might be elementary, but there was a desire to create furniture that would correspond to fashion as closely as possible (fig. 8); the mounts, certainly imported from France, evidence a concern with style that was universal.

DESIGNERS AND DECORATORS

The client rarely knew how to draw and all too often was vague in his demands; the artisan, for his part, ordinarily preferred routine over efforts that required imagination. Two groups of intermediaries came to their aid: the first, including architects and upholsterers, were capable of conceiving grand ensembles; the second, including *ornemanistes* and decorators, invented novel fantasies. The part that each played can be seen, respectively, in architectural furniture and furniture for comfort and amenity; a few remarks on each seem pertinent.

There was no want of people interested in the construction of a grand residence or the renovation of an old house and eager to advise a client who had some money. First came the architect, who took in a percentage on his works: Robert de Cotte, Oppenord, Boffrand, the Gabriels, Soufflot, Ledoux, Belanger, to cite only the greatest (figs. 137, 153). They did a great deal, not only in terms of the layout of apartments, but also in contributing to the evolution of style in the decorative arts, designing paneling and furniture. They designed, proposed, and imposed.

The upholsterer also played an important role. He often sold furniture and occasionally rented it. He prepared draperies and fabrics as well. His choices could determine the character of an entire interior.

Engravers contributed to the creation of furniture and the development of new styles. They designed models and popularized them through their images (fig. 12). The artisans and their clients wanted to be able to review engravings before deciding on a paneling, a piece of furniture, or a detail of decoration or ornament. The need was answered by a category of designers and engravers, sometimes termed *ornemanistes*. Berain, Audran, Roumier, Meissonnier, Pineau, Slodtz, Babel, Neufforge, Delafosse, Liard, Lalonde, Ranson, Prieur, Dugourc left their mark on French furniture in different ways. We will see in the following chapter how the painter and gilder Watin made use of engravings in conducting his business.

The ambitions of a newcomer, the decorator, were encouraged by the importance interior decoration and furniture had gained in the social and artistic life of the eighteenth century. *Ornemaniste* of a special character, the decorator corresponded to a new need: in designing, he assumed a position between the architect and the upholsterer, and through engraving he popularized his work. His title, applied to furniture and taken in the modern sense [of designer], was defined in the last years of the reign of Louis XV.

The *Encyclopédie* still did not acknowledge his function: in its fourth volume, which came out in 1754, decoration was considered to pertain primarily to the domain of theater, spectacles, and illusions, although its importance in architecture and sculpture was recognized and a relevance in interiors was conceded. A few words apropos of some large Parisian town houses are revealing regarding the new genre: "One finds in their apartment the wealth of materials, the magnificence of furniture, the sculpture, the painting, the bronzes, the mirrors, distributed with such taste, selection, and intelligence, that it seems as if these palaces were so many enchanted places." They went no further than the word *distribution,* but they associated with it the qualities that were going to make great decorators. No articles on the decorator or decoration appeared in the 1776 supplement to the *Encyclopédie*.

Let us turn to the poor man's, or artisan's, encyclopedia, which is the publication (or reissuing, to be more precise) of the *Dictionnaire . . . des arts et métiers* (Dictionary of Arts and Crafts), edited by the abbé Jaubert, in Bordeaux in 1773. In volume 4, but note, in the supplement, an article entitled "Décorateur (l'art du)" was presented; it covered theater and singles out Servandoni for praise; it mentioned public festivities and princely palaces and gardens; it clearly defined the importance of this new taskmaster who had insinuated himself into the decoration of interiors:

> The decorator is the only person who knows how to use the talent of each artist to best advantage, *to arrange the most elaborate pieces of furniture, to position them to best effect.* . . . To excel in *this art, which has been born before our eyes,* it is necessary to have a good eye, to have a good knowledge of design, to understand perfectly the merits of each piece

of furniture, to show them in their true light, and to create an ensemble that will *give a pleasing impression;* he should know which are the *appropriate ornaments for each season. . . . the number of Decorators is still very small,* and there is good reason to believé that they will never form a large community, unless luxury is taken to an ultimate destructive extreme.

One notes, in conclusion, that in 1768, Delafosse, in his *Nouvelle Iconologie,* credited himself "architect, decorator, and teacher of design," and, a little later, Lalonde styled himself "decorator and designer" when he published models "for artists and persons who want to decorate with taste."

THE MARCHANDS-MERCIERS

The *marchands-merciers* (dealers in decorative arts) comprised a major guild in Paris that we are just beginning to understand better. Even though they did not work with their hands, they contributed to the transformation of Parisian furniture, particularly the small pieces. The *ébénistes* were the principal beneficiaries of their creative and inventive talents.

The dealers were by definition men of commerce. Among their many activities, they made a specialty of fashionable furniture. They were importers of exoticism; notable among their wares were lacquer and a variety of chinoiseries. They were to be the great propagandists of Sèvres porcelain. Under these diverse titles, they occupied an important place in eighteenth-century Paris.

They unfailingly provided for their clientele's appetite for novelty. Among the *marchands-merciers* who contributed to the development of French furniture, both in its fabrication and diffusion, were Hébert, Duvaux, Bertin, and Julliot (who, like many others also called himself a jeweler) under Louis XV; Tuard, Deseutre, and Poirier in the transition period; Granchez, Darnault, Delaroue (who sold mirrors), and Daguerre (who took over Poirier's business, and whose successor was Lignereux) under Louis XVI (figs. 15, 20–23, 25, 84, 116, 119–22, 136, 145, 146, 151, 165).

Their role could have been limited to coordinating different crafts, for example the *ébéniste* and the bronze maker, but they extended it to the devotee's exploration of the potential of furniture. Since their interest was to attract and sell, they instigated the creation of unprecedented novelty. By the nature of their business, they were accustomed to the widest variety of techniques. They sought to incorporate diverse materials in a single piece of cabinetwork ordered from an *ébéniste.* Duvaux, Darnault, and others made use of antique lacquers they imported from China or took from coffers or screens for modern pieces of furniture; they also had them imitated or added to by Parisian japanners, foremost among whom were the Martin brothers. Two dealers, Poirier and Daguerre, assumed a quasi monopoly of furniture embellished with porcelain; the plaques, panels, or trays that they purchased or commissioned at Sèvres assured the success of "their" furniture.

Retailers and not artisans, although one could call them "embellishers," the great Paris dealers had the virtue of innovating in a century that was avid for renovation in furnishing. They gave their commissions to *ébénistes* of top rank, such as B.V.R.B., Joseph, Saunier, R.V.L.C., Carlin, and Weisweiler. Court and town came to their establishments: foreigners visited them or corresponded with them. Increased vitality and expansion were among the immense benefits French furniture derived from the commerce of the *marchands-merciers*.

Chapter 3

THE DEVELOPMENT AND DIFFUSION
OF FRENCH FURNITURE

Paris and Versailles were able to impose with ease their style and taste in the art of furniture, even more than their techniques, in the provinces, parts of Europe, and even the Americas. A way of living and furnishing was propagated. Sales and shipments of furniture, as well as local copies or adaptations, evidence the influence of the French court and attest to the success of the *menuisiers* and *ébénistes* of the capital. Areas of uncertainty remain in the attempt to trace the major lines of this expansion, but the breadth of the phenomenon can be outlined.

PROVINCES AND FRENCH COLONIES

The authority of Paris, if one can employ this term, was exercised on the French provinces through purchases made directly from Paris and through more or less accurate local copies of Parisian products.

It was normal for great residences to be furnished with major commissions carried out in Paris. Hence the same names of Paris *menuisiers* or *ébénistes* on the furniture that one finds throughout those rare châteaus that have had the good fortune to be preserved intact. Shipments came by land or water, or both, the chairs having been taken apart and marked before crating (figs. 164, 169). Upholsterers and other intermediaries made offerings to the residents of the provinces. A 1781 prospectus published by Havard gave the address on the rue Saint-Andre-des-Arts of an agency where all kinds of furniture, "tapestries, chairs, armchairs, beds, casepieces, room decorations . . . clocks, gaming tables, etc." could be obtained.

One continuously encounters the importance of Parisian models in regard to provincial *menuiserie* and *ébénisterie:* in some cases Parisian pieces were copied, but Parisian models were also made available through prints and drawings. The painter and varnisher Watin, who seems to have been active in this trade, revealed its workings: "Linked by friendship or interest with the most skilled artists, dealers, and workmen of the capital . . . , it would be a pleasure to send with his [the client's] shipment [of colors] everything that is wanted from Paris by way of furniture . . . , fabrics, etc." He also offered to cover the cost of sending albums of engravings "after drawings by the greatest masters," notably Delafosse, Neufforge, Liard or Lalonde. It was appropriate to include with the print of a piece of furniture "on separate sheets, the most precise details of the overview, measurements, cross-section of the frame and its contours, and the carved decoration, which result in the effect of a perfectly finished piece of furniture." He recognized the opulence and the excessive imagination of certain models and suggested a simple solution: "retaining the grace, elegance, agreeable forms, and commodious and graceful contours of all these designs, in order to make them easy to execute and accessible to everyone, it is only a question of sacrificing a few ornaments."

Identical procedures appear, on a more modest scale, in the majority of French colonies in America in the eighteenth century, Canada, Louisiana, Martinique, Guadeloupe, Santo Domingo. Imports from France furnished the houses of governors, officers, or the richest merchants; for example, the two "console tables with their marble tops and gilded bases" that were in the

New Orleans home of Claude Villars-Dubreuil, captain of the militia and builder of the roof of the hospital, in 1757; or the "bidet monté, garni en peau de mouton, tout neuf" (equipped bidet, decorated with sheepskin, entirely new) which was in the Santo Domingo home of Leon de Motmans in 1787 and must have come from a town in the west of France, if not Paris. Such pieces could then become the subject of crude or simplified copies made by the immigrant *menuisiers,* black slaves in the islands or Louisiana, jack-of-all-trades colonists, or by ships' carpenters during their winters on land. No *ébéniste* can be identified, but the imitation of French furniture, especially in the Louis XV style, seems to have been widespread in French territories in America (fig. 8). Jean Palardy even cited the case of Jean Baillairgé, a *menuisier*-woodcarver of Quebec, originally from Burgundy, who specialized in church furnishings, sending his son François to France for three years around 1780 to learn the new styles.

FOREIGN COUNTRIES

The success of French furniture was manifested abroad in much the same manner as in the provinces and colonies, but it was less persistent and presented more variations. Despite the recognition of the supremacy of French furniture throughout the Western world, there were limits to its expansion that varied according to the country. While it found favor with cultivated court circles, local traditions could provoke resistance. The surest method was the purchase of furniture from Paris itself; the movement was so strong that a value-added tax imposed at certain times in France on luxury products, and notably decorative arts that were sent abroad, did not diminish the volume of exports. Exemplars were supplied through the circulation of drawings and prints; the desire to keep up with Paris fashion entailed either an integral copy or, more often, an interpretation in terms of particular habits. Almost everywhere in Europe we see, to the degree that the historians of each country inform us, the indigenous furniture styles transformed and more or less standardized in imitation of French furniture.

There were many different agents of this dissemination: ambassadors who returned home, enthusiastic about what they had seen at Versailles and in Paris, who bought back furniture or models, like Bernstorff of Copenhagen; kings who returned conquered after a trip to France, like Gustave III of Sweden or the Grand Duke Paul, (who was to become Czar Paul I), and Maria Feodorovna in St. Petersburg; important figures of the empire, who established residences in France, such as Prince Xavier of Saxony or the princes of Salm; innumerable travelers, who came first as sightseers, then as purchasers, such as the Russians Razoumovski in 1765 and Demidoff in 1772, or the great English tourists like William Beckford. Coming and going through Europe, perhaps even more frequently, were the artisans themselves.

It seems that almost everywhere this movement was more profitable to the Parisian *ébénistes* than to the *menuisiers*. One should note that these exchanges are not accurately reflected by the current distribution of the principal collections of French eighteenth-century furniture, outlined in one of the last chapters of this book, with the exception of England and Germany.

England illustrates rather well the evolution of French styles in the eighteenth century, from Louis XIV and the Régence to Louis XV and Louis XVI. Periods of popularity alternated with periods of disfavor. An established tradition in the art of furniture and an avowed particularism constituted an obstacle to the infiltration of French styles. The admiration that the court and aristocracy felt for the Versailles of Louis XIV, however, followed from the start of the eighteenth century by the presence of Huguenot refugee *ébénistes* in London, helped to prepare the way for French furniture with such approaches as incrustations of copper and tortoiseshell, floral marquetry on dark grounds, supple forms, gilded bronze and copper, tables, candlestands, and mirrors of richly carved and gilded wood.

Certain great families who maintained contact with France, through travel, embassies, and friendships, introduced Parisian furniture into England in the intervals between the wars, especially in the second half of the century. Richard Arundale, in Yorkshire (fig. 167), the dukes of Northumberland and of Buccleuch, the British delegates who came to the court of Versailles in 1762–63 when the Treaty of Paris was signed, like the duke of Bedford (Joan Evans has studied his mission's expenditures in Paris on furniture) and the duke of Richmond (whose furniture is preserved at Goodwood, fig 115), as well as Horace Walpole (Francis Watson has given special attention to Walpole's trip to Paris in 1766)—these are only a few of the names.

The furniture imported from the Continent contributed to the craze and inspired imitations and adaptations. Thomas Chippendale, whose first edition of the *Gentleman and Cabinet-maker's Director* is dated 1754 and dedicated to the duke of Northumberland, presented models of "French chairs" and what he called a "French commode table," all generally inspired by Louis XV models. An *ébéniste* whom one could call French-English, Pierre or Peter Langlois, knew how to take advantage of this trend; various studies undertaken over the last twenty years, notably those of Anthony Coleridge, Peter Thornton, and William Rieder, have enabled us to learn more about him. Certainly

27

of French origin, he was established in London by 1759 at the latest; he had a superior clientele and made superb furniture, especially commodes, of French inspiration but not quite French in style. His business card, printed in English and French, stated that he "Makes all Sorts of Fine Cabinets and Commodes, made & inlaid in the Politest manner with Brass & Tortoiseshell, & Likewise all rich Ornamental Clock Casses, and Inlaid work mended with great Care, Branch Chandelier & Lanthorns in Brass, at the Lowest prices" (published and reproduced by Thornton and Rieder).

At the end of the reign of Louis XV an unexpected reverse occurred: England, under the influence of Robert Adam, adopted the neoclassical style before France, and English cabinetmakers began providing more elements of novelty to their French rivals than they received from them. The third edition of Chippendale's *Director* was accompanied by an edition in French (1762). It is remarkable that, around 1770, the count of Coventry and the marquess of Zetland went to English chairmakers for the frames of seats for which they ordered tapestry covers from the Gobelins. In 1787, according to the research of Francis Watson, the count of Shrewsbury bought *menuiserie* pieces in Paris but had them gilded in England. A French gilder, Dupasquier, worked for the duke of Argyll in the castle of Inverary. He used Parisian techniques to gild chairs made for the duke in Scotland, for which tapestry covers were woven at Beauvais. While Anglomania spread in France, a fashion for a "cosmopolitan outlook" developed in England. Whenever they could, the English crossed the Channel, and one would like to know in detail what contacts the bronze maker Matthew Boulton made when he visited Paris.

It is interesting to observe the rise in popularity of mahogany. Although the modern French word is *acajou*, the original term was an English cognate, *magahon* or *magahoni*. It was considered one of many woods whose qualities should be tried out and was mentioned more and more often around 1760: the influence of the new furniture from England had much to do with it, as did the austerity sought in the neoclassical style. The furniture ordered by Mme de Pompadour for her châteaus of Menars and Auvilliers shortly before her death in 1764 was almost all of mahogany. This wood, which would triumph in France under Louis XVI, was used largely for furniture inspired by English models, especially dining room furniture, large tables or serving tables; they even went as far as making chairs of mahogany following the English example (figs. 26, 35, 36). A proliferation of small tables, the *guéridons* termed *à l'anglaise,* followed the adoption of serving *thé à l'anglaise.* Mme Du Barry, who owned a particularly precious Parisian example decorated with Sèvres plaques (fig. 136), had purchased three beautiful tables decorated with silver in London in 1770 through the intermediary of a Paris dealer. A Chippendale folding dressing table, lately in the Leverton Harris collection, bears the marks of just such a strange journey; its silver fittings are hallmarked for London 1771 and Paris 1772.

The activity of the *marchand-mercier* Granchez follows closely the course of this development. This dealer, first established at Dunkirk, then in Paris, and soon after appointed "jeweler to the Queen," advertised in 1767 that he received "first pick of the daily output of useful and fascinating products of England's arts and industries"; in 1775 he seemed less exclusive and declared that he had "the large and fascinating store of French and foreign merchandise, with all the newest products of the arts."

By the time of the signing of the Treaty of Versailles in 1783 and the trade agreement of 1786, French furniture had come back into fashion. Every year until well into the Revolution one of the leading dealers of Paris, Daguerre, made selling trips to London with his partner Lignereux. Some French princes like the comte d'Artois and the duc d'Orleans let themselves be seduced by English models, but many more nobles and wealthy Englishmen came to Paris to select beautiful furniture. The Revolution presented only a temporary interruption as emigration and Revolutionary sales actually served to increase the tide. The regent, William Beckford of Fonthill, Lord Yarmouth, Lord Harewood, and many others contributed to the outflow of some of the best and often the most recent Parisian examples of the art of furniture (figs. 17, 129).

Paris exerted a strong attraction on Germany, birthplace of many of the leading exponents of Parisian *ébénisterie*. The procedure remained the same: purchase of furniture in Paris, copies of these pieces, adaptation of French styles. During the eighteenth century, the electors of Bavaria and the Palatine princes practically never stopped buying or commissioning what was most in fashion in Paris, surrounding themselves with the works of the leading *ébénistes* and *menuisiers* of the period (fig. 82). (In removing the marble top from a commode in the Munich Residence, I discovered the label of the dealer Granchez still glued to the carcass.) Dresden and many other German courts followed the same pattern; and, at first glance, one hesitates over whether to attribute certain armchairs or commodes to Parisian or local craftsmen. In Berlin and Potsdam, on the other hand, Frederick II preferred to furnish in his own style, which was Louis XV modified and embellished according to his fancy.

The great book on German furniture by H. Kriesel and G. Himmelheber makes it possible for us to understand better the success enjoyed by Parisian furniture craftsmen. Confronted with similar names on both sides of the Rhine, and closely related works, one is led to raise questions. A commode that appears French but, we are told, is German could, in its bronze mounts, at least, have come from Paris. Could its *ébénisterie* be a faithful copy? Conversely, could several similar commodes preserved at Ludwigsburg, where Rosemary Stratmann has turned up the stamps of different Paris *ébénistes,* correspond to a model created for export, or a specific commission by the elector (fig. 86)? Might not Kambli or the Spindlers, who figured among the leading *ébénistes* of Frederick II, along with many others, have had early contacts with the *ébénistes* and bronze makers of Paris who influenced their work? Why did the famous David Roentgen, who established himself in Neuwied-am-Rhine feel it was necessary to be received into the Paris guild of *ébénistes?* And what of Nicolas Valois, responsible for carving some of the most beautiful chairs created for Marie-Antoinette? We lost track of him in Paris in 1790. But he reappears propagating the Louis XIV style at the court of the landgrave of Hesse-Cassel. The relocation of artisans could have had consequences to German furniture equally as important as the purchase of furniture from Paris.

The influence of Versailles on Europe, and especially on francophile courts throughout the eighteenth century must be kept in mind. It was no accident that the stools of the Gallery at Schoenbrunn were made in Austria, but in the Louis XV style with moldings painted red and gold, just like those of the Hall of Mirrors at Versailles, when Maria Theresa ruled the empire. The greatest families of Austria and Hungary were in frequent contact with Versailles and seem to have purchased furniture of high quality in Paris, judging from the examples known to us (fig. 83).

Even in Switzerland they caught the reflected light of the French court when officers in service to the French king returned to their native country. Much furniture in Berne Basle, Soleure, and in many small châteaus in western Switzerland is in the Louis XV or Louis XVI style. Banking also contributed to these exchanges: there is a beautiful Louis XV lacquer commode which belonged to the Thelusson family; another banker from Geneva ordered numerous chairs, still owned by his descendants, which bear the stamp of Nogaret.

The Netherlands had continuous exchanges with France and supplied Paris with skilled *ébénistes.* The carved furniture of areas around Liege, Namur, Maestricht, and even Aix-la-Chapelle, had many similarities to the Régence, Louis XV, and Louis XVI furniture found in the French provinces. Chapuis (an *ébéniste* who had been confused with a Parisian of the same name until he was correctly identified, on the basis of the form of his mark, by the recent research of Mme Bonnefant) worked in Brussels in the early nineteenth century, in the Paris style of the late eighteenth century. Archduchess Maria Christina, governor of the South Netherlands, who came to Versailles in 1786, surrounded herself in Brussels with decorative arts that were probably bought through the dealer Daguerre. Many more examples could be given; I give just two more: a superb clock by Latz, preserved in a Belgian château, is said to have been the gift of Louis XV, who stayed there at the time of the battle of Fontenoy. A beautiful ensemble by the Parisian *menuisier* Chevigny is in the château of Modave near Namur, which was inherited by the duc de Montmorency in the second half of the eighteenth century.

Holland had submitted to English influence too often not to show some resistance to French incursions. Still, proof exists of French inroads: Lunsingh Scheurleer, while studying in 1948 the Stadhouder thrones, and in 1958 the furniture imported into Holland from France between 1650 and 1810, has revealed aspects of this penetration.

In Denmark, as in Sweden, the court and the ambassadors together contributed to the introduction of French models. Important evidence was destroyed in the burning of the château of Charlottenburg in 1794, but one can again refer to the ambassador Bernstorff, who went to the very suppliers of Louis XV for the decoration of his own palace in Copenhagen (fig. 161). The diplomats that the king of Sweden sent to France, Carl Gustav Tessin and the count of Creutz, played the role of art scouts. The court of Sweden (fig. 97) was more inclined toward French than English furniture. The *ébénistes* of Stockholm were francophiles: they tackled marquetry and bronze mounts; they stamped their furniture in accordance with the French practice. Perhaps their success at imitating French furniture checked the French invasion. The most famous among them, Georg Haupt, had worked in Holland, England, and France, and his style was closely related to that of Oeben and Leleu. Swedish and Parisian furniture intermingles harmoniously, even blends, in the royal residences of Sweden.

In the eighteenth century Poland provided Parisian decorators and artisans with well-informed clients (fig. 85) who were avidly interested in their innovations and bought and commissioned important works. Stanislas Lorentz and François-Georges Pariset have thoroughly researched the role of the architect Victor Louis and the designer and bronze maker Jean-Louis Prieur in the decoration and furnishing of the Warsaw palace for King Stanislas Augustus Poniatowski. The wealthy nobility of Poland followed suit. It is amusing to find in Cracow a curious chair commissioned locally by one of the

Czartoryska princesses, which opens like a jewel case to reveal a French chair; a modest chair of ash and straw such as one sees in old churches; a chair that was venerated because it had belonged to Jean-Jacques Rousseau (fig. 48).

Russia was open to various influences, English and German, as well as French. It was a sign of the times, however, that there was a difference of spirit between the first and second half of the century. Peter the Great was primarily interested in tapestry weavers, whom he summoned and tried to induce to take up residency in his capital. Fortunately the great czarinas, Elisabeth and Catherine II, had more "frivolous" tastes, and kept an eye on French fashion. Furniture was sent from France to St. Petersburg directly by sea. The publications of Denise Roche and later Tatiana Skolova on French and Russian furniture emphasize the quantity of furniture bought in the eighteenth century by the imperial court (fig. 119), the nobility, and wealthy merchants. Louis XV gave Czarina Elisabeth a magnificent writing table of purple wood with floral marquetry, ordered from the dealer Hébert. The Hermitage Museum has a superb *cartonnier* bearing the stamps B.V.R.B. and Joseph and the label of the dealer Darnault on the back, which came from the Palace of Oranienbaum (fig. 165).

Catherine II showed a particular predilection for the German *ébéniste* Roentgen, and she, together with members of her court, purchased an astonishing quantity of his works. She was capable of exercising exquisite taste in her choices, if indeed the green japanned writing table and *cartonnier* stamped Dubois in the Wallace Collection were among her purchases. Her son Paul's trip to France in 1782 had visible repercussions, especially on the furniture of Pavlovsk.

The Bourbon dynasties of Madrid and Parma, the marriages that linked the houses of France and Savoy, the presence of a sister of Marie-Antoinette in Naples, the personal attraction Louis XV exerted on the court of Portugal, all provided opportunities for the insinuation of French furniture and styles. In Spain under Philip V imports were certainly considerable, but we can only learn of the decorations and furniture of Madrid's Royal Palace through drawings, plans, and documents (many of which have been published by Yves Bottineau), because of the fire in 1734. Subsequently a vigorous Spanish national style developed, in which the *casitas* of the royal family were furnished. Finally, Charles III, until 1791, ordered furniture in the Paris taste decorated with porcelain plaques, through the intermediary of his French clockmaker Godon; and he commissioned the *ornemaniste* Dugourc to draw up plans for the decoration, the furniture, and the silks of the Throne Room of his Madrid Palace.

The duchess of Parma, wife of the infante Don Philippe, who was by birth a princess of France, surrounded herself and her husband with French furniture at Parma and Colorno (figs. 6, 164). The furniture, which arrived in convoys, was often paid for by Louis XV himself. The chairs were reassembled by craftsmen resident in Parma, several of whom seem to have been of French origin.

In the eighteenth century the court of Turin benefited from a school of brilliant *menuisiers,* woodcarvers, *ébénistes,* and bronze makers. Some furniture was bought in Paris, but a great deal was made in Turin, and it was very beautiful, especially the interpretations of Louis XV and Louis XVI styles by the *ébéniste* Piffetti and the woodcarver Bonzanigo.

When further studies are undertaken, perhaps more will be known about the development of French furniture in Turkey (fig. 166), India, and China. There are traces of the Louis XVI style in the United States in the eighteenth century; but apart from the former French colonies in America, English cabinetmakers dominated that sector of the world, both in sales of furniture and in their influence on local imitators. French furniture returned with a vengeance in the nineteenth and twentieth centuries. During the French Revolution, one saw an American businessman, James Swan, buying pieces of the highest quality in Paris (many of which belong today to the Boston Museum of Fine Arts). One must not overlook the importance of travels of artisans even to such distant countries as America. Lannuier, *ébéniste* of Paris, became Lannuier, cabinetmaker of New York; his case was exceptional in 1800 but it became a trend in the first third of the nineteenth century.

Imitations and interpretations demonstrate the hegemony of Parisian furniture, even over local production. The takeover was peaceful and the achievement was astonishing. The extent of the phenomenon and its variation are being clarified as research progresses on European furniture of the eighteenth century. It becomes necessary to modify our opinions: doubt sometimes arises as to the origin of a piece, and one ought to write in terms of possible origins. It seemed pertinent to outline the diffusion at this point, because it brought about permutations that could cause errors of attribution. Paris, the provinces, and foreign countries constituted progressive stages in the development of French furniture, where models can be recognized in derivations of varying proximity to the originals.

Chapter 4

GENERAL STYLISTIC
EVOLUTION

F RENCH FURNITURE automatically followed the general rhythm of decorative arts in the eighteenth century. It will suffice to review the major styles, cite some of the artists and artisans who shaped them, and summarize the principal characteristics.

Menuiserie and *ébénisterie* followed the same course with a few minor, predictable deviations based on the popularity of *ébénisterie* furniture, on one hand, and the rather conservative attitude of the dynasties of *menuisiers,* on the other.

A stylistic division by reigns may be artificial, but it provides a convenient and fairly accurate context.

THE REGENCE STYLE

In the history of styles the period between the end of the reign of Louis XIV and the start of the reign of Louis XV, approximately 1700 to 1730–35, has usually been dubbed Régence. The political regency of the duc d'Orleans lasted only from 1715 to 1723, but the style called Régence originated in the research and innovations that characterized the furniture made for the Sun King, Louis XIV (who had to replace the silver furniture he had melted down, and experienced changes in his personal taste) and for his son the grand dauphin. Fiske Kimball carefully traced the first manifestations of this style, which lasted almost a third of a century but was somewhat overshadowed by the vitality of the Louis XIV style and the prodigious development of the Louis XV style. In some provinces, notably Burgundy and the Franche-Comté, the Régence style lasted until the middle of the eighteenth century. Even in Paris, the term *à la Régence* continued to be used into the Louis XVI period to describe massive commodes that were *en tombeau* (sarcophaguslike) and recalled those made at the start of the century.

In *menuiserie* furniture (figs. 10, 50) this period was dominated by the personalities of a few important *menuisiers* and woodcarvers who began working during the lifetime of Louis XIV and were influenced to a degree by Robert de Cotte: Du Goullon, who signed the choir stalls of Notre-Dame in Paris and those of the Sainte-Croix cathedral in Orleans; Potain the elder, who delivered to Versailles buffets, wardrobes, and, in 1735, beautiful chairs that were carved by Gervais and gilded by Bardou; Foliot the elder and Mathelin, who, together with the woodcarver Guyot, executed new works for the prince de Condé; Nicolas Tilliard, who worked for the Crown; and Denis Bazin, who furnished the young Louis XV with carved and silvered stools in 1722. As always, the style of these leaders spread through all the Paris workshops and little by little was picked up in the provinces.

The shapes remained heavy, ample, and monumental (fig. 60). They did lose some of their austerity, however, thanks to the rapid development of subtle undulations: the pediments of wardrobes began to curve, the legs of chairs and tables ended in goat's feet or sometimes volutes, the line of chair backs undulated more or less in an embrace, while seats took on a slight barrel curve. Women's fashions alone would have forced *menuisiers* to revise their formulas, even if they hadn't wanted to: the fullness of the hooped skirts that came into fashion in 1718 obliged *menuisiers* to alter the location of the arms of their chairs, setting them back from the two front legs (figs. 138, 156). X stretchers between the legs tended to disappear, giving chairs a less constrained, lighter appearance from about 1720–30. More wood was left exposed on chair backs, providing a field for the decorative fantasies of the following period. Fine-gauge caning, adopted in imitation of the Netherlands and England, was used increasingly on chairs of this period, notably those supplied by the *menuisier* Heron; it was to remain popular for a long time.

Decoration evolved less quickly: pronounced moldings, rosettes, crossed motifs, gadroons, oves, shells, stylized flowers with tendrils, and the strictest symmetry were retained; but crooks, volutes, and S curves (fig. 38) as well as deeper cutting and lively carving made a tentative appearance as signs of the luxuriance to come. The *campane* (a regularly festooned, fringed, and tasseled silhouette) carried over from the Louis XIV tradition could still be seen on the chairs Tilliard delivered in 1731–33.

Color remained opulent with gilding and silvering used with accents of vivid colors on the most costly chairs, beds, and tables. While on the whole conforming to seventeenth-century usage, color schemes tended to become gayer and more diversified. Especially in the provinces, large *menuiserie* furniture and many chairs were left in the traditional natural wood, treated only with wax or varnish.

In *ébénisterie* furniture (figs. 15, 81), the two figures in the transition from the seventeenth to the eighteenth century who are outstanding for their fantasy, imagination, and taste for sumptuous decoration are Jean Berain I and André-Charles Boulle. In addition to the influence of Gilles-Marie Oppenpord, who worked for the regent, the little-known roles of the Godrons, *ébénistes* to Louis XIV in the last third of his reign, and the Poitous, *ébénistes* to the duc d'Orleans, must be recognized. When A.-C. Boulle died in 1732 at almost ninety years of age, it was not Boulle's own sons who assumed his eminence and carried on his tradition during the Régence and Louis XV period but Cressent.

The shapes of *ébénisterie* furniture retained much of the majestic, imposing, and massive character of the 1680s, but at the same time, curves appeared to attenuate their rigidity. Curved legs raised and freed the silhouette of the piece of furniture. The commode, the large flat-top desk, and the small movable table were developed and popularized in this period.

In marquetry complicated compartments with scrolls and flowers in loose bunches or compact bouquets remained in use but became lighter and brighter. *Singeries* (decorations featuring monkeys) inspired by Berain appeared in Boulle marquetry. An extremely simple geometric lozenge decoration developed in the Régence, mostly executed in rosewood and amaranth, either in an overall pattern of contrasting shades of wood or in reserves (fig. 82).

The use of bronze mounts remained the exception rather than the rule, but, when present, they were almost always of beautiful quality. Mounts retained a monumental character and were often figural, with masks, busts, and even full figures. Bases terminated in goat's feet, lion paws, and occasionally volutes. Handles resembled goldsmith's work with many symmetrical projections, and they were still mobile, pivoting on two hinges. The seventeenth-century term for handles, *mains,* continued to be used (as opposed to the modern *poignées*).

THE LOUIS XV STYLE

The Louis XV style was not only the most vital and successful of the styles of French eighteenth-century furniture, it was also the style that most deserved to bear the name of the monarch. It corresponded in date to the personal reign of the king who died in 1774. It was formed during the Régence and blossomed around 1730–35. The style lasted until around 1770–75 in Parisian *menuiserie* but was transformed somewhat earlier in *ébénisterie* by the transition to the Louis XVI style. In provincial *menuiserie* it lasted well into the nineteenth century (fig. 74).

Parisian *menuisiers* reflected court taste (figs. 2, 11, 40, 57, 150): the Tilliards, the Foliots, and Heurtaut, assisted by sculptors like Roumier and the Slodtz brothers, exerted a powerful influence on the development and success of the Louis XV style within their discipline. The archives of the Royal Garde-Meuble provide an example of stylistic evolution in carved table bases of the same general type, documenting successive deliveries to Versailles and Compiègne in 1731, 1737, 1739, and 1757. The evolution was slow in most of the workshops that specialized in chairs. Roubo accused the *menuisiers* of lack of originality and laziness.

Undulating forms became the rule (fig. 143). The legs of tables, beds, and chairs were not only curved but followed the apron or bedrails in an unbroken line, which, in the case of chairs, often continued from the seat-rail into the arms and back. Occasionally, reverse curves carried over from the preceding era interrupted this sinuous line. At the same time furniture took on convex shapes that could be said to go as far as plumpness. The base on such pieces would be nothing more than a symmetrical serpentine cutout dissolving into the arch of the legs. Feet took the form of volutes, especially at the start of the period, or still more frequently, goat's feet.

Decoration changed with surprising speed, transforming itself in the space of scarcely a decade, then remaining the same for more than a quarter of a century. It can be characterized by two words: *rocailles* and flowers (fig. 147). The *rocaille* consisted of motifs without exact contours or precise names, derived from cut-up foliage, palm fronds, wrinkled skins, deformed shells, and twisted volutes, as well as simulations of rocks, mosses, and foam. The flower was usually stylized, arranged in garlands, pendants, scrolls, and bouquets, or presented singly on a stem with leaves. Together with the *rocaille,* the flower constituted an ever-present element of decoration. Some emblems, including trophies and lively animals or figures, were used as were C-curves and cartouches; but, remarkably, no elements from the decorative vocabulary of classical antiquity, with the exception of the gadroon, was to be found before about 1770. One must also note the importance of relief decoration. Comparing an armchair of the Louis XIV or Régence style with one of the Louis XV style, it is astonishing to see the total change of character in so few years; following the same evolution that was already seen in tables and *guéridons,* the decoration of chairs took on an accent, a rich relief, and an unprecedented animation.

Colors became less harsh and intense, and polychromy came into use. While colors remained vivid, they were used with more refinement, and a new effort was made to harmonize upholstery materials. In Paris chair frames were rarely left in natural wood (fig. 45) unless the chairs were to be caned (fig. 42). Gilding or silvering was frequently employed with carved elements accented in different colors, but varnish was preferred because it permitted a light ground against which reeds, flowers, and palm fronds could be picked out in their natural colors (fig. 14). Two-tone combinations were favored where the ornaments, stringing, and moldings were contrasted to the ground (fig. 43); red and gold or yellow and red might still be used, but yellow and silver, blue and white, green and blue, green and gold, green and lilac, pink and white, and burnished gold with lead white were preferred.

Ebénistes (figs. 3, 21, 22) conveyed a still more sumptuous aspect of aristocratic taste. Cressent introduced the style with his commissions for Louis d'Orleans, son of the regent, and Gaudreaux demonstrated its full flowering in 1738–39, assisted by the bronze maker Caffieri and the models designed by the Slodtz brothers for Louis XV's private apartments at Versailles. In more modest works, masters like Migeon and Roussel realized the charming and whimsical potential of the style. The encouragement of a few great dealers, and the example of an *ébéniste* like Joubert, gave impetus to the elegance of a group of famous *ébénistes,* B. Van Risen Burgh, Joseph, Latz, and Dubois (figs. 84, 96).

The term *serpentine* serves as the best description of the accentuated movement that characterizes the shapes of French *ébénisterie* during this period (fig. 87). Exceptions to the curvilinear rule are few: certain *encoignures* (corner cabinets) and wardrobes, for example, may be rectilinear in shape, but curves are introduced in their bronze mounts, marquetry decoration, or in the design of their feet. The curves of French furniture are full-bodied but remain controlled and noble, avoiding the complicated bulges and bloated effect that one finds in the furniture of some other countries. Among the most perfect creations of Parisian *ébénistes* was the commode (fig. 88), in which they achieved a perfect harmony of contours, and the small table (fig. 166), which they raised to a tour-de-force of elegance.

Movement (figs. 20, 90) also pervaded the decoration of furniture. Veneers of amaranth, rosewood, purple wood, or satinwood were often applied with symmetry, especially on the most elaborate furniture where they formed lozenge or quatrelobe motifs; but marquetry also took on undulating contours, complementing the capricious design of the bronze mounts. The contrasting tones and the occasionally vivid marquetry of flowers and foliage in bunches or boughs enlivened the surfaces of furniture. For the most costly pieces more complicated decorations were created using oriental lacquers (fig. 78) or Western japanning. As the lacquer panels were usually of somber colors and the style of the period was bright and gay, varnishes were invented that permitted a white or colored ground on which animals, scenes, figures, or fantasy motifs amid *rocailles* and flowers were painted in the manner of the artists then most in fashion, Huet and Boucher (fig. 97).

Bronze mounts (figs. 100, 102, 127) had the same characteristics. More and more mounts were used, but on ordinary pieces of furniture they could be quite mediocre in quality: on luxury furniture they were used in profusion—*rocailles,* tangled moldings, lengths of flowers or vines, fixed handles of S-shape, sinuous crooks, undulating motifs, waves, coagulations, blisters, and any other motif that would furnish an element of movement.

THE TRANSITIONAL STYLE

The period of transition between the Louis XV and Louis XVI styles was quite short, lasting from 1760–65 until about 1775. Svend Eriksen's research on the rise of neoclassicism in France has identified the contributing factors: the reaction against rococo excesses; a thirst for novelty among amateurs and aesthetes; English influence; a wave of enthusiasm for classical antiquity around 1765, known as the *goût grec* (fig. 39); and nostalgia in certain parts for the grandiose style of Louis XIV (figs. 17, 154). There were elements of each of the above and some curious mixtures. Apropos of the practice of looking to history in search of novelty, an anecdote recounted by Peter Thornton in his study of the cabinetmaker Pierre Langlois comes to mind: when the Swedish *ébéniste* Carl Petter Dahlström applied to become a master on his return to his homeland after working in the Paris studio of J.-F. Oeben, the Stockholm guild found fault with his marquetry, which they said was in the out-of-date Louis XIV style; in fact, it represented the latest Paris fashion! The rejection of the Louix XV style was slow and gradual, especially among the *menuisiers*. Roubo, in his 1772 treatise on *menuiserie*, illustrates more Louis XV than Louis XVI examples, stressing that the latter are "currently in fashion." Around 1768 the *ornemaniste* Delafosse popularized the Transitional style, which remained somewhat hesitant in its classicizing, often awkward and confused, but, occasionally superbly well resolved.

One audacious figure, whose talent has been analyzed by Eriksen, stood out in Parisian *menuiserie*—Delanois (figs. 58, 137). His clients wanted the most aggressive modernism, and he worked with the architects Ledoux and Louis, who were apostles of the new wave. Other *menuisiers,* like Gourdin (fig. 158), the Foliots, and Jacob, in collaboration with woodcarvers, who were often more progressive, tried to achieve a balance between old formulas and new theories. On occasion the results were superbly successful.

Forms became more rational with less complicated curves (fig. 135). Chair backs took on a more regular outline, either oval or in the shape of a basket handle. The supports for the arms of chairs simply unrolled instead of twisting. Legs, if still originating in the seat-rail, descended in an almost straight line, or if the seat-rail was defined as a separate entity, legs of bracket shape could fit underneath. In 1776 frequent reference was made to baluster legs, and from 1770–72 Foliot and Delanois used straight or baluster legs on chairs for Versailles and Louveciennes.

For decoration (figs. 144, 152) the same recourse was made to elements borrowed from classical antiquity in reaction to rococo exuberance that was to have such significant consequences. This all came about in a general climate of infatuation with classical antiquity, in which the *menuisiers* and woodcarvers were among the very last to participate. In the beginning it seemed that they would only become involved to the extent of reviving Louis XIV ornaments and that their neoclassical themes would be limited to reusing a few decorative motifs that survived in their workshops: straighter and more pronounced moldings, acanthus leaves, gadroons, palmettes, fillets tied with ribbons, lion masks, rings and draperies, cassolettes and trophies, all mixed in with accurately rendered flowers that became more and more profuse. The archives of the Royal Garde-Meuble help us establish the evolution. On the chairs destined for the king's apartments at Versailles in 1763 and 1764, Foliot and Babel used cartels and crooks; and on the bases of console tables, palmettes, which did not alter the Louis XV character. In 1769 they used florets and pearls that accompanied floral crowns. The following year the vocabulary of the same *menuisiers* and woodcarvers demonstrates the evolution of the decorative grammar: split leaves and classical florets in the midst of jasmine and stock; finally in 1771, for the Trianon, leaf tips, pearls, and twisted ribbons.

Color schemes tended to be simpler (figs. 44, 159) and less polychromy was used; all-over gilding and white varnish without any other touches of color were common; in 1767 all the beds and chairs ordered for the Petit Trianon were painted with lead white. At the same time some fantasy pieces announced what would become a trend; in 1776 Marie-Antoinette had the chairs for Choisy painted straw color.

Parisian *ébénisterie* (figs. 4, 19, 113, 154) possessed in Oeben its key personality. More than Joubert, who was *ébéniste* to Louis XV and who tried timid forays into the modern, and more than Garnier, whose successes with amateurs like Lalive de Jully and Marigny have been studied by Eriksen, Jean-François Oeben seems to have played the decisive role in the *ébénisterie* of the period, in matters of construction, marquetry, and bronze mounts. With his progressive abandoning of the Louis XV style, his influential clientele, his relationship to other masters like the Lacroix, and his great pupils, Leleu and Riesener, Oeben had insured the passage to the Louis XVI style by the time of his death in 1763. Choiseul, the prince de Condé, and Mme Du Barry with their new installations at Chanteloup, Palais-Bourbon, and Louveciennes, respectively, contributed along with Oeben, Leleu, and others to this transformation. Louis XV, who had little enthusiasm for it, and Fontanieu, the intendant of the Garde-Meuble who may have been more intrepid but was, after all, not the boss, also played a part in this movement when they called upon someone like Oeben or Riesener.

Forms (figs. 27, 31, 79) hovered between the curvilinear (retained in furniture legs) and the rectilinear (already dominating uprights). The hesitation led to a certain heaviness, which was not without nobility (figs. 24, 28). Although it suggests a later date, the expression *gros Louis XVI*, which has been used by some foreign authors to describe this period, evokes its character rather effectively. The weight that would be a recurring characteristic in the era to come went well with stylistic elements held over from the preceding era, and the combination defined the Transitional style. The result was furniture of original character, virile but not exempt from awkwardness.

In general the use of wood polychromy increased, although a few *ébénistes* experimented with mahogany veneers. The lack of imagination in shapes was almost always compensated for by picturesque elements introduced into furniture decoration. Lozenges, Greek frets, interlaced motifs, and rosettes were used (fig. 115), and going beyond these geometric and classical motifs, entire pictures as well as friezes were depicted in marquetry. Flowers in bouquets, bundles, vases or baskets, trophies, and utensils, sometimes of Chinese inspiration, such as teapots and writing pens, contributed to the wide range of decorations.

Bronze mounts (figs. 23, 80, 93) were included in the antirococo reaction, and floral motives were abandoned, at least temporarily. Corner mounts became plaques decorated symmetrically with classical ornaments. Laurel garlands, Greek frets, rosettes, cassolettes, rams' heads, and lion masks became part of the new vocabulary of decoration inspired by antiquity.

THE LOUIS XVI STYLE

The seeds of the Louis XVI style germinated in the Transition. They surfaced shortly before the end of the reign of Louis XV and they grew in the fifteen years before the Revolution of 1789. So many of the queen's caprices and expenditures on furniture were so beneficial to the development of the Louis XVI style that it could just as well have been called the Marie-Antoinette style. Together with the Louis XIV and Louis XV styles, it was one of the greatest in the history of Parisian furniture, and its effects continued to be felt long after 1800.

Menuisiers and woodcarvers (figs. 41, 71) enjoyed a favorable climate for the evolution of their work. The Foliots worked for the court until about 1784, as did the Babels until about 1778; their new models were designed by Gondoin. As architect of the Medical School, Gondoin had already invented classical chairs that were executed by Delanois and have been identified by Eriksen. As designer to the king, he created the model for the armchairs for the Salon du Rocher (or Belvedere) at the Petit Trianon in 1782. The most outstanding *ornemanistes, menuisiers,* and woodcarvers were part of the queen's circle. Jacob and Sené will be dealt with here, but the clientele of *menuisiers* like Lelarge, Boulard, or Blanchard should be studied further. The architect Belanger worked for the comte d'Artois and so did the *menuisiers* Nadal and Georges Jacob. The latter certainly had the most brilliant clientele in Europe, with Marie-Antoinette heading the list. Sené was, however, the official royal *menuisier,* and with the assistance of woodcarvers like Hauré and Valois, he created for the queen in the last years of the ancien régime some of the most beautiful chairs of the Louis XVI era, covered with carved flowers. Jacob's work was subtly different from Sené's in that it was more stylishly neoclassical. His influence lasted longer because of the models he created, and because his descendants worked into the nineteenth century. It was Jacob who was asked to execute the mahogany chairs for the Laiterie (Dairy) of Rambouillet to the designs of Hubert Robert. The architect Le Queustre, a student of Soufflot, who designed astonishing Egyptian chairs for the town house of the president de Montholon on the Boulevard Poissoniere, entrusted their execution to Jacob, whose son revived some of the models in the Consulate period, presenting them as novelties inspired by the Egyptian campaign. The role of the *ornemaniste,* or decorator, grew more important day by day. To the list of names already cited, including Richard de Lalonde, the name of Dugourc must be added. This prolific and skilled designer, and the brother-in-law of the architect Belanger, was an avid partisan of neoclassicism. Dugourc's designs for furniture and interiors for the comte de Provence at Brunoy, for Madame Elisabeth at Montreuil, and for Charles III and Charles IV in the Madrid palaces, all prefigured the Empire style. He was appointed designer to the Royal Garde-Meuble during the period of the French Restoration, and was one of those who succeeded in continuing aspects of eighteenth-century style in nineteenth-century furniture.

Shapes and forms were predominantly, but not exclusively, rectilinear (fig. 62). Although the gracefully slender curves of the Louis XV style were abandoned, the desire for movement and lightness, though stemming from the same principles, constituted the essential difference between the Louis XVI and Empire styles. That is not to say that some of the massive Louis XVI armoires, square, octagonal, or basket-handle chair backs, or conscientious copies of classical furniture were not heavy, but sensitive proportions and moldings gave a refinement to most furniture. Whether or not they were made in Paris, there was an awkwardness to chair legs placed at oblique angles, as well as to legs where fluting of round or square section could not disguise their massiveness (fig. 70). Most chair legs of the period were elegant, however, round, slender, and carved with spiral or, more often, straight fluting. The refinement of the joining of the arms of a chair, the thin detached colonettes flanking the chair back, the rounding of the seat-rail, and the contour of the chair back demonstrated the greatest delicacy. The same concern with the curve can be seen in the crosier-form armrests tilted outwards on some of the best chairs by Séné and Jacob, or the convex seat backs that can be found on cherrywood chairs made by provincial or Parisian lathe turners as well as on more expensive chairs, or even the "Etruscan" legs of chairs dating between 1788 and 1790. After continuing for a dozen years using the Louis XV receding curved supports for the arms of their chairs and settees, *menuisiers* were brought up short by the change in women's fashions which included the disappearance of wide petticoats: the most innovative *menuisiers* on the eve of the Revolution decided to return the handrest to alignment with the front legs, supporting it with a colonette or a figure.

Classical antiquity was the prime source for decoration, but it was adapted with such grace that, with only a few exceptions, austerity and pedantry were avoided. Leaf tips, palmettes and acanthus leaves, Vitruvian scrolls, interlaced motifs, pilasters and rosettes, pearls, oves, gadroons, fluting, cornucopias, bundles of arms, quivers, capitals, trophies, lion heads and paws (fig. 64), eagles, chimeras, Egyptian women, genies, and classical terms comprised the principal decorative elements, but they were all mixed with fantasy: fantasy derived from the flourishing art of the upholsterer (fig. 51) (simulated draperies, festoons, dentilation, twisted ribbons, cockades, cords and motifs from basket weaving); fantasy in the choice of animals (like the dolphins or the Pekinese dogs decorating the arms of chairs made for the boudoir of the queen); fantasy from exotic sources (figs. 37, 142) (inspiring furniture whose decorative details or droll forms were intended to give it a Chinese or Turkish look); fantasy especially in the profusion of flowers (fig. 148) (carved realistically with exquisite sensitivity, embellishing furniture with flower-laden classical decorative schemes); fantasy even in the treatment of classical antiquity, which became in many cases no more than an inspiration handled with as much casual freedom as the *rocaille* had been. At that moment enthusiasm for classical antiquity was running high. The *menuisiers* were almost unique in their desire to maintain the eclecticism and freedom to which their attachment to the Louis XV style bears evidence. It was more than complacency on their part; in 1776 François Foliot II delivered a *bergère* with lathe-turned legs and classical ornaments, but two years later he made splendid chairs for Madame Adélaïde at Fontainebleau with the collaboration of the woodcarver Babel in which the classical elements combined with beautiful Louis XV contours in perfect harmony. Another manifestation of eclecticism was the acceptance by the *menuisiers* and their clients of the style popularized in England by Chippendale: soon after 1785 chairs and even beds were frequently executed in mahogany with pierced and carved backs.

Sobriety was also expressed in color schemes. Furniture was still gilded (fig. 52), and in some cases green gold was even combined with yellow or pink gold on the same chair, but white painted furniture was prevalent (fig. 53). The deliveries made by the painter and gilder Chatard to the Royal Garde-Meuble in 1786 are typical: only two or three ensembles were gilded, all the rest remaining white. Walnut and beech could be stained to resemble mahogany for certain chairs, but walnut, oak, and fruit woods were left in their natural color in the provinces, while ash was often painted for certain lathe-turned chairs, like the blue painted chairs delivered for the Crown in 1779. There were a few exceptional pieces painted vivid colors, like the furniture made by Foliot for the Cabinet des Coquillages (Shell Room) at Rambouillet, where the frames were fashioned as reeds and shells and painted in naturalistic colors, or the furniture of the Chambre due Treillage (Trellis Room) at the Trianon where wheat, flowers, and pine stand out vividly on a ground simulating basketry. Delicate color harmonies were, however, the rule, like the lilac and white of the large set of furniture made for the comte de Provence at Versailles.

Ebénistes and bronze makers (figs. 94, 103, 106) were marvelously productive during the rather brief span of the Louis XVI style. The influence of Marie-Antoinette and her entourage, the appetite of foreign courts, the expenditures of financiers like the *fermiers généraux* (tax collectors), the commissions from actresses and the wealthy bourgeoisie, the power of the decorators (some of whom have been mentioned in the discussion of *menuisiers*), and the prestige of the Parisian dealers, all followed in the same direction. Names that have remained famous, Leleu and Riesener among the *ébénistes,* both of whom were students of Oeben, and Gouthiere, Forestier, and Thomire among the bronze makers, were proponents of the style. The leader was Riesener, who had married Oeben's widow and settled in the Arsenal. He was a supplier of furniture to the court for a decade (1774–84). His successor was Benneman, and his competitors, Carlin, Saunier, Weisweiler, and Topino, were the *ébénistes* who worked primarily for the *marchands-merciers*. The influx of German *ébénistes* was greater than ever: Stockel, especially, seems to have had a more significant role than has been previously recognized; Roentgen, although he did not become as French as the others, played a part in the evolution of Parisian *ébénisterie*. The expenditures of the comte d'Artois, whose *ébéniste* was Teuné, of the comte de Provence, and of Marie-Antoinette especially on the furniture designed by Lalonde for the château of Saint-Cloud, accentuated the sumptuous elegance of the Louis XVI style.

Furniture was occasionally rather bulky (figs. 94, 99) with large forms on exaggeratedly slender supports (fig. 109), but the proportions of most examples were well balanced (figs. 101, 103, 113). The rectangle was the most popular shape, with a line of drawers at the frieze. Horizontality was emphasized by defining the block with a flat top, usually of marble, and a molding on the bottom. A slight recession on either side of a central projection modulated the form and prevented it from becoming simplistic.

Lacquer and polychrome wood marquetry continued to be used to depict rustic trophies or scenes with figures that became more complicated than ever with the influence of Roentgen. Networks of geometric or fretted marquetry were formed by small-scale sycamore lozenges sometimes bordered with fillets of contrasting wood (fig. 146). Rosettes, scrolls (fig. 94), flutes, and framing motifs in contrasting woods were still in use. *Ebénistes* of this period, however, increasingly favored mahogany (fig. 145), which was used in large sheets of veneer cut to show off a spotted, gnarled, or variegated figure, or flame or satinlike shimmer. Since a degree of austerity was not considered unpleasant, ebony was used more often than it had been in the Louis XV period (fig. 99).

What marquetry lost to simple veneering was gained back by bronze mounts. Never before had finely chased and magnificently gilded bronze mounts attained such sumptousness on luxury furniture. On some pieces fruits, and especially flowers in garlands, pendants, scrolling friezes, or bouquets covered all the structural lines. Mounts depicting draperies, cords, and tassels reflected the influence of upholsterers. Lion paws were often used on feet. As in the preceding period, frequent use was made of classical motifs, palmettes, leaftip moldings, Vitruvian scrolls, rosettes, symbols of love, etc. On many pieces, mahogany was enlivened by simple copper moldings. Solid bronze was used, sometimes with moldings, for simple ring capitals, turned feet, and handles, which again became mobile, and ring pulls, which were chased as laurel wreaths on the most costly pieces.

THE END OF THE CENTURY: THE DIRECTOIRE

It is debatable whether the Directoire (1795–99) should be counted among the styles of eighteenth-century France. It could be considered a period of transition between the termination of one society and the imminent regeneration of the Consulate. The fate of old furniture changed radically as large quantities entered the secondhand market or were used to decorate official buildings. At the same time there was a conscious effort not to abandon the principle of original creation; exhibitions brought these final products to public attention.

La Mésangère offered furniture based on the art of the eighteenth century in the illustrations he published in the year X (1801–2), but a few years earlier the architect Berthault designed interiors for Mme Récamier, which, while not devoid of grace, belong in the context of nineteenth-century decorative arts. The furniture created by the painter David from the time of the Revolution, both for himself and for Philippe-Egalité, as well as Percier and Fontaine's projects, published in prints by Krafft and Ransonette, introduced the more studied classicizing that would characterize the Empire style.

Furniture took on stripped-down forms and was drier and more austere, except for a few chairs that retained something of the earlier slender elegance. Mahogany was prevalent, as the use of marquetry declined, and flowers disappeared almost entirely from woodcarving and bronze mounts (figs. 95, 124).

The lines between *menuiserie* and *ébénisterie* became blurred, leading to a more generalized production. Some names from the past reappeared, but their work became increasingly denatured. The Jacob family achieved a position of overwhelming importance. A furniture industry replaced the artisanry of the eighteenth century.

24. Night table fitted with a bidet that pulls out from the side. Mahogany veneer and gilt bronze mounts, with traces of casters under the feet. An ingenious piece of furniture that G. De Bellaigue has noted occurring several times in Topino's accounts at prices ranging from 108 to 140 livres. Stamped by Topino. Circa 1775. (Waddesdon Manor, Bucks)

25. The traveling and bedroom chest of the comte d'Artois. Probably the one designed for the prince's bedroom at Bagatelle and referred to as his strongbox. The body of the piece is decorated with beautiful bronze mounts, some of which may have been altered under Charles X. It was originally covered with blue leather, not marquetry. Furnished by the dealer Delaroue for 1,578 livres. The stand was made by G. Jacob and J.-B. Rode for 42 and 140 livres for the *menuisierie* and carving, respectively, not counting the gilding. Formerly in the Demidoff collection, Pratolino, Florence. 1778. (Private collection)

26a-b. Folding table with eight legs, four of which slide out to support the two extensions. The use of mahogany underscores the Anglophile nature of this approximation of an English gate-leg table. Stamped by P. Garnier. Circa 1775. (Château de Bouges, Indre)

27. Secretary with drawers above the fall-front. A monumental piece of furniture with a matching armoire with two doors and four drawers. On short cabriole legs; marquetry of rosettes with radiating surrounds; and scrolling gilt bronze frieze on the superstructure. A secretary and commode, also signed by Carlin, but a little more Louis XVI in the form of the feet and the design of the marquetry, is in the Huntington Art Gallery, San Marino, Calif). Formerly in the Polès collection (sale, Ader, Galerie Charpentier, Nov. 17, 1936, no. 211, 210,000 f), and Meyer-Sassoon and Fitzgerald collections (sale, Christie's, London, Mar. 23, 1972, no. 89). Stamped by Carlin and Pafrat, the latter having finished or restored it. Circa 1775. (Private collection)

28a-b. Traveling desk. Solid mahogany carved with moldings, with two handles on the sides. The exterior of the fall-front is a mock drawer and bookshelf with the spines of books simulated in leather. The interior has compartments and drawers of different sizes, two of which are fitted for writing equipment and bottles. A leather-covered writing surface can be raised to reveal a mirror on the reverse. With the stamp and paper label of Teuné (fig. 171). Circa 1775. (Private collection) ↘

← 29. Traveling table. Carved oak. Legs that fold up and a top that opens out; with hinges, pulls, hooks, and feet of gilded copper. A piece of princely refinement. Circa 1720. (Musée des Arts Décoratifs, Paris)

← 30. Game table made to be dismantled. Mahogany. The top is covered with felt on one side and leather on the other and has a brass rim. It removes to reveal the board for backgammon inside. The four legs are removable and there is a handle on each side of the table. Stamped by Pafrat. Circa 1785. (Château de Bouges, Indre)

31. Serving table. Veneered in tulipwood with a marble top and metal compartments for cutlery and bottles, gilt bronze handles and feet and pierced galleries on the shelves. Inventory mark of the comte d'Artois at the Palais du Temple in Paris. Stamped by Teuné. Circa 1770. (Private collection)

32. Small *guéridon* with two candle arms. Veneered in tulipwood except for the tripod base, which is solid tulipwood. The top shelf is of Sèvres porcelain, the lower shelf has marquetry in scrolling pattern. Chased gilt bronze mounts and pierced galleries. Stamped by Carlin. Circa 1770. (Private collection)

33. Low mahogany screen. Adjustable counterweighted panels with gilt bronze handles and hinges. In 1771 Joubert delivered for Madame Adélaïde at Versailles a mahogany screen with similarly pierced panels *à la grec* but it was taller and had *papier de la Chine* panels and 224 gilt bronze rosettes. Stamped Canabas. Circa 1775. (Musée des Arts Décoratifs, Lyon)

34. Embroidery frame. Solid tulipwood with a tambour-top box on each side and gilt bronze accessories. Mid-eighteenth century. (Musée des Arts Décoratifs, Lyon)

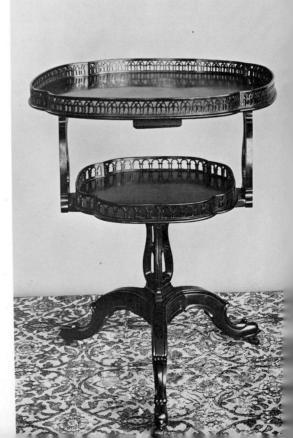

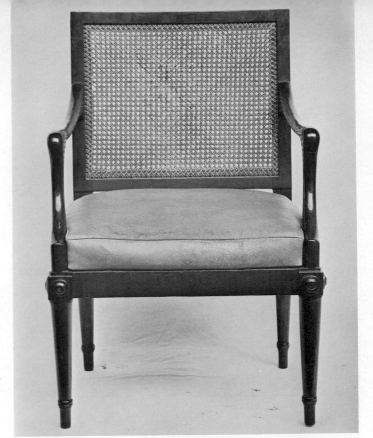

36. "English" armchair. Mahogany and caning. According to the correspondence published by S. Eriksen, the marquis de Marigny ordered from the *ébéniste* Garnier a set of thirty-six armchairs, at 72 livres each, for the dining room in his residence on the Place des Victoires, and this is probably one of them. Stamped by P. Garnier. Circa 1778. (Davezac sale, Champetier de Ribes, Paris, Mar. 15, 1974, no. 102, 15,500 f)

37. "Chinese" armchair. Exoticizing polychrome painted wood. Created for the Marquise de Marboeuf (see fig. 170) for her residence near the Chaillot gate and the Etoile hill where she had a room decorated by the architect Legrand in 1790. Stamped by the *menuisier* G. Jacob. Circa 1790. (The Bowes Museum, Barnard Castle, County Durham)

◄ 35. Two-tier work or tea table. The lower tier turns. Solid mahogany, with pierced mahogany galleries in the English manner. A tripod form used by Canabas and Carlin as well as English cabinetmakers. Stamped by J.-P. Letellier. Circa 1785. (Victoria and Albert Museum, London)

38. Console table. Wrought iron with repoussée and gilded tole. A fine example of the consoles constructed without visible wood for religious or civic use, which are especially numerous in Provence and in the Comtat and also occur in Paris. By Alexis Benoît, a locksmith in Avignon (according to information from G. de Loye). Circa 1725. (Musée Calvet, Avignon)

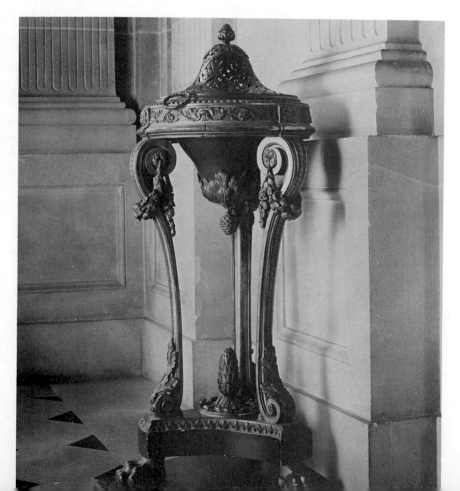

39. Neoclassical tripod, termed an *athénienne*. Carved wood, chased and gilded bronze, and pierced, patinated, and engraved ironwork. A variety of materials were used to create this fashionable little piece that was part of the neoclassical vogue and whose "inventor," according to a document published by Emile Dacier, proposed it be used as a perfume or incense burner, a dish warmer, a brazier, or a plant stand. Circa 1775. (Musée Nissim de Camondo, Paris)

PART TWO

Menuiserie Furniture

Chapter 5

MENUISERIE: THE TECHNIQUE OF MAKING SOLID-WOOD FURNITURE

INTERESTING DOCUMENTATION of the work of furniture *menuisiers* at the end of the reign of Louis XV was published both by the editors of the *Encyclopédie* and by Roubo, who was a carpenter himself. Roubo's volumes, like those of Diderot's encyclopedia, contain technical illustrations that by themselves are informative. Roubo did not hide his disapproval of the profession, accusing particularly the *menuisiers* specializing in large furniture of being stubborn and lazy, and, with few exceptions, of producing mediocre work. He reproached them with not knowing how to design and with letting themselves be exploited by dealers who had little concern for quality. This

hapter is partly based on Roubo's writings, and one should note at the start
hat his harsh criticism was published in 1772.

TOOLS

The *menuisier's* equipment was not extensive. It is reproduced in detail in
plates 7 and 8 under the heading "Menuiserie en Batiments," (Paneling), vol.
7 of the *Plates* of the encyclopedia (Paris, 1769) to which we refer here.

It was composed first of saws: ripsaws of all sizes for cutting lengthwise,
crosscut saws, tenon saws, hand saws, a peg saw, and a saw *à araser* for scrib-
ing tenons.

Then came the range of planes: trying and rabbet planes, and, for finishing, chisels, gouges, mortise chisels, files and rasps.

When a square, a compass, a mallet, a hammer, a bit brace, and a pot of
glue with its tripod were added, the inventory of the *menuisier's* tools was
complete.

The craftsman worked at a joiner's bench with holes in it for the shaft of
an iron clamp and two or three other projecting elements to hold the work in
place. The tools were arranged either on a lower shelf or on a rack attached
to the bench.

THE CHOICE OF WOODS

The *menuisiers* used indigenous woods exclusively. Only regional cus-
toms or added ornaments provided exceptions, which will be discussed later.
The use of mahogany by Parisian *menuisiers* specializing in chairs was quite
common by the end of the reign of Louis XVI. Previously, under Louis XV,
even if screens were made of solid amaranth and tables of solid mahogany,
they were still the work of *ébénistes* such as Gaudreaux, Migeon or Oeben.

Roubo (vol. 3, pt. 2, p. 603) corroborates what we can deduce from
surviving furniture about the use of woods. Beech and walnut were preferred.
Beech was unsuitable for large panels and was used primarily for chairs (fig.
43). Either light or dark walnut did not have to be painted or gilded like
beech. With its fine grain, it was attractive when polished and grew more so
with time, an effect well demonstrated by a number of armoires and chairs
(fig. 45). Roubo advised against the use of oak as it did not take polish well,
recommending that it be reserved for the backs, bottoms, and drawers of case
pieces. He conceded that some armoires were being made entirely of oak, but

stated that "these are only the ones used as wardrobes" and recommended that the wood be painted or gilded. His severity is somewhat surprising because there are eighteenth-century oak buffets (fig. 65) which may not have the luster of walnut pieces but which have taken on a warm patina that Roubo might have foreseen had he looked at medieval examples. Even in Paris certain *menuisiers* seem to have made a specialty of this wood, delivering commodes (fig. 66) and buffets with moldings and carvings made of oak with a clear finish in a style particular to the capital.

For structural reinforcement, particularly of legs, the bills of Parisian *menuisiers* indicate that they made use of *bois cormier*, or *cornier*, service wood, which, according to Valmont de Bomare, was "the hardest of all woods" indigenous to France.

Roubo pointed out the use in the provinces of fruit woods such as sorb and pearwood, which in fact were already used by Paris woodworkers in the eighteenth century along with oak. In this category cherrywood, as well as pearwood, quickly took on a beautiful golden glow.

Roubo was not interested in what went on in the provinces. A few studies that have been published on regional furniture allow us to list and generally identify the woods that were used most frequently in the different provinces: oak in Normandie, Brittany, the Basque region, Gascogne, Lorraine, Artois, and Picardie; walnut (figs. 71–74) in Provence, Dauphiné, Lorraine, the Basque region, Auvergne and Brittany. In Auvergne and Brittany chestnut was also used, which with time attained a dark red patina resembling mahogany. In addition to the numerous Parisian examples of the use of mahogany for chairs at the end of the Louis XVI regime, it was used early on for *ébénisterie* (fig. 77) in the principal western ports, Bordeaux, Nantes, and Saint-Malo. The use of cherrywood, or wild cherry, was widespread in the countryside, and these woods were often associated with panels of burled elm and ash (fig. 76) in at least two areas quite far removed from each other, the provinces of Burgundy and Bresse and the distant Vendée region. In some provinces local sources provided special woods to the *menuisiers*: olive wood in Provence; pine in Auvergne; red cedar, cyprus (fig. 8), and all the varieties of mahogany and various species of pine in the Antilles and in Louisiana, where mulberry was also available; and finally pine (fig. 75), cherrywood, yellow birch, soft walnut, and maple (or plaine, the Canadian equivalent). Ash was widely used in France by lathe turners for common seats (figs. 47, 48).

Whatever the species, the *menuisier* tried to use only wood that was sound and well dried. Under "Menuiserie" in vol. 10 of the *Encyclopédie* it is noted that "intelligent *menuisiers* who can afford the expense take care of picking [the wood] up at La Rapée or l'Hopital docks in Paris and storing their provision in their wood yard in piles, one piece on top of the other, interspersed with laths, so that air can circulate inside and moisture can evaporate easily." They left it to dry in this manner for five or six years. If they selected a wood that was too old they were liable to have wormholes (which, not being forgers, they did not want). For curved pieces, especially chairs, they selected wood that had no splits or knots, so that it would not give or break. The guilds devoted special care to their inspection of the quality of wood being used even in the provinces: Salverte found record of a *menuisier* from Tours, René Renault, who had twice served as a warden of the guild in his city but nonetheless had oak and walnut buffets and commodes confiscated because they were made of defective wood.

PREPARING THE WOOD

The plates of the *Encyclopédie* show, in the detail one expects of its illustrations, the work conducted in the wood yard and the workshop of the *menuisier* (see pl. 1 of "*Menuiserie* en Batimens" and pl. 1 of "*Menuiserie* en Meubles").

After the wood was purchased in the warehouses along the Seine indicated on Turgot's map of Paris, it was sawed lengthwise, and the boards thus obtained were piled up for drying. The *menuisier* drew what was needed for the workshop from this constantly replenished stock. On the workbench the wood was first sawed. Working with a saw was the essential skill of the furniture *menuisier,* who, according to Roubo, was competent in handling his numerous small saws but too negligent to then plane the wood.

It is possible that the author of the *Art du Menuisier* was too quick and general in his disparagement of colleagues that he felt to be inferior. The *Encyclopédie* seems to contradict him, because in the illustration cited above, one can see, beside the workers engaged in sawing, two others busy at their workbenches planing the wood, one using a rabbet plane and the second using a chisel.

Examination of surviving eighteenth-century furniture shows, however, that except for extraordinarily fine pieces, parts that did not show (such as the undersides of chairs and the backs of larger pieces) were not planed down (fig. 168); in many cases saw marks are still visible. Was this true of the parts that did show? Was the time-consuming labor of finishing a piece of furniture, imparting its smoothness and polish, not done before it left the hands of the *menuisier?* It is difficult to believe.

ASSEMBLAGE

The *menuisier* prepared the different parts of his piece of furniture according to type (some of the categories are reproduced in the *Encyclopédie*). Roubo reproached the *menuisiers* not only with infrequent updating of these categories but with being incapable of original creation. This complaint, while certainly unfounded in the cases of Tilliard, Sené, or Jacob, was generally quite legitimate; even in royal furniture we see first-rank *menuisiers* like Foliot using the same models for a period of fifteen or twenty years.

Once the different elements were fashioned, and, if necessary, decorated, the *menuisier* assembled them. That was the most important aspect of his work, where he continued, almost without changes, a centuries-old tradition.

The *menuisiers* making chairs, beds, and tables used the traditional mortise-and-tenon assembly almost exclusively (fig. 43). Two wooden pegs inserted in holes prepared in advance held and consolidated the assembly. The exact models of these pegs were specified in the *Encyclopédie* alongside each piece of furniture illustrated. They could be replaced by long iron screws for beds (fig. 51), especially alcove beds, which were often moved; and also for some wardrobes and billiard tables.

The *menuisiers* making large-scale furniture used techniques similar to those of *menuisiers* making paneling. Like their predecessors in the Middle Ages, they inserted panels in frameworks (fig. 65). One of their favorite techniques was tongue-and-groove assembly, which they used along with mortise-and-tenon and dovetailing, which was used for the drawers of *ébénisterie* and *menuiserie* furniture.

The solidity of assembly is one of the most remarkable characteristics of antique *menuiserie*. Even in simple but sound shapes, the frame, pegged without glue, was allowed play and could eventually be dismantled like a simple ingenious mechanism. One has only to examine these Louis XV or Louis XVI chairs, which have proved so durable despite their apparent slenderness of line, to see that the assembly of the legs gives them sturdy support. Elements of the seat-rail are sunk by mortise and tenon into the leg itself, which is surmounted by a large cube of wood and secured by two pegs on either side. Upholstery covered the upper pegs, leaving only the lower ones visible, and *menuisiers* from the Louis XV period on strove to make these less obvious.

DECORATION

Among the innumerable charges that Roubo leveled at the furniture *menuisiers* was "leaving the decoration of their work to the woodcarvers, who not only made the required ornaments but even executed moldings, the *menuisiers* doing no more than assembling and giving the general contour to their products." This reproach seems aimed more at *menuisiers* making large furniture than those specializing in chairs, but it could explain the number of pieces, especially armchairs, where moldings intersect unevenly. Nevertheless the records of the Royal Garde-Meuble, which admittedly reflect the very best *menuisiers* working in the period, do show *menuisiers* as having made and delivered chairs with moldings (fig. 56), a few unimportant Louis XV flowers, or a routine Louis XVI rosette. When the decoration became more significant, however, the *menuisiers* only executed the unfinished frames and then sent them on to a woodcarver.

Carved Ornament

The woodcarver could assist the *menuisier* in two ways. First, for unique original pieces, generally commissioned for a specific location, the *menuisier,* or often the architect, asked the woodcarver to execute a model either in wax or wood. Often this sketch was presented to the client for his ideas. We have examples of this in royal furniture, and three models published by Hector Lefuel, two in wax and one in wood, are cases in point. Like the *ornemanistes'* drawings and engravings, one side of the model was different from the other, presenting two possible options.

A woodcarver could also make a model in clay, sometimes even using a soft wood like lime for some of the details. The clay model would then have a plaster mold made from it, and from that mold a plaster model would be made, not only to judge the final effect, but also to serve as a guide to follow in the execution of the piece.

The woodcarver was called upon again for the finishing of most *menuiserie* furniture, as we have just cited Roubo, who claimed that in his day even moldings were done by the woodcarver. There is no doubt that furniture of any quality was finished by the woodcarver (fig. 40), the *menuisier* having fashioned the frame (called the *gros bois*) and assembled it. Even for furniture with what seems standard ornament (fig. 44), for chairs with insignificant decoration of Louis XV flowers or *rocailles,* or Louis XVI acanthus leaves, the participation of a woodcarver seems to have been the norm. Occasionally one comes across a mark on a chair other than the *menuisier's* stamp that could be interpreted as the woodcarver's mark. The records of the Royal Garde-Meuble give valuable information on this obscure point: some members of the Foliot dynasty were *menuisiers,* while others were woodcarvers; at the start of the reign of Louis XVI, Babel also decorated chairs by the Foliots, while Valois decorated those of both Boulard and Sené.

Plagiarism and imitation were accepted among these ornament sculptors, and some of their practices are surprising. In 1785 the frames of two X-stools of a model designed by Hauré were executed by Sené. The ornament on one stool was carved by Vinceneux for 66 livres, while the second, identical but cheaper, was done by Cherin for 30 livres. The cost of the gilding also went from 88 to 77 livres. What was true of royal furniture (and one could cite many other examples) was true elsewhere: Rode (figs. 25, 142) worked for Jacob at Bagatelle, and Rascalon (fig. 148) for Blanchard at Bellevue. Each *menuisier* seems to have had, not far from his establishment, woodcarvers he regularly patronized.

Roubo (p. 601 footnote) had nothing but contempt for the woodcarvers who assisted the *menuisiers,* finding them mediocre; he said they worked "by routine, tracing their sketches from patterns often without knowing how to do original designing." This remark could explain the banal, hasty, and endlessly repetitious character of the decoration of much furniture of the eighteenth century. But, on the other hand, what of those admirable works, which could only have been created by woodcarvers whose skill was matched by love of their profession (figs. 57–59)!

Painting and Gilding

After a piece of furniture had been assembled by the *menuisier,* it went on to the painter-gilder unless, as in many cases, the wood was to be left in its natural state (fig. 45). Then it was only waxed and polished by the *menuisier.* Roubo draws a distinction between two categories of furniture; ordinary furniture, such as armoires, and beech or walnut commodes, which could be polished with a mixture of two parts yellow wax to one part tallow, and "beautiful works," for which he specifies that "one must use a nice white wax, even though it is not the usual practice." Walnut was more often left in its natural state and simply waxed than was beech; however, the latter wood "carved with ornaments and varnished" is found in numerous caned chairs delivered by Tilliard between 1730 and 1736. Sometimes beech was given a walnut stain, as in the armchairs ordered by the Garde-Meuble in 1727 and 1728. We again encounter the division between *menuisiers* and *ébénistes* when we see that Sené made armchairs in mahogany—true, not run-of-the-mill

57

armchairs, but ones ordered for the library of Louis XVI at Versailles—but the *ébéniste* Benneman polished them.

When it came to painted furniture, the work was more or less complicated according to the extravagance of the piece. A single color could be used, blue, which was often used for furniture made of ash, or white, which was popular from around 1770 to the end of the century (figs. 44, 53). Two-tone color schemes (fig. 43) were more popular in the Louis XV than in the Louis XVI era. Moldings and grounds matched the color of the upholstery. In 1786 Chatard did chairs for Compiègne in gold and white, and we know how this formula was favored abroad in the Napoleonic era.

Polychrome varnish could raise *menuisierie* furniture to the level of importance of *ébénisterie* and lacquer. We have lost sight of its importance because too many examples have been stripped, gilded, or painted, destroying the vivid colors that were so much appreciated in the eighteenth century. Even those pieces that seem the best preserved have suffered with time. Flowers, fruits, and ornaments were rendered in their natural colors throughout the eighteenth century, but the practice reached a height around 1730–40 (fig. 14), when colors were even added to gold. The technique of polychrome varnish is described in the 1773–74 treatise *l'Art du Peintre Doreur Vernisseur* written by the painter-gilder Watin. He gives the formula of the varnish for chairs as a mixture of shellac, colophony, and sandrach (both resins) in alcohol and turpentine. The varnish was applied like lacquer in one or successive coats according to the quality of the chair to give a soft polish. It is likely that the Martin brothers and their Parisian predecessors, imitators, and competitors applied their Chinese-style lacquer and varnish to *menuiserie* furniture just as they did to *ébénisterie* and paneling, but we have no record of it. The popularity of varnish diminished under Louis XVI but did not completely die out. A rather recent discovery reveals that, on a piece of furniture executed for the comte de Provence at Versailles now belonging to the Louvre and Versailles, the lilac and white painting was done in watercolor and covered over with a light varnish to preserve its brilliance. Chatard employed the same method on chairs for Mme Thierry de Ville d'Avray in Paris which were "white picked out with pale lilac, after they have been painted white, smoothed, tooled and varnished." Chairs which were entirely white could be varnished and tooled as painstakingly as gilded chairs; on the other hand there were examples of pieces painted "in varnished white after having been tooled with slight care."

The gilder belonged to the same guild as the painter, although his technique required more expertise and was more costly. Beautiful gilding was a

Parisian specialty, and Watin, in the treatise just referred to, devoted considerable space to the different methods.

Oil gilding was rather unusual on furniture, at least in France. By this method the mixture to which gold was to adhere was spread on after several coats of lead white and ground yellow ochre in thick oil were applied, allowed to dry, and polished with pumice and horsetail reeds. Gold leaf was then laid on and varnished.

Distemper gilding, or gilding on a gesso base, was the prevalent method in the eighteenth century (figs. 40, 41). It peeled off easily, but it was favored because it allowed delicate tooling and beautiful effects in the contrast of burnished, mat, and shadowed areas: in Watin's words, "it lives and breathes." It was used by Bardou for the royal commissions of Louis XV, and by Cagny for Mme Du Barry (fig. 137). It was again the issue in 1786 when, following a competition between the gilders Guintrange, Houet, Dutems (fig. 148), and Chatard (figs. 140, 162), the Garde-Meuble experts expressed their preference for Chatard as follows: "His gilding is beautiful and carefully executed and the tooling is well done; the price of 116 livres 3 sols (for a folding stool) that he asks is a reasonable price." A great deal of attention was devoted to tooling, an area in which Parisian gilders demonstrated remarkable finesse and sensitivity. Of the seventeen steps that Watin described for this kind of gilding, tooling was the most important. After applying absinthe glue and preparing several layers of Bougival or Meudon white (gesso) by rubbing with hide and pumice, details of the decoration were brought out by recarving or chasing with a tooling iron. This work was so essential and so skillfully done by the gilder that soon the woodcarvers recognized that, if a chair was to be gilded, the details could be left to the gilder. In that light one can appreciate how wrong it is to strip the gilding from a beautiful chair and how deformed it becomes. Once the tooling was done, the piece was covered with a coat of reddish yellow liquid before the gold leaf was applied. Most often it was yellow gold, but it could also be green, if, for example, a contrast between the two tones was wanted. Finally, the gilder finished his work by burnishing with agate and matting according to the desired effect. The work involved in creating one of these beautiful gilded eighteenth-century pieces, which could withstand the rigors of time, can be seen in the bill submitted by Jacob for the armchairs he delivered to Saint-Cloud in 1787 for the salon des jeux (gaming room) (the chairs are now in various collections, among them the Louvre). The text of the bill is reproduced here because it explains the technical perfection that can be seen in the chairs today: "The frames . . . had been planed and treated with absinthe, then given twelve coats of gesso, pumiced and softened with water, all the ornament tooled and defined with the greatest care in order to make the most of the carving; then gilding was applied to the ground in every area with the finest and the strongest gold available; the parts that could be were burnished in accord with the carving in order to emphasize the relief of the flowers, the overall was finished with the greatest perfection."

Gilding *à la grecque,* (Greek, or in the neoclassical style), outlined by Watin is mentioned several times in the descriptions of chair frames in the inventory of Mme de Pompadour. The method seems to have been relatively popular over a period of twenty years and presumably can be seen on Transitional (Louis XV–Louis XVI) chairs, but with the restoration to which even the best-conserved pieces have been subject, it is difficult to identify. It seems the technique allowed greater differentiation between burnished and mat surfaces. Burnished areas, after sizing, received a preparatory coating comprised of red chalk, white lead, and talc, which had been reduced to powder through heat in order to grind it with glue and gesso; the tooling, the base coat, and the application of the gold followed the normal pattern. The mat areas, which had been reserved, received three or four coats of shellac, which were polished with horsetail reeds before mucilage and gold leaf were applied, as in the oil gilding technique; finally, alcohol and oil varnish were used. Watin, in describing this technique of gilding, underlined its advantages: it was washable and did not peel off; the mat areas were very beautiful; and since the preparatory coats were fewer, and less tooling was required, "Greek" gilding was more economical; on the other hand, the burnished areas were not as brilliant, and, most importantly, the fumes of the oxidation made the workers seriously ill, leading to the discontinuance of the method.

Silvering, which was more common in the first half of the century, had similar preparatory steps to gilding, and the silver was also laid on in leaves. The primary problem was tarnishing, which they attempted to retard with an alcohol varnish. On occasion a combination of gold and silver was used on the same piece, notably for Marie-Antoinette. The technique reached extreme refinement in the eighteenth century, which makes one regret all the more the fact that most surviving furniture has lost its original appearance. This is true of painting and gilding, and alas, even more so when it comes to upholstery.

Upholstery

The upholsterer, according to Roubo, was the principal vendor of *menuiserie* furniture; and his was almost always the final step in its fabrication.

The invaluable little volume by Bimont, master upholsterer and dealer in Paris, which appeared in at least two editions (1770 and 1774), provides information on the fabrics, the arrangement of beds, chairs, and curtains, the measurements, and the prices of various items. In it we see something we are barely aware of today, the concern that was shown in the eighteenth century with this indispensable finishing of the piece of furniture. A piece with its tapestry covering untouched (figs. 135, 163) gives us a singular impression of harmony, a balance between mass and void, and between wood and textile. Pieces covered in silk (figs. 40, 41), with a very few exceptions, have been reupholstered, and it is rare to be able to reconstruct the original coverings with accuracy.

It was on coverings for *menuisierie* furniture, however, that the eighteenth-century upholsterer poured out his talents. Recorded in dessicated sheaves of old bills and little known today, the role of great upholsterers to the Crown, must be stressed as much as that of the *menuisiers:* during the reign of Louis XVI, Lallié, Sallior, Le Queustre, and especially Capin exerted an influence on the art of furniture that has been overlooked. The more importance the furniture frames and their carving took on, the more the upholsterers worked at emphasizing and equaling them in the disposition of fabric and trimmings. In collaboration with ornament designers and silk weavers, they sought the ideal scale to suit each different part of the chair, the back, the borders, and the arms. Surviving examples, especially those in needlepoint on canvas (fig. 53), provide a pleasant surprise in the care that was taken in the arrangement of motifs and in the composition of borders. The ladies who executed these embroideries were assisted by specialized merchants.

Every grand residence had a valet employed to take care of upholstery, making minor repairs and changing the upholstery for summer and winter. Seasonal changing of seat covers spurred the *menuisiers* and upholsterers to create chairs whose coverings were easily removable and interchangeable. Having slip seats and backs and armrest pads with stops and bolts made it possible to have various coverings on a single frame (figs. 43, 135).

The upholsterer figured importantly as a trimmer. His basic materials were: webbing (fig. 168), nails, horsehair, down, and linen. He used a wide range of textiles for chair coverings and bed hangings: silks, velvets, calicoes and printed cottons, imberline (heavy satin), tapestry, velvet, Savonnerie carpet, etc., also embroideries, and, for beds and dressing tables, all kinds of muslin. Leather was often used on chairs. The color could be varied by piping; for example, lemon yellow leather could have red piping. There was also embroidered leather; and some silk cushions were covered first in leather to prevent the feathers leaking out.

The practice arose of supplying easychairs with "handkerchiefs" to serve as head rests. The dauphine Marie-Josèphe de Saxe had taffeta handkerchiefs put on the backs of the chairs in her drawing room at Versailles in 1766; and Biver noted the concern with this trifle shown by Mesdames (the daughters of Louis XV) on the eve of the Revolution. Under Louis XVI the role of the upholsterer extended still further; draperies and flounces were added below the seat-rail and on the backs of luxury chairs, and even around the aprons of certain tables. All through the century the reverse of chairbacks was covered with silk or linen of a color chosen to harmonize with the fronts.

The upholsterer went to the *passementier* (lacemaker) for all trimmings. Some trimmings served to hide seams, while others were absolutely necessary: braid, tufts, piping, and nails. Heights of luxury were achieved under Louis XVI in the area of pure decoration; cord, tassels, rosettes, ribbons, etc. In 1781 Marie-Antoinette ordered "*cartisane* [strips of paper wrapped in silk, used for stiffened trimmings] in two different lengths imitating the carving of the chairs, in pearls and almonds, of Paris gold thread" from the lacemaker Saporito, for her Salon du Rocher (or Belvedere) at the Trianon. Today it is difficult to imagine the extravagance required of upholsterers by their clients in what appears to us to be superfluous detail. The loss of these embellishments considerably modifies the architecture of a piece of furniture. When one does find them today—as in the furniture for the boudoir of Marie-Antoinette at Versailles, formerly in the Berlin museum, which has lost only the tassels on the cushions; the blue and white furniture in the Rijksmuseum; or the chairs made for the duc de Penthièvre which are in the Metropolitan Museum (fig. 41)—one is surprised by the perfection and harmony that these small ornaments bring to the furniture.

The upholsterer generally delivered slipcovers, which could be of matching color and quite sumptuous, along with his furniture.

The upholsterer was sometimes associated with a feather merchant, who not only supplied but installed plumes for the canopy of a bed or dais, and maintained them. These panaches consisted of bunches of ostrich feathers with an aigrette at the center. They are known to us through engravings, and their use was not restricted to the court.

It was rare indeed that a chair escaped the upholsterer. Even for caned chairs, the upholsterer supplied loose cushions (fig. 138). The *menuisier* could execute the caning on this type of chair himself (fig. 42) and Salverte found records of the strife between the *menuisiers* who wanted to legitimize the practice and the basketweavers who claimed exclusive privilege. Pragmatism led the *menuisiers* to turn to specialists in caning, who were, according to Roubo, "attached to the *menuisier* who keeps them busy all year long."

There remains one essential contributor among all the professions accessory to the making of furniture, the blacksmith. The screws and wheels of beds, the ironwork of columns and canopies, the hinges and screws for the assembly of armoires, buffets, and commodes, the axes of folding stools, the rollers and frames for swivel chairs used at the dressing table (fig. 159) or desk, and the ratchets for reclining chairs are just a few of the fittings *menuisiers* needed from blacksmiths.

Today we find the collaboration of so many different professions in the making of a single chair or bed, and the mutual interdependence of these professions, surprising. The condition in which surviving pieces come down to us gives little indication of the successive labors that went into them. Careless amateurs in a hurry, or decorators looking for an easy solution, believe it sufficient to cover a chair in old fabric to restore its original character. The cutting and placement of the fabric, the role of the trimmings, the color of the wood, and the harmony between the wood and the fabric that was sought in the eighteenth century too often escape modern understanding. One should note the important role of technique in both form and color before passing judgment on the furniture of a bygone era. If the technical manuals of the eighteenth century were better known to amateurs, restorers, and experts, they would certainly lead to greater prudence and veracity in the treatment and handling of antique furniture.

CHAPTER 6

The Principal Types of Furniture

So many difficulties are encountered in even the most summary attempt to classify the types of furniture used in the eighteenth century that rigid divisions cannot be established. It is possible, however, to divide *menuiserie* into six broad categories: chairs, beds, and screens; tables; chests and commodes; armoires; clocks; *guéridons* and mirrors.

CHAIRS, BEDS, AND SCREENS

Seats without backs include: *tabourets* (fig. 11), four-legged stools, with or without stretchers, which were popular all through the century; *pliants,* folding stools of **X** form with an iron bar, which was sometimes decorated, providing the axis, found in only those eighteenth-century apartments where the most formal etiquette was observed; a rigid version of the **X** stool, still called a *pliant* even though it did not fold, became popular at the end of the century thanks to the influence of classical antiquity; *banquettes,* benches usually with eight legs, which could have stretchers between them for added strength.

Since most seats had backs, the term *chaise à dos* (chair with a back) used to designate chairs without any other distinguishing features, was abandoned after the Régence period. The form of the chair back served as a criterion by which side chairs and *fauteuils* (armchairs) could be separated into two general groups: *à la Reine* (figs. 43, 150) designated a flat chair back, but this qualifier was often dropped; *en cabriolet* (fig. 44) indicated a rounded back, on which the so-called basket or basket-handle crest rail occurred more frequently. Chairs of either type were identified by their placement in a room as *sièges meublants,* which formed part of the architectural scheme (fig. 5), or *sièges courants,* which were comfortable and informal in character (fig. 69).

If the format was larger, the chair was called a *confident* or *tête-à-tête,* in modern parlance, a *marquise.* This was really little more than a very big *bergère,* a chair having enclosed and upholstered sides and a loose seat cushion (some side chairs and armchairs reserved for ladies also had a loose cushion). The *fauteuil de commodité* was what we would call a wing chair. The *fauteuil de malade* (invalid's chair) was a wing chair with a back that could be lowered to a reclining position by iron ratchets and a seat that could be fitted as a toilet. There were numerous intermediary forms between the *fauteuil* and the *bergère,* ranging from the *fauteuil en demi-bergère,* and *demi tête-à-tête,* to the *fauteuil en confessional* with a high embracing back (some twenty examples of the last were listed in the inventory of Mme de Pompadour). If the crest rail scrolled over on a Louis XVI *bergère,* the chair was dubbed "Turkish." In 1787 Marie-Antoinette commissioned for her cabinet at Versailles *"une bergère en cabriolet en confessional avec des joues"* (a high rounded-back wing chair) that is now in a private collection. The term *chaise longue* indicated an extension of a chair to allow the occupant to stretch out his or her legs. In the eighteenth century this was usually referred to as a *duchesse,* or if the leg rest was separate from the chair, a *duchesse brisée* (fig. 55). The *tabouret de pied* (footstool) can also be mentioned here (fig. 67). If it had a back and raised sides and resembled a smaller version of the end of a *chaise longue,* it could be termed *en chancelière.*

What we now call a desk chair (figs. 143 and 144) had a wrap-around back and usually a leg at the center front supporting a projecting front seat rail. This shape was sometimes called *en bidet,* but toward 1780 it became known as *gondole*. The dressing-table chair had a revolving seat and a low back sometimes with an extra dip to it (fig. 159). If a chair had a seat that was higher than usual it might have been one of those rare chairs reserved for the king's use in the private apartments he frequented. If the back was low it could have been a harpsichord chair. If it had a footrest it could have been a choir stool; with or without a back such stools, which were placed in the chancel of a church, could be very beautiful. Not to be confused with ecclesiastical furniture, the *voyeuse* (fig. 46) was a chair intended for gaming, with its back padded at the top to form an elbow rest. It came in side chair, armchair, and *bergère* format. Today these are dubbed smoking chairs, gambling chairs, or *prie-Dieu* (prayer stools). The man's *voyeuse* had a seat of normal height on which a spectator sat astride. A *voyeuse à genoux* had a low seat on which the spectator knelt. Of course there was the true *prie-Dieu,* which often had an open back. Roubo illustrated a church seat of X form where the position of the back could be reversed to form either an armchair or a prayer stool, a model that was more functional than it was elegant. Bidets had backs of cane or leather where the crest rail formed the lid of a sectioned compartment. Like the *chaise percée* (toilet) (fig. 68), which was usually supplied with armrests, the bidet also came in the form of a stool. The bowls for both were of faience (tin-glazed earthenware) or pewter. The exteriors of some toilets were made of Morocco leather to look like large folios.

Any chair could be constructed in an *encoignure* (corner) format. The inventory of Mme de Pompadour lists several including a settee, a bench, a long bench seating five, and two small armchairs. In 1785 Marie-Antoinette had a *sultane* of *encoignure* form made by Hauré and Sené for Saint-Cloud.

The shape of the back provided a means of differentiating types of settees and beds. Eighteenth-century authors warn us of the inconsistencies in the language covering this subject because of fashion and the imagination of dealers. Nonetheless it seems that the term *canapé* (fig. 47) signified a piece of furniture with a back, armrests, and sometimes wings, in essence an enlarged armchair or *bergère,* ranging in length between 39 and 78 inches. There were variants like the *canapé à billard* with a high seat and a footrest, and the *canapé à confidents* (figs. 147, 148) with a corner seat at each end. If the form comprised two upholstered sides or a continuous embracing back, the *canapé* became a daybed and took on exotic names: *ottomane* (fig. 56), where the form was an elongated oval; *turquoise,* which had a clearly differentiated back and sides; *sultane,* which, under Louis XVI at least, had no back and only sides; *paphose,* whose name alone suggests its romantic character; and *veilleuse* (fig. 56), where one side was higher than the other (Roubo indicated these were generally used in pairs positioned symmetrically on either side of a chimney-piece). The sofa, sometimes identical to the *canapé,* was commonly uphol-stered with no wood left visible. It usually stood in a mirrored niche. In Provence, expecially in Marseille, it was termed a *divan à la turque* (Turkish divan) and covered with oriental carpets and many cushions. It could become so long that it required masonry support. Most settees were part of the archi-tecture of a room: usually placed under a mirror opposite a chimneypiece, they followed the design of the wall paneling. The more bizarre and compli-cated the back of a settee may appear to us, the more certain we may be that the explanation lies in the surroundings for which it was designed.

Beds can be divided into two overall categories: on one hand the *lit à la française* (French bed); and on the other, all the rest that were given the names of foreign nationalities. A French bed had a headboard that was placed against the wall and a rectangular canopy of the same dimensions as the mattress frame. The most prevalent type of French bed was the traditional *lit à colonnes* (four-poster bed) (fig. 54), which was always popular in the provinces (fig. 49) and colonies. Around 1700 small, better heated rooms allowed the intro-duction into fashionable interiors of the *lit à la duchesse* (see Marie-Antoinette's bed at Fontainebleau) with a canopy that had supports at the head of the bed and attachments to the wall or ceiling, leaving the foot of the bed unencum-bered. Other beds had two or three enclosed sides and were often placed in niches or alcoves with the long side attached to the wall. The term *lit à la polonaise* (Polish bed) (fig. 51), frequently used in the eighteenth century, de-scribed such beds when the uprights that supported the canopy consisted of curved iron bars hidden by curtains. Contrary to current belief, the type of bed that had curved scrolling ends without any visible columns was termed, according to Roubo, *lit à la turque* (Turkish bed). It should be noted, however, that Louis XVI's bed at Saint-Cloud, which had straight ends, was listed in a pre-Revolutionary inventory as a *lit à la turque.* The type of bed that was placed obliquely and had an independent canopy attached to the wall from behind was authoritatively designated by Roubo as a *lit à l'italienne* (Italian bed), but termed by various ornament designers *chaire à prêcher* (preacher's chair) or *à la romaine* (Roman), and also known as *à la d'Artois.* The principal varieties of these beds were illustrated in the plates published by Lalonde on the eve of the Revolution.

The daybed (figs. 50 and 52) usually had a headboard and resembled a small-scale French bed without canopy or curtains. As discussed above, it could be little more than another variety of settee.

As for cradles, Parisian examples usually had sides covered with fabric, while in the provinces they were simply wood, carved, engraved, or painted. Roubo illustrated a model of cradle where the lines of the rockers were as elegant as those of contemporary sleds.

Fire screens (figs. 57–59) were made to match the rest of a set of seat furniture. The supports took the form of two skids, with rare exceptions like the pivoting or tripod screen of classical or English inspiration. An upholstered panel was generally mounted in a frame; it slid between the channels of the uprights on either side and was raised or lowered by means of a cord and counterweights. Folding screens (figs. 33 and 163) might be constructed of several similarly framed panels if they were low, but usually the wooden framework was covered over with fabric or paper.

Over the course of the eighteenth century the various items described above became increasingly interrelated. The term *un meuble* (figs. 54 and 135) came into use meaning an ensemble comprising chairs, fire screen, folding screen, and bed, unified by similar carved ornament and color coordination between wood and upholstery, and even with the same fabric used to cover the walls.

TABLES

The bases of tables (figs. 2, 63, and 64), often executed with the collaboration of skilled woodcarvers, ranked among the most highly prized products of eighteenth-century *menuisiers*. The form of these supports was rectangular under Louis XIV, often *en console* during the Régence and Louis XV period (figs. 60 and 61), and again rectangular or semicircular under Louis XVI (fig. 62). The table tops were made of marble, stone, granite, slate, or stucco. The tradition of sumptuousness in these beautiful gilded bases, originating in the Louis XIV era, continued in the customary decoration of the *noix,* a virtuoso motif at the center of the base in the form of a perfume burner, bouquet or vase of flowers, a trophy symbolic of military might, music or love, demons, or *rocailles* (curvilinear rococo motifs). Except in the smallest examples, stretchers forming an X between the legs continued to be required for structural reinforcement in the lower section of the piece. The bases of tables, which were meant to attach to the wall rather than being free-standing, must almost always have been made by the *menuisiers en batiments,* who specialized in paneling. It is only in exceptional cases that one finds the stamp of a furniture *menuisier,* like Chollot under Louis XV, or Georges or Henri Jacob, Rabaudin, or a few others under Louis XVI, on such pieces.

Dining tables could be *menuiserie*. They could be extendable (Roubo documents several models, but none appear to have survived). If they were intended for the country or to be used by servants, the workmanship could be so crude that it was little more than basic carpentry.

Menuisiers made economy versions in solid walnut, cherry, or pearwood of most of the pieces created in veneered woods by *ébénistes:* writing tables and desks, bed or bedside tables, dressing tables, gaming tables, secretaries, sliding-top, cylinder, and slant-top desks (which can be found in all the provinces), lecterns, serving tables, etc.

CHESTS AND COMMODES

Chests, trunks, and storage boxes with domed lids have a long history. They were manufactured mainly by box makers. In Paris both utilitarian and luxury chests were made, some with wood veneers, some covered in tooled leather with gilt bronze mounts. They were supplied with carved and gilded wood stands. *Coffres de toilette* like those that belonged to Juan V of Portugal and the comte d'Artois (fig. 25) were probably of the most lavish type, intended for the bedroom rather than the closet.

Chests continued to be made and often, as in the case of marriage chests, decorated with great care in the provinces of Normandy, Alsace, Burgundy, Lorraine, Brittany, and the Basque region. Simple pine cases or hutches were brought to the capital on rafts by peddlers from Auvergne and the Bourbonnais. These products were stamped on arrival by wardens of the guild of *menuisiers-ébénistes*. Thus it would not be too surprising to encounter the Paris mark on a crudely made box, totally lacking in style. On the other hand it seems likely that Parisian *menuisiers* made kneading troughs, less extravagant than those made in Provence, but of excellent construction. The number of granaries with their projecting pulleys, on top of the old *hôtels* (town houses) of Paris supports this supposition.

In Burgundy, especially in the region around Mâcon, kneading troughs assumed the commode form, with a top that could be raised and simulated drawers (for instance the so-called *patière* of the Tournus hospice). The enormous popularity of the commode as a piece of *ébénsterie* furniture in the early years of the eighteenth century led to innumerable replicas and variations in *menuiserie* (figs. 66, 71, and 77). No matter which French town these were made in, they almost always corresponded to the commode form known as *à la Régence,* having three equally large drawers, one above the other. The tops were usually made of wood. I firmly believe that a closer study of the *menu-*

iserie commodes of the eighteenth century, which have been rather too quickly dismissed as "rustic," will reveal that a number of them bear the stamps of Parisian *menuisiers*.

At the end of the eighteenth century another type of commode was frequently executed in *menuiserie:* this was the Louis XVI commode having two large drawers below a narrow frieze drawer. Instead of the usual mahogany, the *menuisiers* made it of walnut which they could give a mahogany stain.

ARMOIRES

An armoire could be made by either a *menuisier* specializing in paneling or one specializing in furniture (figs. 73 and 74). Roubo concentrated on this essential piece of furniture, showing us how functional considerations led the *menuisiers* to equip armoires with sliding shelves fitted with handles or with rods to hold clothes hangers.

The buffet (fig. 75) was closely related to the armoire. It was called a *bas d'armoire* or *bas de buffet* (figs. 65 and 72) if it did not have a superstructure above the stone or marble top. Roubo noted how *menuisiers,* at least in Paris, made the doors open in two stages by means of a second set of hinges mounted on pilasters. The doors could be completely opened up, which was usual at mealtime when, Roubo said, "they always remain open, more, however, for ostentation than by necessity." The buffet, continuing the medieval tradition of the dresser, served not only for the arrangement but for the display of dishes. In the countryside it can be seen in the primitive and rudimentary dish rack, and in some provinces the open cupboard (fig. 76). Roubo specified that if poor folk had to be content with small buffets serving for the storage of food, having doors fitted with wire mesh and lacking pilasters, the middle class used buffets to decorate dining rooms even when they owned no dishes of great value to display on the wood or marble shelves. We have already taken note of the unusual system by which the doors opened. Roubo also described notches and grooves for the upright mounting of the dishes that were so much the object of the bourgeois pride, and the visible or interior drawers where the silver place settings were arranged. Such vanity extended to provincial furniture. Buffets could be with or without dish racks, a superstructure having sliding doors as in Provence or small decorative doors on the sides of the dish rack as in Burgundy and Bresse. They would have a narrow drawer above each of their doors (which were rarely limited to two) as in the Vendée, Brittany, Burgundy, Bresse, and the Basque region, or drawers below the doors as in Alsace. In the large buffets of Lorraine, Picardy, and Artois, the drawers were located in the midsection of the piece, one above the other. Iron sliding bolts and wood stops were used instead of locks in Canada and Louisiana for simple buffets with doors, with or without a superstructure.

Finally, in conjunction with this type of furniture one should consider the bread box, which could take the form of a cabinet or a set of shelves; the salt box and the flour bin, which in Provence could be incorporated with the kneading trough in a piece of furniture that would occupy a place of honor; and the *encoignure* of triangular format to fit in a corner, which in Paris could be treated as a low cabinet, with or without a superstructure of shelves, or in Provence constructed in two parts, one atop the other, and termed a *cantoniero*.

CLOCKS

People who lived in the country, especially at the very end of the century, became as proud of their *menuiserie* clocks as the princes a few decades earlier had been of the costly and complicated clocks decked out in veneers and bronze mounts.

Tall clock cases were made everywhere, of rectilinear or "violin" shape, with an oculus in the middle of a long door on the front through which the pendulum could be seen. At the top the clockworks, which could themselves be fairly primitive, were contained in a housing of wood and glass.

A clock was incorporated in the center of a buffet or dresser in some regions such as Bresse and sometimes Lorraine; it could be at one end of a large buffet in Picardy.

GUERIDONS AND MIRRORS

The pier table with a mirror above and two *guéridons* (candlestands) on either side formed an integrated ensemble of carved and gilded wood fashionable in the Louis XIV era. The elements became dissociated in the course of the eighteenth century and the custom disappeared.

The base of the table became a console and is included in our discussion of tables.

Only in a few palaces could one still find the tall, richly carved *guéridon* serving as a candlestand. The low *guéridon,* or circular table, could have a simple turned-wood base and remain the product of a *menuisier,* but more often it was transformed by the talents of *ébénistes* and dealers.

The mirror (fig. 10), on the contrary, with a wood frame that was carved and often gilded, and having a pediment that was more or less exuberant, enjoyed uninterrupted popularity. It was the pride of the home, from the most modest to the most luxurious where the hanging mirror was to be found along with pier glasses. The numerous examples stretching from the Régence to the Louis XVI period and the innumerable twentieth-century imitations attest to the volume of production.

Chapter 7

SOME DISTINCTIVE CHARACTERISTICS

I T IS NOT EASY to sort out valid distinctions between the various workshops active at the same time, particularly in Paris. We have already discussed the conservatism, closed-mindedness, and family orientation of the *menuisiers:* these characteristics made them more faithful to their traditions than were members of other professions. Their evolution came about by virtue of the pressure of trends that were already widespread in other branches of the decorative arts by the time the *menuisiers* decided to follow. Once they adopted new formulas, *menuisiers* clung to them.

By the same token there seems to be uniformity within each period. The eye does not pick up the nuances of differences between two Louis XV *fauteuils-cabriolets* from two different workshops or between two Louis XVI armchairs with moldings that may have come from regions of France far distant from one another. *Menuisiers,* however, employed patterns that were not exactly the same in each workshop. A meticulous study accompanied by precise measurements should permit us to reconstruct some of them. Cross-checking these with the stamps on pieces of furniture, we should be able to identify workshops despite their similarities. For now, only occasional characteristic details are evident. Some stronger personalities, some bolder and more inventive *menuisiers,* generally those working for the court, were able to leave their signature in certain specific accents not present in the work of their colleagues.

A separate category will be established for furniture classified as "rustic Parisian." There appear to have been *menuisiers* who made it their specialty. They cannot be called second-rate masters because their furniture is robust, with good moldings, and sometimes embellished with carving. Their names are included among the masters registered with the guild and their stamp is sometimes found on furniture together with that of the Paris guild wardens. They were especially devoted to a tradition that was not without a certain grandeur. They remained obscure, almost peasants in the heart of Paris. For want of a more intensive study of the subject, an alphabetical list will have to suffice, drawn from the names stamped on buffets, armoires, and commodes that must be classed with Paris furniture: Boulogne, Duval, Franc, Laurent, Mouzard, Saddon, Thuillier (figs. 65, 66).

In the provinces, strong local traditions resulted in easily definable characteristics. Luxury more pronounced in one place than another, certain furniture types, relative proximity to stylistic developments in Paris, and the use of certain woods characterize the products of different regions. The boundaries may be vague, but regionalism is a valid principle of grouping.

THE PRINCIPAL PARISIAN WORKSHOPS

Jean-Baptiste Tilliard (figs. 44, 57) as supplier to the Royal Garde-Meuble during the first half of the reign of Louis XV must have figured importantly in the adoption of the Louis XV style by Parisian *menuisiers* specializing in chairs. He was in his fifties in 1737–39 when he made the frames for the most novel furniture at Versailles, destined for the queen's apartments and the bedroom and cabinet of Louis XV. These frames were all carved by Roumier and gilded or silvered by Bardou. It is difficult to determine Tilliard's exact role because we cannot establish his chronology: his masterworks date before the use of the signature stamp, and his son, Jean-Baptiste II, almost always signed with his father's stamp. The Louis XVI pieces and works in the Transitional style between Louis XV and Louis XVI, *à la grecque* (neoclassical), certainly postdate the death of the father in 1766 and must be attributed to the son, who seems to have been more a follower than a leader. On pieces that could date between 1743 and 1766, one sees a tendency to give emphasis to the ends of the crest rail with an ornament or a slight dip, and a predilection for a sort of pleated palmette at the top of the legs. This form of decoration, with optional flowers, was not exclusive to Tilliard, but it is found frequently in his work.

The Foliots (figs. 40, 152, 157, 161, 164) played an analogous role with son succeeding father over forty years in the service of the Royal Garde-Meuble: Nicolas (d. 1745 or 1746), then his two sons, Nicolas-Quinibert (d. 1776) and François I (d. 1761), and finally François Foliot II, who was probably the son of the last and worked for the court until 1785. The works of Nicolas-Quinibert and François I were among the most ample expressions of the Louis XV style, and this characteristic continued in some of the furniture made by François II under Louis XVI; an elongated curve in the crest rail and a noticeable undulation in the lower edge of the chair back, as well as shoots flanking the triangle at the top of the leg, were typical of their style. Two furniture ornament carvers, notable Toussaint Foliot and François III (who moved to Toulouse) were part of this family which the royal archives and the recent research of Svend Eriksen have allowed us to become better acquainted with.

Nicolas Heurtaut (figs. 46, 147), who also belonged to a family of *menuisiers* and woodcarvers, has been overlooked until now. His stamp is found only on chairs of the highest quality, occasionally of somewhat heavy but ample form, of such luxuriant *rocailles* and flowers that we may presume that he worked for the most important figures of the second half of the reign of Louis XV.

Louis Delanois (figs. 43, 58, 137) influenced the transition between Louis XV and Louis XVI in the same way that the *menuisiers* discussed above influenced the Louis XV style. He is the subject of a serious monograph by Svend Eriksen. He worked for Mme Du Barry, the prince de Condé, and wealthy patrons both French and foreign, but not for the king. Around 1765 the designs of his chairs were sometimes ample, at other times graceful, with the standard decoration of little flowers, or with heart-shaped cartouches at the center of the seat and crest rails, and a sort of Y at the top of the legs, offering the main element of originality. Around 1770 he was drawn into the neoclassical movement and he tried several chairs loaded with garlands and pendants, but with the same cartouches on the crest rail. Then for Mme Du Barry, who paid him considerable sums in 1770 and 1771, he made chairs whose frames were already Louis XVI in style: they had circular seats, straight, tapering legs that abutted the line of the seat-rail, and large-scale chair backs of almost medallion shape with the slight bulge at the bottom that we have noted in the work of Foliot and was later adopted for certain models by Boulard and Sené.

The Gourdin brothers (fig. 158) worked along the same lines as Delanois, without evolving as far or achieving the same renown. The son of a *menuisier* specializing in chairs, Jean-Baptiste became a master in 1748, and Michel, the younger brother, became a master four years later. At first both made fine Louis XV chairs with flowers and *rocailles;* then, between 1770 and 1775, they began to make beautifully designed pieces of relatively large scale with console-shaped Louis XVI armrests and well-defined seat-rails. The legs, which terminate in volutes, seem Louis XV if one overlooks their acanthus-leaf ornaments, shallow curve, and the rectilinear blocks above them. This attempt to transform Louis XV lines without totally abandoning them is found on a number of their armchairs, and it seems unique to the Gourdins.

The Nadals (fig. 141), Jean Nadal and his two sons, Jean-René, who signed himself J. Nadal *l'aîné* (the elder), and Jean-Michel, called *le jeune* (the younger), who died in 1800 and seems to have worked all his life in the rue de Cléry, were typical Parisian *menuisiers,* moving from the Louis XV to the Louis XVI style with an assured elegance that allowed for a degree of daring. One could even wonder if some of the models created by Jean-René Nadal, who worked for the comte d'Artois at the Temple, were not copied by Georges Jacob.

Georges Jacob (figs. 25, 37, 41, 52, 56, 124, 142, 159, 169, 170) quickly surpassed the artisans listed above in audacity and notoriety. Although he became a master in 1765, very few Louis XV chairs by him are known, because he seems to have abandoned this style almost immediately in search of novelty. There are a certain number of armchairs bearing his stamp, however, which are *en cabriolet* with a coved back: their console legs, which terminate in top-shaped feet, support a separately defined seat-rail bracketed by arm-rests of reverse console shape. (One of these chairs has colonettes, demonstrating that Jacob continued to use the model at a later date.) Most of these pieces have a rosette on the triangular area where the arm joins the chair back, and a rosette on the block on the seat-rail above the leg. This block was to become standard at the intersection of leg and rail on chairs and beds for the following quarter century: Jacob would decorate it with a sun or gadrooned rosette and Sené would give it an elegant concave contour. The device may be credited as the invention of Georges Jacob or Delanois, who appears to have been his teacher. Spurred by his imagination and clientele, Jacob developed a variety of innovative forms and decorations which others were to adopt. Around 1780, perhaps even earlier, he began to carve out the interior underside of the seat-rail to lessen the weight of the chair without diminishing its sturdiness. With the exception of Sené, very few other *menuisiers* went to such lengths, and by passing one's hand underneath a chair, one can often identify the work of one of these two masters from this detail. Georges Jacob was one of the first in France to use mahogany for chairs. After trying to position fluted rear legs obliquely for increased stability, probably at the same time as Sené, he adopted the saber leg *à l'étrusque* (in the Etruscan manner), perhaps under the influence of Hubert Robert. The scrolling consoles, the carved foliate mounds, or ball finials at the top of the stiles often found in his work are devices he can be credited with inventing. Jacob's production was immense, even setting aside works that are of doubtful attribution or falsely stamped. It ranged from the simplest to the most elaborate and even fantastic, and, besides chairs, included screens and beds, tables and consoles which show equal imagination. Jacob was so often copied and imitated, even in his own time, that it is difficult to do him justice, and by the same token, to define accurately the originality in his style.

Jean-Baptiste-Claude Sené (figs. 139, 162) was overshadowed during his lifetime, and in the view of posterity, by the fame of Georges Jacob. The heirs and the firm of Jacob continued to be famous through the first half of the nineteenth century. Jacob's name was synonymous with the beautiful Louis XVI chair: furthermore, he had the good fortune to have had as clients the queen, the comte d'Artois and the comte de Provence. But Sené was a supplier to the king and his châteaus, and new furniture was commissioned for them through the eve of the Revolution. It is time to reattribute to Sené some of the most beautiful Louis XVI furniture, which has long been given to Jacob (and where some authors have even thought they could decipher Jacob's signature). Unlike Jacob, who came from Burgundy, Sené was part of a family of Parisian *menuisiers* with all it represented in terms of the traditions of the profession. He only became a master in 1769 and the four years between his entry into the profession and that of Jacob meant that he never went through a Louis XV period. He may well have been influenced by his famous rival as his mahogany pieces with grille backs or lyre backs, for example, tend to indicate. At least once, for Madame Elisabeth at Montreuil in 1790, he was asked to copy Jacob's chairs, and he may have done the same for Marie-Antoinette at the Tuileries in the following year. Sené's simple pieces, by virtue of their breadth of line especially in the seats and chair backs, figure among the purest examples of the Louis XVI style: they have both finesse and majesty. In his sumptuous pieces, where a crest ornament of a trophy, figure, or monogram often surmounts the chair back, one sees certain features characteristic of his work: detached colonettes on either side of the chair back and an extra ornament making a graceful transition between the handrest and its support.

Jean-Baptiste Boulard (fig. 140) was a supplier to the Garde-Meuble under Louis XVI, but after 1785 he sank to secondary status in relation of Sené. Sometimes they each executed and signed different pieces for a single ensemble. In such cases, which of them should receive credit for the elegance of the proportions and the vigor of the moldings? Boulard was active under Louis XV, and the pleated palmette that we have noted as typical of Tilliard was also found on chairs that bear Boulard's stamp or that of Georges Jacob.

Jean-Baptiste Lelarge III (fig. 51), son and grandson of Parisian *menuisiers* of the same first and last names, became a master in 1775 and worked through the Directoire period. A number of his chairs have medallion backs surmounted by a bow or mound of ornament and two awkwardly curved members connecting the chair back and seat-rail. Associating these with the reputation he enjoyed for chairs that were termed *à la d'Artois,* one tends to think he made a specialty of such armchairs, but there are also rectilinear chairs with moldings by him. Some of them are identical to chairs stamped by G. Jacob, or J. B. Sené, or obscure *menuisiers* like Lenain.

The Blanchards (figs. 67, 148), the father and his two sons, exemplify the evolution of Parisian *menuisiers* of the eighteenth century. They were firmly established in the rue de Cléry from the start of the reign of Louis XV until the Revolution. The last, Jean-Nicolas Blanchard, counted Mesdames (the daughters of Louis XV) and their nephew the comte d'Artois among his clients. The Blanchards' works ranged from serious to charming, from Louis XV to Louis XVI.

I must reiterate how premature and risky it would be to make positive assertions or hasty generalizations in this area, although they might appear sound until contradicted by new information. Caution must remain the rule for a long time to come in the attribution of examples of *menuiserie.*

PROVINCIAL CHARACTERISTICS

Similar uncertainty surrounds the authorship of provincial furniture for different reasons. With only rare exceptions, the furniture makers did not stamp their products (fig. 70). Even dating is difficult to establish: a study by

Suzanne Tardieu has been devoted to furniture bearing date inscriptions. It must be admitted that documentation pertains more to nineteenth- and twentieth-century, rather than eighteenth-century regional furniture. There are still more problems in identifying the region from which a piece comes: sometimes the problem is just to separate pieces that were made in Paris from those that were not.

Pierre Nogaret is the best known of all the provincial *menuisiers:* even during his lifetime his fame spread beyond the region around Lyons where he worked. He belonged to a family of *menuisiers* and woodcarvers. François Canot, whose signature has been found on a number of chairs, was his father-in-law, and both were born in Paris. Furniture bearing Nogaret's stamp consists almost exclusively of chairs in the rococo style, similar in form and decoration to what was being done in Paris in the middle of the eighteenth century, except that Nogaret's carving may have been slightly richer than that of his Parisian colleagues. The consistent use of walnut with a wax finish that has taken on a splendid patina with time is characteristic of his work. Nogaret was the outstanding representative of the Lyons school. His successors, Carpantier, Geny (fig. 69), Parmantier, Lapierre, and still others for whom no stamped furniture is known, also specialized in chairs, and the authors Audin and Vial, Claude Dalbanne, Monique Ray, and Bernard Deloche have provided information on them. The entire valley of the Rhône was influenced by Paris through the intermediary of Lyons. Salverte believed that the taste of Lyons could be seen in the chairs by the *menuisier* and *ébéniste* Pillot, who worked at Nîmes at the end of the reign of Louis XVI.

It is said that the divisions between the professions of *menuisier, ébéniste,* and woodcarver were less clearly drawn in the provinces than in Paris. The consuls' desk dated 1738 in the Palace of the Popes at Avignon and a slant-top secretary in the museum of Lille that appears to bear the hallmark of the town and the date 1769 are both solid walnut with a few marquetry embellishments. Should they be considered works of pure *menuiserie?* Often decorative details of fruitwood inlays (figs. 73, 74), and sometimes large panels of burled wood (fig. 76), as in Burgundy and the Vendée, were incorporated in regional furniture, but it cannot be called *ébénisterie.* The confusion is even greater in some port cities where mahogany was used as a *menuiserie* wood from the middle of the eighteenth century (fig. 77). Finally the carving was usually done by the *menuisier* himself, and, for example, one cannot be certain whether the whist table made of carved walnut and signed M. Froidevaux in the Strasbourg museum is the work of a woodcarver or a *menuisier* by that name.

Each region had its preferred woods which imposed their requirements and their color. Fruitwoods were used almost universally in the countryside, but less in the cities. The degree of influence exerted by Paris varied according to whether a town or a region was in close contact with the capital and whether it was a sizable city or a country village. If the time lag behind Paris grew larger, it was almost always accompanied by increasingly marked regional, if not archaic, characteristics. Court furniture, city furniture, and country furniture, were probably the three principal levels of *menuiserie,* with infinite nuances among them. The travels of *menuisiers* and woodcarvers to this or that center, as well as the degree to which certain clients wanted to imitate what they believed to be a higher class, created considerable variations within the same region.

With these stated reservations, one can, even without going into the different species of wood employed, distinguish some broad regional currents whose character appears sufficiently pronounced.

Vigorous, emphatic moldings dominated other carved decoration in certain provinces: Artois, Picardy, Lorraine (fig. 73), Auvergne, and the Vendée.

In most regions of France carved ornaments, executed in low relief, were of only moderate importance in relation to the decorative role of moldings. These carved motifs of baskets of flowers, rosettes, cockades, and pleated motifs which, although altered, were probably of Parisian origin, could be found in identical versions in areas far distant from each other. We can cite Gascony, Burgundy, and Bresse (fig. 76) as well as the Basque country (fig. 72), where the carving was incised, almost engraved; Brittany, where it could be accompanied by spindles or copper nails; and the areas around Rennes and Vannes, where the crudeness could develop toward elegance or exuberance.

The carving was rich and the ornament abundant, with skillfully accentuated relief, depicting flowers, *rocailles,* and occasional elements of Louis XVI style in at least two provinces, Normandy and Provence (fig. 71).

The extreme simplicity of colonial furniture (figs. 8, 75) is hardly surprising, given what we know of its manufacture. There is, however, often compensating beauty provided by the woods used.

One must keep in mind two of the preceding statements: the Louis XV style largely dominated regional *menuiserie;* and a good portion of the furniture coming from provincial workshops that is eighteenth century in appearance actually dates from the nineteenth century, but the source for both its techniques and decoration lies in the eighteenth century (fig. 74).

40. *Bergère.* Carved and gilded wood. Part of a set of furniture that belonged to the duc de Penthièvre, comprising two *bergères* and six side chairs, with the original embroideries of flowers and vignettes from the *Fables de La Fontaine* (reappliquéed on a modern ground). The set has been identified in the 1794 inventory of Chanteloup by G. De Bellaigue. This *bergère* bears the château marks of Chanteloup and Sceaux. The stamp of N. Q. Foliot is on five of the side chairs in the set. Circa 1745. (Waddesdon Manor, Bucks)

41. Side chair. Carved and gilded wood. Part of a set made for the duc de Penthièvre for the *Chambre du Balustre* at the Hôtel de Toulouse (today the Banque de France). This is one of two side chairs and there are two matching armchairs still covered with the original embroidered silk. The set was probably transferred to the Elysée in 1793 and kept by the financier Ouvrard. It was returned to the duchesse d'Orléans, daughter of the duc de Penthièvre, and is listed in an early Louis-Philippe-period inventory of the château of Bizy (near Vernon, Eure). It then passed by marriage into the Saxe-Cobourg family and was purchased by Duveen. Stamped by G. Jacob. Circa 1785. (Kress collection, Metropolitan Museum of Art, New York)

42a-b. Caned armchair with carved and varnished frame. A chair of this type, with moldings and a few carved motifs, neither painted nor upholstered, was created entirely within the *menuisier's* shop, caning included. On the back, the wood strips that served to anchor the caning can be seen. Four armchairs from the same set remain together bearing the numbers of their original order (1, 5, 11, 13). They were probably dining room chairs. Stamped by Deshêtres. Circa 1750. (Château de Bouges, Indre)

43a-b. Armchair (one of a pair) with a large flat back, termed *à la reine* or *meublant*. Carved wood painted dark and light blue. Slip seat and back allowing for seasonal change of upholstery. The bolts by which the armpads are attached to the frame are clearly visible.

c-d. An elegant design with emphatic moldings conforming to the shape of the arm supports and the crest rail. Carvings of small flowers and light rococo motifs with a scalloped framing of the upholstery panels of the seat and back in imitation of trimming braid. Stamped by Delanois. Circa 1765. (Château de Bouges, Indre)

44a-b. Armchair with curved back, termed *en cabriolet* or *courant*. Carved wood painted white. A light chair, both comfortable and fashionable. The shape of this chair (one of a set of four) is still Louis XV, but the decoration already hints of the neoclassical movement: cartouches, laurel garlands, acanthus leaves replacing *rocailles,* and no flowers. Stamped by Tilliard. Circa 1765. (Musée Gérard, Bayeux)

45. Armchair termed *meublant*.
Natural carved wood. Part of a set
comprising eight armchairs and
one settee. Covered in needlepoint. From the château of Juil-
lenay, Côte d'Or. Stamped by
Louis Cresson. Circa 1750. (Mi-
ron gift, 1959, Musée des Beaux-
Arts, Dijon)

46. Gaming chair, termed *voyeuse*. Natural wood carved with
moldings. A narrow seat to be
straddled in the reverse sense
while leaning on the armrest at the
top of the back; elegant front legs
but sharply canted rear legs for
stability. Stamped by Heurtaut.
Circa 1755. (Musée Gallé-Juillet,
Creil)

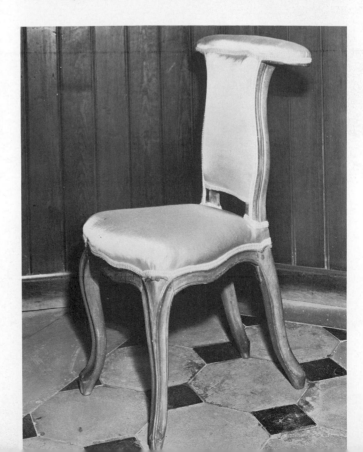

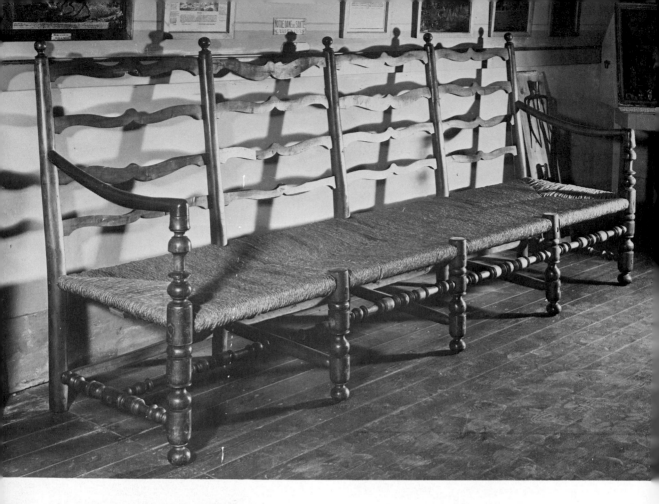

47. Settee. Turned wood with a straw seat. Extremely long (2.92m, or 9 ft., 7 in.), it takes the form of four chairs with four separate chair backs. Part of the furniture of Mgr. d'Inguimbert, bishop of Carpentras (1735–1757), who was as learned as he was charitable. Mid-eighteenth century. (Musée Duplessis, Carpentras)

49. Four-poster bed. Carved and waxed wood. A form passed down from the Middle Ages. Turned posts. Louis XV decoration in low relief with an attractive contour emphasized by moldings at the base. Dated: 1837. (Musée Lorrain, Nancy) →

50. Daybed. Carved and gilded wood. The ends decorated on both sides and carved with the lozenge emblem of the Rohan family. It appears to come from a hunting pavilion of the Rohan cardinals in Alsace. Circa 1720. (Gros-Hirschler gift, Musée des Arts Décoratifs, Paris) →

48a-b. Jean-Jacques Rousseau's chair. Turned wood with a straw seat. Part of the writer's furnishings in Switzerland. Purchased by the princess Isabel Czartoryska, who had the casing in which it has since been enshrined made for it around 1800, probably in Warsaw. Mid-eighteenth century. (Czartoryski Museum, Krakow)

53. Chair *en cabriolet*. Wood, →
carved with moldings and painted
white. Oval coved back. The original gros point embroidery covering demonstrates the importance
of the upholsterer: the border
bands emphasize both the frame
and the fabric. Part of a set of six
similar chairs with their numbers
written under the seat-rails (see
fig. 168). Stamped by Othon.
Circa 1780. (Château de Bouges,
Indre)

51. Bed termed *à la polonaise*.
Carved wood painted white. The
canopy is smaller than the bed
rails and is connected by wood
and iron uprights. Bows imitating
pleated ribbon are carved on the
ends of the bed, the rails, and the
crown. From a château in the So-
logne area. Stamped by Lelarge.
Circa 1780. (Château de Bouges,
Indre)

52. Alcove bed. Carved and
gilded wood. Enclosed on three
sides. Finely carved decoration of
guilloche and rosette bands, flowers, leaves, wreathes, ribbons, and
torches. The uprights are carved
in the form of quivers. Stamped
by G. Jacob. Circa 1785. (Victoria
and Albert Museum, London)

Chapter 8

LIST OF *MENUISIERS*

ONLY *menuisiers* who are of real interest in the study of French eighteenth-century furniture today figure in this listing. Those who specialized in frames or "borders" for pictures (some of whom adopted the practice of stamping their names on the back) are not included; nor, in general, are most of those whose names do not correspond to any work that it has been possible to identify. The names of woodcarvers, some of whom have been mentioned in the text and are known to us through archival documents rather than by a stamp, are not included here.

The *menuisiers* listed below belonged to the Paris guild unless otherwise indicated. The year in which each became a master (*m.*) is taken from the

54. Four-poster bed with no visible wood. The printed fabric probably manufactured by Wetter in Orange. The skirt panels that went to the floor on the sides are missing. It seems to have been in the same second floor bedroom at Montgeoffroy since 1775, when it was inventoried there: "233. Hangings of Horange fabric in latticework pattern. Four-poster bed with its coverlet and skirt in the same. 5 *à la reine* armchairs with beautiful lattice-work fabric." Circa 1771. (Château de Montgeoffroy, Maine-et-Loire)

guild records or more often from the "Register for the recording of certificates of mastery for the City and Suburbs of Paris." These two sources, which are complimentary but not always in exact agreement on dates, also served as the source for the publications of Molinier, Vial, and Salverte. There is a certain empiricism here, as in everything that concerns the eighteenth-century Parisian trades. I have decided that it would be superfluous to include the month and day in the dating. In some cases birth and death dates (drawn mainly from Salverte and Vial) precede the date of entry into the guild.

When the *menuisier's* stamp (*st.*) is reproduced in the next chapter, its number there is given here.

Achard, Pierre (end 18th c.), in Grenoble (?), *st.* 128

Aguette, H., c. 1780, *st.* 106

Amand, Henri, *m.* 1749

Annest, Crépin-Claude, *m.* 1756

Aubert, Charles-François, *m.* 1768, *st.* 147

Aubert, François, *m.* 1749, see *st.* 147

Audry, Jacques (1743–1784), *m.* 1777, *st.* 79

Avisse, Guillaume (b. 1720), *m.* 1743, *st.* 137

Avisse, Jean (1723–after 1796), *m.* 1745, *st.* 70

Avisse, Michel, c. 1740

Bara, Charles-Vincent, *m.* 1754, *st.* 117

Bara, Pierre, *m.* 1758, *st.* 130

Barnon, Jean-Baptiste, *m.* c. 1727, *st.* 126

Baron, Gilles, *m.* 1751

Baudin, Noël (1719–c. 1784), *m.* 1763, *st.* 21 (see also *st.* 115)

Bauve, de (or Debauve), Mathieu (d. c. 1786), *m.* 1754, *st.* 124

Bazin, Denis (1st half 18th c.)

Bazin, Jean-Denis (mid-18th c.), *st.* 47

Belanger, Antoine (d. 1776)

Belanger, Antoine, II, *m.* 1773

Bellangé, Pierre-Antoine (1758–1827), *m.* 1788, *st.* 113

Bergez, Clément (d. 1780), *m.* 1720, *st.* 150(?)

Bernard, Pierre (c. 1730–1788), *m.* 1766, *sts.* 26 and 155

Bertet, Joseph, *m.* 1788

Bessierre, c. 1800, *st.* 143

Bizet, Michel-Philippe, *m.* 1741, *st.* 48

Blanchard, Jean-Nicolas, called the younger (b. c. 1730), *m.* 1771, *st.* 83

Blanchard, Nicolas, *père, m.* 1738

Blanchard, Sylvain-Nicolas (b. 1725), *m.* 1743, *st.* 84

Blanchon, P.-J. (?), c. 1780

Bondat, Georges, *m.* 1743

Bonnemain, Antoine, *m.* 1753, *st.* 42

Boucault, Jean (c. 1705–1786) *m.* 1728, *st.* 72

Boucault, Guillaume, *m.* 1766, *st.* 6

Boulard, Jean-Baptiste (c. 1725–1789), *m.* 1755, *sts.* 50 and 97

Boulard, Michel-Jacques, c. 1800

Boulogne (Boulongne), Jean-Baptiste, *m.* 1758

Boulogne (Boulongne), Jean-Charles, *m.* 1768

Bouvier, Guillaume-Eutrope (d. 1784), *m.* 1733

Bovo (?) (mid-18th c.), *st.* 125

Bremant, Etienne (d. before 1774)

Bremant, Etienne-Crépin, *m.* 1765

Bremant, Etienne-François, *m.* 1785

Breton, Valentin-Noël, *m.* 1787

Briois, Jean-Claude (d. 1782), *m.* 1766, *st.* 61

Brion, Pierre, c. 1800, *st.* 110

Brizard, Pierre (1737–1804), *m.* 1772, *st.* 82

Brizard, Sulpice (c. 1735–after 1798), *m.* 1762, *st.* 27

Brocsolle, Jacques (d. 1763), *m.* 1743, *st.* 86

Brocsolle, Louis, *m.* 1755

Burgat, Claude-Louis (1717–before 1782), *m.* 1744, *st.* 49

Cagnard, Claude-Antoine (c. 1715–after 1798)

Caillois, Jacques-Antoine, *m.* 1748, *st.* 1
Caillois, Jacques-Nicolas, *m.* 1760, *st.* 2
Caillois, Simon, *m.* 1769
Camus, Barthélemy (1737–1803), *m.* 1774
Canot, François (1721–1786), in Lyons, *st.* 157
Carpantier, Sébastien (1733–1813), in Lyons, *st.* 85
Carpentier, Louis-Charles (d. c. 1787), *m.* 1752, *st.* 121
Catherinet, Jean-Baptiste (1738–c. 1795), *m.* 1776
Caumont, Jean (1736–after 1800), *m.* 1774, *st.* 23
Cercueil, Joseph, *m.* 1787
Chantereau, Jean-Charles (b. 1735), *m.* 1772
Chardon, Barthélemy-Denis, *m.* 1764, *st.* 52
Charles, Claude, *m.* 1738
Charpentier, Paul-P. (mid-18th c.)
Chaumont, Bertrand-Alexis (1741–after 1790), *m.* 1767, *st.* 7
Cheneaux, Jacques (d. c. 1782), *m.* 1756, *st.* 112
Chenevat, Jacques, *m.* 1763, *st.* 111
Chevigny, Claude, *m.* 1768, *st.* 41
Chollot, Edme (c. 1695–after 1774), *m.* 1723, *st.* 88
Corbisier, Pierre-François-Joseph (1737–1809), *m.* 1768
Courtois, Jacques-Marin, *m.* 1743, *sts.* 66, 159, 161
Courtois, Nicolas-Simon (1724–after 1789), *m.* 1766, *st.* 102
Craisson, Louis, *m.* 1772
Cressent, c. 1800, *st.* 142
Cresson, Jean-Baptiste (d. 1780), *st.* 138
Cresson, Louis, I (1706–1761), *m.* 1738, *st.* 32
Cresson, Louis, II, *m.* 1772
Cresson, Michel (1709–after 1773), *m.* 1740, *sts.* 19 and 136
Cresson, René, called the elder (c. 1705–before 1749), *m.* 1738, *st.* 92
Crouen (Grün), Jacques (1735–1797), *m.* 1765
Cudot, Louis-Médéric, *m.* 1773

Decant, Denis, *m.* 1764, *st.* 75
Delaisement, Nicolas-Denis, *m.* 1776, *st.* 69

Delanois, Louis (1731–1792), *m.* 1761, *st.* 39
Delaporte, Antoine-Nicolas, *m.* 1762, *st.* 45
Delaporte, Martin (d. 1756), *sts.* 90 and 152 (?)
Delaporte, Martin-Nicolas, *m.* 1765
Delaunay, Jean (d. 1778), *st.* 38
Delenoncourt, Charles, *m.* 1752, *st.* 44
Delenoncourt, Joseph, *m.* 1764
Delettre, Jean-Jacques, *m.* 1782
Delion, Claude (d. 1759), *m.* 1757
Delion, Jean, *père* (2d quarter 18th c.), *st.* 145
Delion, Louis-Hyacinthe (1721–1793), *m.* 1766
Dellenooz, Lambert (d. 1754), *m.* 1737
Demay, Jean-Baptiste-Bernard (1759–1848), *m.* 1784, *sts.* 62 and 162
Deplaye, Pierre-Edme, *m.* 1786
Deseine, Claude (1726–1796), *m.* 1754, *st.* 4
Deshayes, Louis, *m.* 1756, *st.* 146
Deshêtres, Jacques, *m.* 1747, *st.* 100
Destrumel, Guillaume-Antoine (2d quarter 18th c.)
Destrumel, Jacques-Philippe (mid-18th c.)
Dieudonné, Charles (mid-18th c.)
Dieudonné, Claude (1739–c. 1780), *m.* 1765, *st.* 89
Dieudonné, Etienne, I (2d quarter 18th c.)
Dieudonné, Etienne, II, *m.* 1740, *st.* 76
Dieudonné, Etienne, III, *m.* 1768
Drouilly, Claude-François, *m.* 1748
Dubois, Adrien, *m.* 1741
Dufour, Louis, *m.* 1764
Dulin, Antoine, *m.* 1763
Dulin, Louis, *m.* 1761
Dupain, Adrien-Pierre, *m.* 1772, *st.* 156
Dupont, Jean-Pierre, *m.* 1769, *st.* 51
Dupré, Jean-Auguste (b. 1707), *m.* 1743, *st.* 118
Duval, Nicolas, *m.* 1743, *st.* 158

Epaulard, Etienne (1736–1803), *m.* 1772, *st.* 5
Evrard, Charles-François, *m.* 1752, *st.* 53

Falconet, Louis, *m.* 1743, *st.* 67
Falconet, Pierre (1st half 18th c.)
Ferré, c. 1728

Fligny, Jacques, *m.* 1764
Foliot, François, called the younger (d. 1761), *m.* 1749, *st.* 107
Foliot, François-Toussaint, called François II (b. 1748), *m.* 1773, see *st.* 107
Foliot, Nicolas (d. 1745)
Foliot, Nicolas-Quinibert (1706–1776), *st.* 116
Fonbonne, François, *m.* 1762, *st.* 24
Forget, Pierre (1723–1789), *m.* 1755, *st.* 14
Franc, François (1722–1799), *m.* 1756, *st.* 129
Francastel, Jean-Baptiste (1725–1758), *m.* 1743
Francastel, Jean-Baptiste-Antoine, called the elder (1749–1787)
Froideveau, René (1727–1802), in Strasbourg
Fromageau, Jean-Baptiste, *m.* 1755, *st.* 46

Gaillard, Antoine, *m.* 1781, *st.* 33
Gascoin, Vincent, *m.* 1753
Gauthier, François (1st half 18th c.)
Gauthier (Gautier), Jacques-Alexis (d. 1767), *m.* 1748
Gauthier (Gautier), Jean (d. 1785), *m.* 1754
Gautron, Marc, *m.* 1785, *st.* 31
Gautruche, Jean-Pierre (1744–after 1792), *m.* 1772
Gautruche, Pierre, *m.* 1743
Gautruche, Pierre-Claude, *m.* 1771
Gay, Jacques, *m.* 1779, *st.* 123
Geny, François-Noël (1731–1804), *m.* in Lyons 1773, *st.* 80
Gérard, Ponce, *m.* 1778
Gérardin, Jean-Baptiste (mid-18th c.)
Gerboud, Claude (1736–1800), *m.* in Lyons 1765, *st.* 160
Germain, Denis, *m.* 1774
Gillier, Pierre, *m.* 1749, *st.* 132
Girard, François, *m.* in Lyons 1741, *st.* 65
Girardot, Jean, *m.* 1738
Girardot, Jean-Baptiste, *m.* 1776
Giroux, Jacques (1736–1801), *m.* 1766
Gorgu, Claude, *m.* 1770, *st.* 18
Götz, Martin (1745–1802), *m.* 1784
Gourdin, Jean (mid-18th c.), *st.* 141
Gourdin, Jean-Baptiste, *m.* 1748, *st.* 71
Gourdin, Michel, called the younger, *m.* 1752, *st.* 20
Grivet, Benoît (1737–1792), *m.* 1774

Héron, Charles, *m.* 1725
Héroux (early 18th c.)
Heurtaut, Nicolas (1720–1771?), *m.* 1755, *st.* 30

Jacob,. called Desmalter, François-Honoré-Georges (1770–1841), *st.* 163 (from 1796 to 1803)
Jacob, Georges (1739–1814), *m.* 1765, *sts.* 16 and 149
Jacob, Georges, II (1768–1803), see *st.* 163
Jacob, Henri (1753–1824), *m.* 1779, *st.* 17
Jacquet, E. (end 18th c.)
Jean, Paul-François,. *m.* 1784, *st.* 8
Jean, Simon, *m.* 1787
Jullien, Martin, *m.* 1777
Jullienne, Denis, *m.* 1775, *st.* 37

Kohl, Pierre-Nicolas-Joseph (1743–1798), *m.* 1779

Labry, François, *m.* 1777
Langlois, Pierre-Eloi (1738–1805), *m.* 1774, *st.* 58
Langon, Jean-François-Marcoul, *m.* 1769, *st.* 3
Lapierre, François (1753–1823), *m.* in Lyons 1784, *st.* 93
Laroque, Pierre, *m.* 1766, *st.* 36
Laurent, Jean (1706–1766)
Laver, Christophe, *m.* 1788
Lebas, Barthélemy, *m.* 1771
Lebas, Jean-Baptiste (1729–after 1795), *m.* 1756, *st.* 13
Lebas, Jean-Jacques (1750–1795), *m.* 1772
Lechartier, Jacques (1754–1809), *m.* 1773, *st.* 40
Leclerc, Claude, *m.* 1785, *st.* 34
Leduc, Pierre (c. 1685–1765)
Leduc, Pierre (1721–1792), *m.* 1778
Lefèvre, Louis-Michel, *m.* 1749, *st.* 57
Lelarge, Jean-Baptiste, I (1st half 18th c.)
Lelarge, Jean-Baptiste, II (1711–1771), *m.* 1738, *st.* 119
Lelarge, Jean-Baptiste, III (1743–1802), *m.* 1775, see *st.* 119
Lelibon (Le Lisbon), Pierre (early 18th c.)
Lenain (?) (late 18th c.), *st.* 64
Lerat, Claude, *m.* 1785, *st.* 12
Lerouge, Jean-Baptiste, *m.* 1749, *st.* 139
Leroy, Félix, *m.* 1749, *st.* 135

Leroy, Louis (mid-18th c.)
Leroy, Louis-Gabriel (b. 1730), *m.* 1754
Lerpsher, c. 1800, *st.* 68
Letellier, Jacques-Pierre, *m.* 1747, *st.* 99
Lexcellent, Nicolas, *m.* 1764, *st.* 43
Lheureux, Denis, *m.* 1748
L 'Hoste, Jean-Mathieu, *m.* 1757
Louis, Jean-Pierre, *m.* 1787, *st.* 144
Lozeray (late 18th c.)

Maclard, Jean-Baptiste (d. 1778), *m.* 1765
Mahé, Jacques-Jean, *m.* 1786
Maillet, Etienne, *m.* 1784
Malot, Jacques, *m.* 1748
Malteste, Sylvain, *m.* 1778
Marcel, Joseph (d. 1788), *m.* 1745
Mariette, Claude-Louis, *m.* 1765
Mariette, Nicolas-Louis, *m.* 1770, *st.* 55
Martin, François-Louis, *m.* 1767
Mathelin (early 18th c.)
Mathieu, Gaspard, *m.* 1778, *st.* 74
Mathieu, Pierre-Jean (2d quarter 18th c.)
Mathon, Augustin, *m.* 1763, *st.* 140
Maucuy, Blaise (1729–1798), *m.* 1758, *st.* 78
Mayeux, Louis-François, *m.* 1757, *st.* 25
Mayot, Louis-Etienne, *m.* 1787
Menant, François-Claude (1757–1792), *m.* 1786, *st.* 54
Mercier, Jean, *m.* 1743
Meunier, Antoine (b. 1690)
Meunier, Antoine, *fils, m.* 1752
Meunier, Antoine-Luc, *m.* 1782
Meunier, Etienne (mid-18th c.) *st.* 109
Meunier, Jean-Baptiste (b. 1714), *m.* 1739
Meunier, Simon (mid-18th c.)
Michard, Claude-Etienne (1732–1794), *m.* 1757, *st.* 81
Migeon, Antoine (1745–1793), *m.* 1769
Moreau, Jean-Joseph (d. 1756), *m.* 1742
Moreau, Pierre (1722–1798), *m.* 1765, *st.* 29
Mouette, Jean-Baptiste (b. 1697), *m.* 1740
Mouzard, Antoine, *m.* 1755, *st.* 28
Mutel, Charles-Louis, *m.* 1756

Nadal, Jean (mid-18th c.), *st.* 131
Nadal, Jean-Michel, called the younger (1734–1800), *m.* 1765
Nadal, Jean-René, called the elder (b. 1733), *m.* 1756, *st.* 91

Nauroy, Etienne, *m.* 1765, *st.* 108
Nicolas, Antoine (?), *m.* in Paris 1765 and in Nantes (?), *st.* 114
Nogaret, Pierre (1720–1771), *m.* in Lyons 1741, *st.* 9
Normand, Charles-François, *m.* 1746, *st.* 98

Othon, Pierre, *m.* 1760, *st.* 63

Parmentier, Nicolas (1736–1801), in Lyons, *st.* 10
Paturaux, Gilbert, *m.* 1777
Petit, Nicolas (1730–1798), *m.* 1765
Pichard, Barthélemy (d. before 1749)
Pillot (end 18th c.), in Nîmes, *st.* 148
Pissart, Jean-Baptiste-Pierre, *m.* 1765
Planet, Antoine (d. 1756)
Plée, Pierre (1742–1810), *m.* 1767, *st.* 127
Pluvinet, Louis-Magdeleine (d. c. 1785), *m.* 1775, *st.* 101
Pluvinet, Philippe-Joseph (d. 1793), *m.* 1754, *st.* 35
Poirié, Noël (d. 1753)
Poirié, Philippe, *m.* 1765, *st.* 94
Porrot, Noël-Toussaint, *m.* 1761, *st.* 95
Potain, François, *père* (d. c. 1735)
Potain, François, *fils* (1688–before 1773)
Pothier, Jean-Jacques, *m.* 1750, *st.* 73
Poussier, Louis (1st half 18th c.), *st.* 77

Rabaudin (3d quarter 18th c.), *st.* 22
Rascalon, Barthélemy-Mammès (2d half 18th c.)
Rémy, Pierre (1724–1798), *m.* 1750, *st.* 133
Reuze, François (1716–1799), *m.* 1743, *st.* 122
Rhenon, Jacques, *m.* 1746, *st.* 87
Richard, Pierre, *m.* 1777
Roussens, J. -I. (end 18th c.), *st.* 103

Sabatier, Théodore, *m.* 1746
Saddon, J. (mid-18th c.), *st.* 15
Saint-Georges, Etienne (d. 1756), *st.* 105
Saint-Georges, Jean-Etienne (1723–1790), *m.* 1747, *st.* 120
Sarrazin, Antoine, *m.* 1777
Sefert (Cephert), Pierre-François, *m.* 1780, *st.* 56
Sené, Claude, I (1724–1792), *m.* 1743, *st.* 134

Sené, Claude, II, called the younger, *m.* 1769, *st.* 11

Sené, Jean, *père* (1st half 18th c.)

Sené, Jean-Baptiste-Claude (1748–1803), *m.* 1769, *st.* 96

Serrurier, Charles-Joseph, *m.* 1783

Theron, Mathieu, *m.* 1740

Thuillier, Jean-François, *m.* 1752, *st.* 60

Tilliard, Jean-Baptiste, I (1685–1766), *st.* 104

Tilliard, Jean-Baptiste, II (d. 1797), *m.* 1752, see *st.* 104

Tilliard, Nicolas (1st half 18th c.)

Turcot, Pierre-Claude, *m.* 1734

Upton, Jacques, *m.* 1782

Vibert, Jean-Baptiste, *m.* 1776

Vinatier, Gilles-Hyacinthe, *m.* 1784, *st.* 59

Yon, François-Antoine (b. 1729), *m.* 1783

Chapter 9

MENUISIERS' STAMPS

Dictionaries of *menuisiers* and *ébénistes* publish the stamps in alphabetical order. I have chosen here another formula, first used in the earlier edition of this book, which was welcomed by collectors and dealers as facilitating research.

The stamps are organized according to their dimensions, height and length, and general style: no initial, one initial, or two initials. Stamps with the same or similar groups of letters which lead to easy confusion are juxtaposed (e.g., M. Gourdin and N. Boudin, I. Cheneaux and I. Chenevat, P. Bara and I. Nadal, etc.).

The height of the letters in a mark serves to narrow the scope of research. Without claiming absolute precision in reproduction, I have divided the stamps into six different sizes:

1. Stamps less than 4 mm high
2. Stamps approximately 4 to 5 mm; these are the most numerous
3. Stamps approximately 5 to 6 mm, also numerous
4. Stamps approximately 6 to 7 mm
5. Stamps approximately 7 to 8 mm
6. Stamps measuring 8 to 10 mm
7. Unusual types of stamps: with fleurs-de-lys, probably indicating that the *menuisiers* enjoyed royal appointment (Deshayes, Aubert); framed (Pillot of Nîmes); composed just of initials (whose interpretation is often ambiguous); circular (one of these, the stamp of Dupain, is sometimes accompanied by two initials, V. F., which can also be found alone, and remain unexplained); finally, stamps of a two-line format.

It is easy to correlate the stamps reproduced below and the names given in the preceding chapter with the marks that one sees or supposes to be on a piece of furniture. When the stamp is clear and easily legible, the *menuisier's* name can be found in the preceding chapter, where a number refers the reader to the corresponding facsimile of the stamp, if it is included. When there is uncertainty and hesitation among several possible names, it is advisable to make a rubbing of the mark with a soft pencil and tracing paper and compare it directly to corresponding facsimile marks on the following pages, which were obtained by the same method. The empirical arrangement that I propose is certainly arbitrary, but it is based on experience. I believe it will avoid a good deal of frustration, error and waste of time.

By way of exception, six marks (nos. 106, 151–54 and 157) found on eighteenth-century chairs are reproduced even though they may be stamps of woodcarvers, or provincial *menuisier*-woodcarvers.

It seemed wise to add an occasional (?) emphasizing the uncertainty which remains in some cases.

MENUISIERS' STAMPS

Stamps less than 4 mm high

JACAILLOIS
1. CAILLOIS (J.-A.)

MCAILLOIS
2. CAILLOIS (J.-N.)

M • LANGON
3

C.DESEINE
4

E • EPAULARD
5

G • BOUGAULT
6

B • A • CHAUMOND
7

P • F • JEAN
8

NOGARET·A·LYON
9

PARMANTIER·A·LYON
10

Stamps approximately 4 to 5 mm

C • SENE
11

C • LERAT
12

I • LEBAS
13

P • FORGET
14

J • SADDON
15

G • IACOB
16

H • JACOB
17

C • GORGU
18

M·CRESSON 19	L·CRESSON 32
M·GOURDIN 20	A·GAILLIARD 33
N·BAUDIN 21	C·LECLERC 34
J·RABAUDIN 22	P·PLUVINET 35
J·CAUMONT 23	P·LAROQUE 36
F·FONBONNE 24	D·JULLIENNE 37
L·MAYEUX 25	J·DELAUNAY 38
F·BERNARD 26	L·DELANOIS 39
S·BRIZARD 27	J·LECHARTIER 40
A·MOUZARD 28	G·CHEVIGNY 41
P·MOREAU 29	A·BONNEMAIN 42
N·HEURTAUT 30	N·LEXELANT 43
Mᵉ·GAUTRON 31	C·DELENONCOURT 44

A·N·DELAPORTE
45

I·8·FROMAGEAV
46

J·D·BAZIN
47

M·P·BIZET
48

C·L·BURGAT
49

J·B·BOULARD
50

J·P·DUPONT
51

B·D·CHARDON
52

C·F·EVRARD
53

F·C·MENANT
54

N·L·MARIETTE
55

P·F·SEFERT
56

L·M·LEFEVRE
57

P·E·LANGLOIS
58

G·H·VINATIER
59

J·F·THUILLIER
60

J·C·BRIOIS
61

J·B·B·DEMAY
62

Stamps approximately 5 to 6 mm

OTHON
63

LENAIN
64

GIRARD
65

COVRTOIS
66

FALCONET 67	B•MAUCUY 78
LERPSHER 68	J•AUDRY 79
DELAIZEMENT 69	F • GENY 80
IAVISSE 70. AVISSE (Jean)	E•MICHARD 81
I•GOVRDIN 71	P•BRIZARD 82
I•BOUCAULT 72	N•BLANCHARD 83
I•POTHIER 73	S×BLANCHARD 84
G•MATHIEU 74	S•CARPANTIER 85
D•DECANT 75	J•BROCSOLLE 86
E•DIEVDONNE 76	J•RHENON 87
L•POUSSIEE 77	F•CHOLLOT 88. CHOLLOT (E.)

C*DIEUDONNE
89

JB·BOULARD
97

M·DELAPORTE
90

CF·NORMAND
98

J·NADAL·LAINE
91

IP. LETELIER
99

CRESSOULAINE
92

I·DESESTRE
100

F·LAPIERREALYON
93

L·M·PLUVINET
101. PLUVINET (L.-M.)

PH·POIRIE·
94

N*S*COURTOIS
102

N T PORROT
95. PORROT (N.-T.)

JI·ROUSSENS.F
103

I·B·SENE*
96

Stamps approximately 6 to 7 mm

TILLIARD
104

St·GEORGE
105

HAGVETTE
106. AGUETTE (H.)

F*FOLIOT
107

E. N A URoy
108

E.MEVNIER
109

P•BRION
110

I*CHENEVAT
111

I•CHENEAUX
112

P•BELLANGÉ
113

A•NICOLAS
114

N-J-BAUDIN
115

N.P*FOLIOT
116

CV•BARA
117

I ADUPRE
118. DUPRÉ (J.-A.)

I*B*LELARGE
119

J•ESt•GEORGES
120. SAINT-GEORGES (J.-E.)

L-C•CARPENTIER
121

FRC•REVZE
122. REUZE (F.)

GAV
123

BAUVE
124

BOVO
125

BARNON
126

J·PLEE
127. PLÉE (P.)

PACHARD
128. ACHARD (P.)

FC·FRANC
129. FRANC (F.)

P·BARA
130

I·NADAL
131

P·GILLIER
132

P*REMY
133

G*SENE
134

F·LEROY
135

M·CRESSON
136

G·AVISSE·
137

I*B·CRESSON
138

I*B·LEROUGE
139

OG*MATHON
140

PERE·GOURDIN
141. GOURDIN (Jean)

Stamps measuring more than 8 mm

CRESSENT
142

J.LOUIS
144

BESSIERRE
143

I·DELION
145

Unusual types of stamps

 DESHAYES
146

 CL·BC
150. BERGEZ (?)

◆ AUBERT ◆
147

N·DLP·S
151 (cf. p. 233)

PILLOT
148

MD LP
152 (cf. p. 233)

 I B
149. JACOB (Georges)

 M✦P
153

C·J·V·M

154 (cf. p. 234)

155. BERNARD

156. DUPAIN

157. CANOT (F.)

158. DUVAL

IM
COVRTOY

159. COURTOIS (J.-M.)

GERBOVD
FAITALYON

160

COVRTOIS
REVDESEINE

161. ÇOURTOIS (J.-M.) ?

D E MAY
RUE·DE·CLERY

162

JACOB FRERES
RUE MESLEE

163. JACOB (F. et Georges II)

PART THREE

Ebénisterie Furniture

Chapter 10

TECHNIQUES OF *EBENISTERIE*

I N HIS *Art du Menuisier,* Roubo devotes a volume of more than 250 pages in folio and more than 60 plates (pt. 3 of vol. 3) to the *Art de L'Ebéniste.* A *menuisier* by profession, but scrupulously correct, Roubo makes a point of stating (p. 895) that in writing about this specialized technique he availed himself of the advice of a journeyman *menuisier-ébéniste* by the name of Chavigneau. (It was not until thirteen years later, in 1787, that Chavigneau was received as a master in the Paris guild.) Roubo thus affirms the importance then accorded *ébénisterie* and the specialization of the *ébénistes* as opposed to those who remained simply *menuisiers.*

Although I have based this chapter almost entirely on Roubo, and refer the reader to the pages and illustrations of his book, I will not follow the order he adopted. After dealing with the materials employed, and the work of the *ébéniste,* our course will lead to a greater emphasis on the finishing of the furniture, and to an expanded consideration of the professions and techniques that contributed to the perfection or the pictorial character of an eighteenth-century piece.

TOOLS

The saws peculiar to the *ébéniste* could be mounted in iron with the only wood being the handle; in some, termed *à l'anglaise,* the blade was held by means of screws. Some of these were for cutting veneer and were termed *scies a dépecer* (pl. 278, fig. 12). Others were exclusively for cutting out pieces of marquetry: these were fretsaws (pl. 292).

The planes, trying and rabbet planes, were the same, or very little different, from those used by the *menuisiers;* as were the chisels. The *ébéniste* used a plane with teeth (pl. 281, fig. 3) which served to avoid splintering as well as to score the wood so that the glue would adhere better; the router planes (pl. 290, figs. 11, 13), that he used to rout the ground of a piece in a direction parallel to the grain were also furnished with notched blades.

The ornamental cutting out of the wood required special equipment: a trim knife (pl. 289, fig. 16, and pl. 293, figs. 11–12), a rod compass (pl. 293, figs. 1, 2) for cutting circular sections, a *tire filet* (a device through which filets of wood were pulled and shaved down) (pl. 289, figs. 3–5), a bench with its vise and pedal (pl. 291), where the operation of cutting out marquetry took place.

For veneers, the *ébéniste* needed a veneering hammer and a heating iron (pl. 294, figs. 3–5, 8–9), a brazier and glue in a double boiler, a sponge, and, once the work was done and dry, scrapers or fine files (pl. 296, figs. 3–5), buffers and reed brushes (pl. 296, figs. 7–12) made of wood or cane, as well as pumice and pieces of smooth sharkskin. Roubo recommended in addition that the *ébéniste* have locksmiths' equipment in his establishment (p. 932).

Already in Roubo's day the *ébéniste*'s workbench had a tail vise on the side (pl. 279, fig 1) and was called a German workbench, "whether" as our author stated, "it was invented in Germany, or, more likely by German *ébénistes* who are in Paris in great number." Clamps and vises accompanied the workbench. In addition, to hold the freshly glued works, the *ébéniste* used either large horizontal presses (pl. 280, figs. 1–4), small presses, or hand screws (pl. 294, figs. 1, 2).

WOODS

Roubo published (pp. 768 ff.) a list of the woods that were used by the *ébénistes* in his day, under the general heading "bois des Indes" (woods from the Indies). This designation of exotic woods under names that are far from precise is complex and difficult to retrace in retrospect. The question remains so important for *ébénisterie* furniture, that, despite the stated reservations and the prudence that I urge on the reader, I will undertake the attempt.

Of the forty-eight species published by Roubo, the following were the most frequently used in the eighteenth century.

Bois rose or *bois de rose* (tulipwood, *Phsocalymma scaberrimum*) (fig. 78), is yellow striped with red, which takes on an attractive yellow color with age.

Satiné, if red and with a pronounced grain, was often confused with *bois de rose* under Louis XV (fig. 114) and later, if less vivid, lighter, and more solid in color, confused with satinwood under Louis XVI. Mme de Pompadour asked Lazare Duvaux to have 778 sheets of a veneer that may well have been satiné cut to be used for the furniture she ordered.

Amarante (purple wood, *Copaifera bracteata*) (fig. 82) is of a vivid purple color that quickly turns brown.

Bois de violet (violet wood), which seems to have been confused with *amarante* on occasion, is today more frequently termed *bois de violette* (figs. 81, 88). Roubo made a distinction between two types of this wood: one that he called simply *violet* (probably kingwood, *Dalbergia greveana*), coming from the East Indies; and the other, *violet palissandre,* also called *Sainte-Lucie* (palissander, *Jacaranda brasiliana*), coming from the West Indies, more specifically the island of Saint Lucia in the Windwards. In the eighteenth century there was even more confusion than there is now between the different categories of wood. The forests of the Americas and the Antilles were exploited in no particular order. New woods arrived in abundance; the trees from which they came had not yet been thoroughly studied by botanists; and the *ébénistes* attached little importance to their exact identity since their only concern was the quality of the wood, its color, and how it cut. *Bois violet* and *amarante,* are, according to some authors, the same wood, taken from the *Copaifera bracteata* of Guyana. Roubo, however, makes a distinction between them. Others confuse purple wood and palissander, but Joubert in 1758 specified that some of the pieces of furniture he delivered to the Garde-Meuble were veneered in purple wood and tulipwood, and others in palissander and tulipwood.

Cayenne, recorded in royal deliveries in the middle of the century, and *bois de Chine,* mentioned at the start of Louis XV's reign, are—like *corail* (coralwood or redwood, *Adenanthera pavonina* or *Pterocarpus indicus*), *amourette,* and *Brésil*—woods that have a bright red color when new. Roubo mentions them as different species. On the other hand he cites a *bois d'Inde* as aromatic laurel from Martinique, although it is certain that eighteenth-century *ébénistes* used the term *bois d'Inde* or *bois des Indes* for any exotic wood that was somewhat rare without taking great pains to research the correct name, which would have been quite difficult to ascertain.

Bois aurore, which Roubo does not list, is mentioned several times in the registry of the Garde-Meuble during the third quarter of the century.

Olivier (olive wood, *Olea europaea*) was used in Paris at least until around 1740, and still longer in the south of France.

Under Louis XVI, the range of woods expanded; some went out of fashion or were put to different uses, others became more frequently used.

Acajou (mahogany, *Switenia mahagoni*) became the most popular of all (figs. 24, 95, 129, 145). It came from the East Indies, and occasionally from the Malabar coast, or from the West Indies, particularly Santo Domingo. This wood, which the English had used for a long time previous, appeared in either solid wood or veneers from time to time under Louis XV. In the Louis XVI era it dominated all other woods and is found on the most beautiful examples of furniture in either plain or figured tones: milky, chenille, speckled, in root or bramble.

Citronnier (satinwood, *Fagara flava* or *Chloroxylon Swietenia*) Roubo distinguishes from *bois citron* (lemonwood, *Citrus medica*), the latter coming from Bermuda, Jamaica, and Santo Domingo. It is likely that certain kinds of satiné were included under this designation (fig. 103). Roubo dealt only with the red variety of satiné, but it could also be a yellow wood with long fibers, cut along the grain or meshed, that is the satinwood, *satinholz,* or *seidenholz* of the English and German *ébénistes.* Satiné was used in large sheets of veneer, for details, or for marquetry backgrounds; but there seems to have been a good deal of confusion surrounding the name. Riesener mentioned satiné in his bills, especially stained satiné (fig. 113), which can be nothing other than a more or less exotic variety of maple. The "yellow wood," usually having no further description, that was used by the dealer Daguerre and the court supplier Hauré in the last years of the Louis XVI reign, could be lemonwood. The rare mention that one finds in Louis XV documents suggests the following tentative interpretation of the archaic terminology: it appears that one should distinguish the *citronnier* (satinwood) that was occasionally used to line the lid of a toilet (1738) from the *bois citron* (lemonwood?) of a leaf of a cabinet door (1745). The latter term was used by Lazare Duvaux in 1758 for "a type of night table in commode form" at a price of 96 livres, and in 1750 for "two bookcases with wire mesh doors" for 120 livres that could, on the basis of their color, resemble the two pieces acquired by the Musée des Arts Décoratifs in Paris from the Paulme sale. Rolltop desks by Saunier have the same yellow color, as does the so-called Robespierre table in the Archives Nationales, which was stated to be in "yellow walnut from Guadeloupe" when it was reveneered in 1787.

Amboine (amboyna) (fig. 22); a few rare examples can be cited from the middle of the century.

Ebène (ebony) (figs. 109, 128) had not gone out of fashion since the Boulle era and was imitated in lacquer and in stained pearwood.

Courbaril (courbaril wood, *Hymenaea Courbaril*) is a superb, heavy wood which, according to Bomare, was found "on the hills of Santo Domingo and the adjacent islands" and whose use seems to have remained limited to the furniture made in the Antilles.

Roubo grouped indigenous French woods separately from the *bois des Indes* and presented them in a comparable alphabetical listing. Some of them, like holly, yew, box, and barberry, were only used for details of marquetry. Others, like walnut (figs. 91, 123) and cherrywood (fig. 125) could be used solid or in veneers; e.g., in 1733 Gaudreaux delivered a secretary "of cherrywood with geometric marquetry of the same wood" for Marie Leczinska. The use of olive wood and pearwood, which did not have to be varnished and were used in *menuiserie,* has already been discussed.

Bois lorrain de Sainte-Lucie (near Verdun) deserves special mention. It was used for delicate work, woodcarving, and *tabletterie* (small, intricate carved objects) as well as *ébénisterie*. Extremely refined accessories, often destined for the dressing table, were made of this wood in the first third of the eighteenth century. They are often, incorrectly, termed *de Bagard:* a scholarly study by Pierre Marot has attributed them in the main to the Foullon family (fig. 16).

In the choice of woods, whether exotic or indigenous, the *ébéniste* naturally looked for solid pieces whose patterning corresponded to the effect he wanted. He avoided clefts and knots, but in order to obtain a lively variegated surface, he made use of gnarls, burls, roots, the natural design of the grain, or the imperfections in the wood. He combined and matched the colors of various woods to achieve, even in plain veneers, the vivid tonalities that were so attractive. After reading the preceding lists it is impossible not to notice that eighteenth-century nomenclature for woods always retains reference to their color (rose, violet, coral, amaranth, lemon, or yellow) with little concern for scientific designations. This reflects the contemporary exploration of the polychrome effects obtainable with exotic woods, and the reaction against the oak and ebony dear to the seventeenth century.

The woods were thoroughly, but not excessively, dried before use. It should be noted, however, that even in this state they changed color. When they were worked, and especially when they were polished, they turned browner. Then, as they aged, a number of the exotic woods altered: the color, which was in some cases strong and even bloodred at the start, toned down to a warm patina.

Wood arrived as logs at the Saint-Nicholas port in Paris. It was sawed into lengths, not by the *menuisiers-ébénistes* themselves, but by specialized workmen who, Roubo noted, "did not work exclusively for the *ébénistes,* but also for musical instrument makers and anyone else who needed thin lengths of wood." In the eighteenth century veneers were nowhere near as thin as they are today thanks to machines by which a continuous layer of wood can be peeled off a rotating log. They were usually cut to thickness of one *ligne* (slightly more than 2mm). Roubo was already protesting, and with good reason, the temptation to try to cut a sheet too thin in order to economize on wood, since the completion of the work inevitably lead to further reduction of its thickness. The wood was usually sawed lengthwise, with the grain, but to obtain certain effects it could be sawed crosswise, or even diagonally.

CARCASS

Oak of a rather soft variety was the wood frequently used in the eighteenth century for the carcasses of the best furniture, even more so under Louis XVI than under Louis XV. Oeben set the example, and his followers, Leleu and Riesener, both specified in their bills for their best pieces that they used "oak from the Voges." The fine grain of oak made for solid structures that were clean and neat.

Pine *(Pinus silvestris, Pinus strobus)* was also utilized a great deal. It is astonishing to see how much fine Louis XV furniture, secretaries as well as commodes, has pine construction underlying veneers and bronze mounts that evidence considerable expenditure. Roubo also mentioned linden *(Tilia europaea).* In regard to the selection of carcass woods it is useful to recall Roubo's words on the subject of carcasses.

With a touch of malice and bitterness, Roubo provided us with the explanation for the surprising mediocrity of construction revealed on the back of certain pieces and the poor quality of the carcass that has caused the marquetry to work loose. Most *ébénistes,* he said, "do not execute carcasses themselves but have them made at the lowest possible cost by other *menuisiers* who do nothing else, and who make indiscriminate use of woods which they consider adequate as long as they are cheap, with the result that they make furniture carcasses with shipbuilding wood, be it oak or pine, barrel staves, linden, poplar, chestnut, and other inferior woods." Although Roubo's remark about the construction of carcasses by people other than the *ébéniste* should not be taken too seriously, Salverte does provide some corroboration in his note on the *ébéniste* Provost: "He constructed carcasses for furniture which was to be veneered."

The construction of a piece of *ébénisterie* did not differ in principle from that of a piece of *menuiserie.* On this subject Roubo showed equal disdain in regard to the construction techniques of the *ébénistes* and the *menuisiers:* "To the poor quality of wood, they add very bad workmanship, most of their carcasses being made with virtually no joinery, except for a few crude ends." In fact, *ébénistes* did use mortise-and-tenon and tongue-and-groove joinery, dovetailing for their drawers and the tops of their furniture, as well as butted edges for areas that were to be covered here by leather, there by veneer; but all of these were rather crude and carelessly made. The sumptuous pieces executed by someone like B.V.R.B. under Louis XV or Riesener under Louis XVI constitute exceptions; it is not at all unusual, even on the furniture of Cressent or Carlin, to discover a curious negligence, almost a sloppiness, when one turns over the piece or removes its marble top. The *ébéniste* always had to be careful to avoid pegs in a carcass because their expansion and shrinkage would dislodge the veneer. He also had to avoid wood cross-cut against the grain because glue would not adhere well to it.

Once his structure was completed, the *ébéniste* allowed it time to dry. The wood could be left solid, especially for small pieces of furniture (mahogany, walnut, and occasionally purple wood were treated this way); but veneering was the true stuff of *ébénisterie.* Before covering his carcass with veneer, the *ébéniste* waited to see if the wood expanded or contracted, and made repairs if necessary. He then outlined the design of the veneer or marquetry on the carcass.

VENEER

After veneer woods were cut, they were grouped and stored according to thickness, grain, and shade so that the *ébéniste* could achieve a homogenous effect on a single piece of furniture. The concern with matching woods was sometimes carried to extremes. For example, in 1788 Benneman delivered a writing table of burled mahogany for the king's study at Saint-Cloud, and because one of the legs was broken in transport, all four were remade "in order that they would be of the same color." It cost 3 livres for turning the feet on the lathe and 5 livres for two days' work of craftsmen who were paid 50 sols, for a table whose total price was 260 livres. In principle, repairs should have resulted solely from alterations, which could be caused by errors in the initial choice of woods. The *ébéniste* could obtain varied effects at will with the same wood, or contrast two or more different woods in large sheets of veneer.

Veneers could be cut with the grain and the sheets placed horizontally, diagonally, or perpendicular to each other. Wood cut along the grain could be cut into pieces and applied in various ways to obtain different effects: diagonals, stripes, lattices (figs. 81, 89), in herringbone pattern, or even to form diamond facets, hearts, quatrefoils, multilobed motifs, or rosettes (fig. 108).

The same wood cross-cut against the grain, or a different wood altogether, could be used for borders in order to create either subtle or strong contrast between the panels and the background (figs. 89, 111). The corners were treated with mitered or bias-cut wood. End-cut wood could also be used to create markedly contrasting borders (fig. 88).

Friezes were usually separated from panels by thin filets, generally of holly (fig. 80), but also, according to Roubo, of wicker specifically prepared for this purpose and sold to the *ébénistes* by the caners. Toward the end of Louis XV's reign and under Louis XVI, friezes were often separated from panels by thin strips of wood cut with the grain with a wood filet on either side.

Roubo's plate 294 shows the technique of veneering, which has remained unchanged to this day. In one hand the *ébéniste* holds a hammer whose use seems to have been less specialized in the eighteenth century than it is today. In the other hand he holds the veneering iron, keeping it hot by placing it on his brazier. He had previously worked over the surface with a rasp to insure an even thickness and striations so that the glue would adhere better. Once the glue was applied, which, if he followed Roubo's advice, he preferred to be a good English glue, the craftsman applied pressure with the hammer and the iron. He immediately removed the excess glue with a sponge. After veneering the piece he "sounded" it, tapping it lightly with the hammer to see if the adhesion was perfect. He put it in a press or, if it was a curved element, under a bag of warm sand. Finally he used a chisel or spatula to remove the glue along the seams.

MARQUETRY

Marquetry involved more complicated procedures. Before the marquetry motifs were cut out, the design was drawn on the wood. The design was generally traced or drawn with the aid of a pounced stencil. Each *ébéniste* had his own patterns, and the same sprays of flowers are found on several secretaries by Delacroix (fig. 114), and the same baskets of flowers on various pieces of furniture by Leleu. Some *ébénistes,* because of the large volume of their production, had patterns cut out in white metal or thin sheets of copper. A special marquetry saw was used for cutting out the pieces. They were glued by the same method as veneers.

Ever since the work of the fifteenth-century Italian intarsists, the aim of marquetry has been to imitate painting. Marquetry woods were therefore subject to special treatments not used for simple veneers. They were stained blue, yellow, red, green, fawn, black, and gray. These stains, which must have endowed furniture with an extraordinary polychromatic effect then (fig. 154), have been darkened and dulled by exposure to light, and also perhaps by varnish. Blue and gray have hardly ever survived, but occasionally one finds, in removing the mounts or the varnish, that the wood underneath has retained a vivid green. In the same way, the marquetry lining the interiors of some pieces can remain fresh. It was to avoid the disadvantages of staining that Roentgen, followed in France by *ébénistes* such as Wolff, tried to nuance his images with the variety of colors of woods used in their natural state.

Marquetry designs were given accents by reworking the woods for effects of shadow and relief. Engraving was done with a burin. Sometimes hollows were filled in with white or red paste. Often the motifs were shaded, and this was accomplished by the use of acids or hot sand, a technique that has always been current. Here too Roentgen avoided the inconvenience by making use of naturally darker areas in the wood caused by irregularities or veins. Marquetry achieved its fullest development between 1760 and 1780, when its range extended from simple flowering branches (figs. 87, 96, 101, 104) to large bouquets artfully arranged in a vase or basket (fig. 154), and from cursory still lifes, composed of a few, occasionally Chinese, utensils, to trophies, large allegorical compositions, or landscapes. Marquetry could be purely geometric (figs. 115, 126) composed of checkers, lozenges, dice, cubes without background, or cubes in projecting perspective, Greek keys, chains, or Vitruvian scrolls. It could also become trompe-l'oeil. Under the rubric "mosaic, or painting in wood," Roubo, who was usually so negative, termed (p. 866) this "kind of *ébénisterie* . . . the most precious of all."

Materials other than wood could be employed in marquetry. Certainly applications of tortoiseshell, copper, pewter, which enjoyed high favor in the era of André-Charles Boulle, although subsequently fluctuating in popularity, continued in use throughout the century (figs. 15, 17). Roubo stated that in his time these materials were used only for small objects and clock cases (fig. 13) "which led to the *ébénistes* calling their colleagues who specialized in such work *pendulistes*" (a coined term, roughly "clockists"). Animal horn, which came from England already prepared and stained green, red, or blue, could be used instead of tortoiseshell. Occasionally silver or gold was used for small inlays. Ivory and mother-of-pearl can also be found, usually in details.

THE FINISHING OF THE PIECE OF FURNITURE

When the veneer and marquetry were sufficiently dry, they were evened off and given a finish. After removing the seams of glue, the panel was gone over with a file. Then it was polished with a scraper, a smooth sharkskin, and finally with horsetail reeds.

Once the surface was prepared in this manner, the actual polishing began. This could be done in a rudimentary way by spreading wax over the wood to be polished and then removing it with a wax scraper. When the wood was sufficiently impregnated, it was rubbed with a cloth. For more elaborate pieces, after they had been gone over with horsetail reeds, they were polished with a solution of ground rottenstone in olive oil. Roubo added that ebony could be polished effectively with charcoal or colophony (a resin).

Ebénisterie furniture was often varnished. After it had been polished with horsetail reeds, rottenstone, or calcium carbonate, called *blanc d'Espagne,* several layers of varnish were applied. This varnish, called Venetian or white varnish, seems to have been a mixture of alcohol, sandarac, mastic, rubber, and oil. After one or more coats, it was polished with a pad of cloth or buffalo hide. Roubo (p. 865) gave an explanation of the purpose of varnish, which, although not entirely accurate, should not be overlooked: "The varnish, by stopping up the pores of the wood, arrests the color, which, since it is unable to evaporate, remains in the same state, which is a great advantage, in view of the fact that much of the beauty of *ébénisterie* lies in the vivacity of these very colors."

RELATED CRAFTS AND MATERIALS

Bronze Mounts

Here I will dwell on two points only: the repetition of models and the mounting of bronzes on a piece of furniture.

Roubo (p. 999) noted in regard to clocks as well as *ébénisterie* in general, that, after casting and varying degrees of chasing, the bronze mounts were gilded with a mercury gilding, or, more frequently, given a golden color by a simple application of varnish [*mise en couleur d'or*]. The same models were reused ad nauseam, because, as he stressed, the creation of new models was expensive: "It is necessary first to make design drawings, then wood models on which the ornamental motifs are fashioned in wax just as they are to be executed in bronze; instead, they would much rather cast ornaments after an already existing model." The problem of repetition is important (figs. 79, 80, 86, 89, 93, 98, 99, 109, 129). *Ebénistes* and bronze makers did not hesitate to plagiarize their neighbors' models: hence many lawsuits, injunctions, disputes, and a good deal of confusion. There is also another reason why identical bronze mounts are found on furniture by different *ébénistes:* with a few exceptions like Cressent, Marchand, Latz, and Riesener, the *ébénistes* did not make bronze mounts themselves. They went to bronze casters and the same model could be sold by a single bronze caster to several *ébénistes*. Thus the same corner mounts with flowers and *rocailles* and the same plaques with *cul-de-lampes* or garlands are found on pieces of furniture bearing the stamps of different *ébénistes*.

For a long time the method of attaching bronze mounts remained rather rudimentary (fig. 83). The *ébéniste,* as was stated earlier, had the right to attach the mounts himself; and, if we are to believe Roubo, to varnish them with so-called English varnish. It is possible that he also had the right to make the copper filets, flat borders, moldings, and flutes that accented the lines of much Louis XV and Louis XVI furniture (figs. 95, 112). It is difficult to see how the *ébéniste* could have had these elements made other than in his own workshop as the application follows strictly the form of the piece of furniture, especially the moldings on the legs of Louis XV commodes and small tables that protect the exposed edges (fig. 97). Roubo indicated that the copper could be cast or drawn out, which must frequently have been the case.

· Roubo noted (p. 1026) that bronze mounts were usually attached with small copper nails or wood screws having gilded round heads "which are placed in positions where they are less obvious, like the background, the underside of leaves, etc." He illustrated (pl. 337, figs. 7, 8), however, a form of threaded pin fixed to the back of the mount which is held in place by a nut on the other side. At just this moment the *ébéniste* J.-F. Oeben was working on the problem of disguising the attachment of bronze mounts. Until then the best *ébénistes* of the Louis XV period had given little thought to the matter, and today we are astonished at the crude attachment of the mounts on so many of even the very best pieces of furniture. The screws are visible and shocking. A few rosettes on some Boulle furniture, and the curve of the leaves or interlaced motifs on pieces by Cressent are hesitant attempts to diminish the harsh effect of a screwhead. B.V.R.B. and the other *ébénistes* of his day made the screwheads as small as possible, but they were still visible. Oeben, who was as much a mechanic as an *ébéniste,* could engage in experiments forbidden to others, in his workshop at the Arsenal (a site exempt from guild regulation). He made great advances in the attachment of bronze mounts that were to benefit his successors in the Louis XVI period. The system of pins lugged from behind illustrated by Roubo was used frequently by Oeben; it had already been employed for the bronze rims on the tops of large writing tables. A device developed by Oeben that was soon widely adopted since it worked well with the construction of furniture consisted of soldering a projecting tab to large decorative moldings with a screw and nut hidden under the drawer or marble top.

Lacquer and Japanning

Lacquer was widely used on furniture in the eighteenth century. Whether the true oriental lacquer or the varnish called japanning used by Western imitators, it was even more popular in the Louis XV than in the Louis XVI period. In his *Art du vernisseur,* Watin described the method of japanning cabinets, usually in black with gold and silver accents, to make them resemble oriental imports. A varnish with a base of amber or *karabé* (yellow amber), or a shellac diluted with alcohol, was applied to fine-grained, lightweight wood that had been thoroughly dried. In Europe limewood, maple, boxwood, or pearwood was used. In the West, as in the Orient, muslin was used to separate the wood from the varnish. It was glued on and polished flat before varnish was applied in numerous successive layers. Each layer was polished over and over, as many as twenty times. Vigorous and repeated polishing with horsetail reeds, with pumice, and with powdered rottenstone gave the final work its smoothness and luster.

The most sought-after lacquer furniture was that decorated by the simplest method, the application of panels of oriental lacquer. Apparently furniture was never sent from France to the Orient to be lacquered, as it was from Denmark, but there are many examples of the application of panels made in China or Japan. In the documentation of royal furniture I have found evidence of the delivery of oriental screens to be cut up for lacquer furniture. The process was not complicated for rectilinear furniture (figs. 78, 93, 112). A screen was cut apart or a panel was removed from a large box, and, if necessary, the lacquering was extended to reach the desired dimensions. If the fur-

55. Chaise longue in two parts, of a form termed *duchesse brisée,* comprising a large easychair and an elongated stool with six legs. The carved ornament and the shape of the frame are in a full but not excessive Louis XV style. Unsigned. Circa 1740. (Musée Nissim de Camondo, Paris)

56. Daybed, of a form termed *veilleuse* because the back is higher at one side than the other and *ottomane* because of its sinuous enveloping contour. Wood carved with moldings and painted white. Folded palmettes carved at the knees. One of a pair, higher on opposite sides as was often the case with such pieces designed to go on either side of a fireplace. Stamped by G. Jacob. Circa 1765. (Private collection)

57. Screen termed *à la française* because the supports are in the form of double skids. Carved and gilded wood of emphatic rococo character. Stamped by Tilliard. Circa 1755. (Wrightsman Collection, Metropolitan Museum, New York)

58. Screen. Gilded wood, carved with flowers, olive branches, and classical ornaments of the greatest delicacy. Appears to have been made for the salon of the pavilion of Louveciennes, built and decorated by Ledoux for Mme Du Barry (see fig. 137). Formerly in the Hoentschel and Balsan collections, then, unappreciated, offered at a very low price on the New York art market. Stamped by Delanois. Circa 1770. (1963 acquisition, Musée du Louvre)

59. Screen. Very finely carved and gilded boxwood. Uprights formed by pillars flanked by colonettes. Attributable to Delaisement thanks to Frances Watson's identification of the model as that of two signed armchairs in the Cleveland Museum. Circa 1780. (Waddesdon Manor, Bucks)

60. Console table. Carved and gilded wood. The front legs carved as two winged sphinxes. Provision was made for a ceramic vase to be placed at the center of the stretcher. Circa 1715. (Louis Guiraud sale, Ader, Galliéra, Paris, Nov. 26, 1975, no. 102, 41,000 f)

61. Console table. Carved natural wood. A true console shape carved with pierced rococo motifs. The *noix* at the center of the stretcher is composed of a large palmette. Circa 1740. (Musée des Arts Décoratifs, Paris)

62. Console table. Carved and gilded wood. Of demilune shape with four fluted columnar legs and an X-form stretcher. Carved with a scrolling frieze, mask, and flower garlands on the apron, and a lyre between laurel branches on the stretcher. Beautiful red griotte marble top. Circa 1780. (Petworth House, Sussex)

63. Table or, more precisely, *pied de table* supporting a rectangular *brèche d'Alep* marble top. Carved and gilded wood. On four robust legs. Excellent carving of rococo motifs and flowers, with a lattice-work and dot ground on the apron. Fine detail in the gesso and brilliant gilding that seems to be original. Circa 1740. (Musée du Louvre)

64. Table, or *pied de table*, supporting a white marble top. Carved and gilded wood of demi-lune shape. Lion heads above four fluted classical legs with paw feet. Finely carved with rosettes on the apron. One of a pair made to go between the windows of the bed-room of Louis XVI at Compiègne. Identified by its decoration and an original paper label. Circa 1785. (Bibliothèque Mazarine, Paris) ↓

65. Cupboard termed *bas d'armoire* or *bas de buffet*. Polished oak boldly carved with moldings. Rounded corners and rectilinear base. Two drawers in the upper corners. The doors are double hinged as is often the case with the armoires of Paris anterooms. Furniture of this type was even sold by so fashionable a dealer as Lazare Duvaux. Stamped by Duval. Circa 1745. (Musée Gallé-Juillet, Creil) →

66. Commode termed *à la Régence*. Polished oak carved with moldings with varnished bronze mounts. Two small drawers above two large ones decorated with a continuous S-shaped molding which can be found on other "rustic" Parisian commodes. Rounded corners and sinuous apron. Stamped by Thuillier. Circa 1755. (Sale, Ader, Paris, June 23, 1977, no. 147) →

67. Doghouse. Wood carved with moldings painted red on a white ground. Simple forms still in the Louis XV style. Upholstered sides. Made in Paris. Stamped Blanchard, possibly Sylvain-Nicolas Blanchard. Circa 1760. (Private collection) ↓

68. Toilet in the form of a box. Natural wood. Louis XV in style but made in the countryside. Preserved with several other rustic pieces in the attic of a château whose original furniture has remained in situ. Eighteenth century. (Private collection) →

69. Armchair made in Lyon but of a style so pure as to be almost Parisian. Carved natural wood. Stamped by F. Geny. Circa 1775. (1967 acquisition, Musée Historique, Lyon)

70. Double armchair from the old presidial in Nantes. Wood carved with moldings and painted white. Part of set of ten double armchairs, one of which is higher than the rest. A more robust version of a Louis XVI model. Made locally around 1790. (Musée Dobrée, Nantes)

71. Commode from the region of → Arles. Carved and polished walnut. Arles was a furniture-making center in Provence which long remained attached to the forms and ornament of the first half of the eighteenth century but finally adpted the Louis XVI style. Laurel branches, rosettes, draperies and tassels, and even Revolutionary motifs. Circa 1793. (Museon Arlaten, Arles)

72. Basque cupboard, or bas d'armoire. → Carved and polished walnut. A strong regional folk tradition survives within a Louis XV framework (moldings on the doors, apron, and scrolling feet). Second half of the eighteenth century. (Musée Dobrée, Bayonne)

73. Combination secretary and armoire from the province of Lorraine. Polished walnut, with inlaid and carved ornament and iron hardware. With arched hood, elaborately contoured apron, scrolling feet, and numerous drawers behind a slanting fall-front. It belonged to a Nancy lawyer, J.-B. Payot (1773–1845). Nancy, 1796. (Musée Lorrain, Nancy)

74. Armoire from the province of Anjou. Waxed walnut, with inlaid and carved ornament and iron hardware. Typical of the armoires made in western France (Normandy and Brittany) in the eighteenth and nineteenth centuries but with less carving than many. Predominantly Louis XV in style, but with some Louis XVI ornament. Carved with the date 1816. (Château de Montgeoffroy, Maine-et-Loire)

75. Canadian cupboard. Pine carved with moldings and painted white, with iron hardware. In the form of a two-part armoire with four doors. Simple Louis XV decoration, notably in the apron. From Saint-Pascal de Kamouraska, Quebec. Published by J. Palardy. Late eighteenth century. (Musée des Beaux-Arts de Montréal)

76. Sideboard from the region of Bresse. Polished walnut carved with moldings and inset with panels of burled wood. Louis XV in its shape and decoration, but probably dating from the early nineteenth century. (Tony Révillon gift, Musée de l'Ain, Bourg-en-Bresse)

77. Commode from Bordeaux. Solid polished mahogany, all in curves and moldings. Second half of the eighteenth century, the handles and escutcheons probably dating from the nineteenth century. (Musée des Arts Décoratifs, Bordeaux)

niture was curvilinear (figs. 83, 98, 100), the adaptation was more delicate. Roubo was well acquainted with this type of work. He described how panels from cabinets or screens were sawed lengthwise to halve their thickness and planed down still further. In the course of these two operations the lacquer was laid out on protective coverings or cushions; it was left at a thickness of only 2 or 3 mm, or one *ligne*. Then the normal veneering procedure was begun, using heat, which is probably the cause of the networks of fine cracks that we see today in the oriental lacquer on Louis XV furniture.

Many imitations of Chinese lacquer were also done in France. Watin even gave formulas for paste relief and mother-of-pearl inlays that made it possible to duplicate the most beautiful oriental work. Silver as well as gold was applied and aventurine grounds were created in French japanning (fig. 109). The Orient remained, however, preeminent in the field; one can even see from the eighteenth-century sales catalogs what efforts were made to distinguish the characteristics of different oriental lacquers. An interesting example is the record of the dealer Hébert's delivery in 1750 of three commodes where one was specified as being of Japanese lacquer, the other Coromandel, and the third Chinese. In Mme de Pompadour's inventory commodes *en ancien lacq* (of antique lacquer) were distinguished from others; and in the 1781 catalog of the sale of the duchesse de Mazarin a notable preference was shown for Japanese over Chinese lacquer, even to a panel-by-panel description of those decorating important pieces of furniture. This competition benefited the ongoing French efforts at imitation.

From the Louis XIV period there had been attempts, notably at the Gobelins, to replicate oriental lacquers, and numerous japanners, like Antoine Igou, Gosse, his son-in-law François Samousseau, and Chevalier, a student of the Martin brothers throughout the century made "Chinese-style varnish" and boasted of the "beauteous black" of their products. Some *ébénistes* had their own japanners, and from 1737 a master like Gaudreaux could be found delivering corner cabinets veneered in pearwood "destined to be varnished." French japanners did not limit themselves to reproducing oriental models. Lazare Duvaux, one of the dealers who encouraged the development of lacquer and varnish in furniture, supplied on repeated occasions furniture of "polished varnish, imitating veneers." Duvaux employed the Martin brothers. These great japanners, whose establishment was authorized in 1748 as a royal manufactory, contributed more than any others to the creation of an original French style which, without losing the allure, hardness, or brilliance of oriental wares, produced bright works in the current taste (fig. 97) that were sought after by Louis XV, Mme de Pompadour, and many others.

Porcelain and Glass

Japanning went further than marquetry in satisfying the taste for polychromy, but the use of porcelain went further still (figs. 21, 22, 119, 121, 122). Certain *marchands-merciers* ordered trays and plaques from the Sèvres factory. These were intended for pieces of furniture that were often also japanned. Porcelain embellishment was used in the creation of some of the most charming furniture, almost always small in scale, full of fantasy and elegance, and sometimes with japanning in harmony with the porcelain. A porcelain tray might form the top of a small table; rectangular or curved porcelain plaques might decorate the apron of a piece of furniture; circular, square, or rectangular porcelain plaques which could run quite large might decorate the front of a commode or cabinet. Two dealers, Poirier and Daguerre, made a specialty of such concoctions, and B.V.R.B., Lacroix, Carlin, and Weisweiler successively worked for them.

On some tables faience or reverse-painted glass was used instead of porcelain. This was the period when an expert in glass decoration by the name of Glomy popularized a technique which, although it had been practiced earlier, came, nonetheless, to bear his name, *verre églomisé*. Since the beginning of the century long strips of glass painted on the back with gold arabesques on a dark ground in the manner of Boulle and Berain were used to border mirrors. In the second half of the century *verre églomisé* (fig. 128) simulated porcelain plaques painted with polychrome flowers, provided a field for arabesque decoration, reproduced chinoiserie figures and landscapes much like the reverse-painted glass pictures that merchants and Jesuits were exporting from China, or, as in the grisaille paintings of the miniaturist De Gault, imitated Wedgwood-type cameos.

Various Metals

A great variety of metals and metalworking techniques were used in the decoration and occasionally the construction of furniture. We have discussed the importance of ornaments as well as handles, pulls, etc. of gilt bronze. In extremely rare cases silver was used, either to represent the height of luxury, or for lack of gilt bronze: silver escutcheons are mentioned in Santo Domingo in the 1787 inventory of Léon de Motmans.

Gilt bronze was the primary component in some pieces of furniture, tripods, braziers, *athéniennes* (a tripod furniture form based on the braziers of classical antiquity) (fig. 39), and bases of the most extravagant of tables—all too often copied in the nineteenth century.

A certain number of consoles and table bases were made of wrought iron (fig. 38) with variations in the color of the iron, blue, white, or gilded. These were sometimes intended for churches, but they were also made for grand galleries or salons. They were particularly popular in Provence, but they were made in Paris too.

There are examples of japanning done on sheet metal (fig. 116) instead of wood. It was more economical and is found in solid color, oriental or French motifs. It was really a type of enamel fired on sheet metal called tole. There was a considerable fashion for painted tole in the Louis XVI era, so it is not surprising to find furniture craftsmen making use of this technique of decoration.

Sheet iron was also used for certain drawers and wardrobes that were thereby transformed into safes. I know of at least two secretaries of this type, which was mentioned several times in the daybook of Lazare Duvaux. Thin sheets of silvered or silver-plated steel or copper formed compartments in small serving tables (fig. 31) and, at the end of the century, in jardinieres.

Steel was also used for ornamentation. Under Louis XVI panels of steel, blued or given a mirror polish, were used as background to set off gilt bronzes.

Finally, locks and mechanical devices (figs. 29, 30, 105, 106, 118, 124, 126, 136, 154) could be made by the *ébéniste* himself or by a locksmith. Roubo advised that the *ébéniste* should have locksmithing tools in his workshop so that he could make the ironwork, pins, hinges, axles, pivots, etc. required for his furniture. It is known that some *ébénistes* employed locksmiths and mechanics in their workshops. Oeben and Riesener made a personal specialty of mechanical furniture with elements that raised or pivoted by means of springs, levers, and compasses. It appears that it was their experiments that led to the cylinder desk and the *table à la Tronchin* (table whose height is adjusted by means of ratchets) among others.

Marble

Most fine pieces of *ébénisterie,* at least those in the commode category, were covered with marble tablets (figs. 87, 91, 93, 99, 100, 146, etc.). The marble came from Italy, the Pyrenees, Flanders, or Brittany, according to the desired quality and the acceptable cost. It usually arrived in Paris from Le Havre or Rouen. The finest marbles belonged to the Royal Marble Depot, and courtiers were avid for it. Marble cutters cut, polished, and customized each tablet to fit the contour of the piece of furniture, giving double moldings (hollowed above and below) to the tops destined for the most expensive furniture. In certain exceptional cases granite, porphyry, recycled antique marbles, stone, slate, and even petrified wood can be found.

Some pieces were made entirely of marble. The unique and magnificent table in the Frick Collection (fig. 153) is of a marble called *bleu turquin* accented with gilt bronze mounts of exquisite quality. Marble could also be used for small objects like tobacco boxes (fig. 9).

Either through conservatism or an interest in saving valuable works, *pietra dura* mosaics, some in high relief, were still used on luxury furniture through the eighteenth century, especially under Louis XVI. The technique had its origins in Florence, but Louis XIV succeeded in transplanting it to the Gobelins manufactory. *Pietra dura* panels were used on furniture by Joseph and Carlin (e.g., the pieces commissioned by the duc d'Aumont which are at Versailles), the casket created by Daguerre for the Crown diamonds, and some beautiful furniture now in Windsor Castle.

Interior Fittings and Other Decorations

Ebénistes turned to a variety of other professionals to complete their furniture. They went to the *tabletiers,* as was mentioned earlier, for various fittings, notably for game tables: e.g., Topino used the *tabletier* Aufrère. They obtained mirror and plate glass from glaziers, bottles from glassblowers, inkwells and candleholders from goldsmiths or bronze makers (figs. 18, 32).

Linings of watered silk, taffeta, tabby, or paper and writing surfaces of velvet or leather made necessary the collaboration of specialists in their application. The false book covers on the doors of tables and secretaries (fig. 28), the cardboard boxes with leather fall-fronts in file cabinets, the drawers with honeycomb compartments in metal cabinets, and the leather trunks that were used in bedrooms and wardrobes were all the work of binders.

It would be difficult to enumerate all the varieties of refinement explored by the furniture makers and dealers of the eighteenth century. Pierre Quarre discovered two panels dating from the middle of the fifteenth century with the arms of the Knights of the Golden Fleece traceable to the Sainte-Chapelle of Dijon, inserted in a Burgundian armoire in the Louis XV style, made immediately after the sales of the Revolution. I was not surprised to discover in a Parisian collection a panel depicting Judith and Holophernes, which had been taken from a French Renaissance buffet and mounted at the end of Louis XV's reign on the door of a *bas d'armoire* in the style of Pierre Garnier. The use of marble mosaics, some of which were taken out of Louis XIV cabinets, was just discussed in the previous section.

In 1770–71 embroidered panels were used to decorate the jewel cabinets made for the dauphine and the comtesse de Provence. There were small pieces of furniture covered entirely with straw marquetry which were the specialty or hobby of collectors like the prince de Conti's master of the hunt, Delasson. The eighteenth was a century of furniture, where everything conceivable was tried out.

Chapter 11

THE PRINCIPAL TYPES

OF FURNITURE

IN FRENCH FURNITURE of the eighteenth century, and particularly in *ébén-isterie,* there is so much diversity and fantasy that any categorization is arbitrary, simultaneously valid and false. In the interests of concise exposition, I group the principal items around five basic types, from which the others more or less derive: the commode, the table, the armoire, the cabinet, and the clock.

COMMODES

The commode could be called the key achievement of the century in the art of furniture. Still undefined in 1700, it was first termed *bureau:* however, the facilities afforded by this type of chest with large drawers were soon recognized and the name *commode* was adopted. In the opening years of the eighteenth century the duc d'Antin himself oversaw the execution of some of these new and precious pieces that were made for the king. The date of 1708, when payment of 3,000 livres was made to André-Charles Boulle for the commodes for the king's bedroom at the Grand Trianon (now at Versailles), is not surprising, considering the awkwardness of the two pieces. While splendid in their execution, they have the conservatism and hesitancy indicative of developmental prototypes.

In the Régence period the commode took on its classic conformation: a carcass defined by the uprights and side panels and containing a variable number of drawers. The curvature and height of the legs varied according to type and period. The *commode à la Régence* (termed such throughout the century, even after the close of the political regency), alternatively called *commode en tombeau* (figs. 81, 85, 86, 89, 94), had drawers extending almost all the way to the floor and consequently very short feet. The commonest version, of which innumerable Parisian and provincial examples survive in *ébénisterie* and even *menuiserie,* was made around 1730–50. The drawers were arranged in three rows: simply three drawers one above the other, or two large drawers with half-width drawers set side by side above, sometimes with a blind panel between them. The commode *à la Régence* was still made under Louis XVI, and Riesener often made use of the form adapting it to his times. On the other hand, the commode with only two rows of drawers (large or half-drawers) set on high curved legs was made as early as the Régence: I believe that a commode of this type (one of those in the Louvre) veneered with violet wood can be attributed to André-Charles Boulle himself.

What we call today a *Louis XV commode* (figs. 82, 83, 84, 87, 88, 132) developed out of the Régence type. There were usually two drawers. The cross-piece that separated them disappeared around 1740 giving a more rounded and integrated look, which was perpetuated under Louis XVI in *Transition* commodes. Mostly dating from 1775–80, these had rectilinear bodies set on curved legs but no Louis XV decoration, and some had only two large drawers (figs. 4, 79, 80, 92, 98, 133). It may have been this *Transition* type that was referred to in the listing of several *commodes à la grecque* in the inventory of Mme de Pompadour which were described as made of mahogany and satiné for the châteaus of Menars and Anvilliers between 1761 and 1763.

The *Louis XVI commode* (figs. 94, 95, 99, 134) could obviously retain a hybrid character derived from earlier periods. However, a new type began to develop around 1770 and soon became well defined: it borrowed from the Régence commode in its short, sometimes top-shaped feet terminating in bronze *sabots* (shoes), its deep, wide drawers, and the occasional figural corner mounts; and from the Louis XV commode in its two larger drawers, one above the other, with or without cross-pieces between them. Above the two principal drawers, the Louis XVI commode had a narrow frieze drawer that could be divided into three drawers. At the same time that the division between the large lower drawers and the frieze drawer or drawers was maintained, a block-fronted shape with a central projection which divided the horizontal drawers accentuated the character that the decoration and marquetry gave to the Louis XVI commode (figs. 79, 92). At the end of the eighteenth and in the early years of the nineteenth century, block-fronting became less pronounced and finally disappeared, principally on simple commodes of mahogany or walnut, but the system of frieze drawers above two large drawers remained.

Early on, it became a practice to make *encoignures* (corner cabinets) (figs. 96, 97) to match commodes. As a rule they were made in pairs, but in exceptional cases they were supplied for all four corners of a room like the game-room of Louis XVI at Versailles. In the Louis XV period the *encoignure* was usually surmounted by a set of shelves, or *étagère,* of matching *ébénisterie;* this set of shelves consisted of two or three shelves of triangular format and graduated size with two small doors on the bottom level. Today these shelves are almost always separated from their original *encoignures.* Some were never intended to surmount corner cabinets but rather designed as hanging shelves that could be attached, for example, on either side of a projecting chimney. In this case they were finished on the underside in *ébénisterie* generally with a console or *cul-de-lampe* motif (fig. 20). Whether it had shelves or not, the *encoignure* resembled a small corner armoire having one or two doors, with an optional extra foot on the front according to its scale, the required stability, and the date. (This extra foot disappeared in the second half of the century.) In the Louis XVI period *encoignures* were furnished with a frieze drawer and some were made in an open format without a door (there are even examples of the latter under Louis XV).

When two commodes were intended to furnish the same room, one of them would often be given doors instead of drawers (this alteration may have been inspired by the *encoignure*). Thus the *commode à vantaux* (with doors) (figs. 22, 90) came into being. Until the middle of the century it remained the exception, or was not clearly distinguishd from the *bas d'armoire*. When, under Louis XVI, the division of the facade into three vertical panels, as discussed above, led to three doors (two opening one direction and the third the other) (figs. 95, 99), the new type became truly defined. It enjoyed great success under the Empire. From the Louis XVI era on, the paradox existed of commodes where the drawers (and sometimes sliding shelves in the English manner) were concealed behind doors that had to be opened to gain access to the drawers.

Lateral compartments (fig. 98), each with a door, could recuperate the space lost when the contour of a piece entailed a difference in width between the front and the back, or the plan was semicircular or semioval as became popular under Louis XVI. From the end of the Louis XV era commodes were constructed with open corner shelves (fig. 99). Too often pieces of this type have been called *dessertes* (sideboards): if the corner shelves were backed with mirror glass, it was to show off gold or lacquer boxes or other collector's objects, not the leavings of a meal.

A piece of furniture did develop out of the commode for use in the dining room: it was the *console* (figs. 101, 153) and it enjoyed immense popularity under Louis XVI. Furnished with a frieze drawer like the contemporary commode, and with optional *encoignure* shelves, it resembled a commode in which the two large drawers had been removed and replaced with two shelves of marble or *ébénisterie*. The source appears to have been the Louis XV *commode in console* (figs. 12, 100), which was a commode reduced in size, having only one drawer, set on high, curving legs and probably intended to be attached under a pier glass. Perhaps, however, one should trace the origin of the *ébénisterie* console, which bears very little relationship to the *menuiserie* console, to certain shelves of palissander or mahogany commissioned from *ébénistes* by Mme de Pompadour: a *commode en bibliothèque* (bookcase) and "a commode without a front, the sides of antique lacquer, furnished with shelves of palissander wood, and a top of *brêche d'Alep* marble."

Commodes came in all shapes and sizes. There were enormous ones that ran 3 meters (9 ft. 10 in.) in length, and there were charming short ones, dubbed under Louis XV *demi-commodes* (fig. 93), which were to become indistinguishable from some small tables under Louis XVI. Some commodes were modeled on Chinese cabinets; others, made up by *marchands-merciers* from lacquer boxes imported from the Far East, had ten or twelve drawers all of different dimensions, like the commode mentioned in the inventory of Mme de Pompadour that must have been the work of B.V.R.B., or like the one signed by Leleu around 1770.

TABLES

The diversity and innumerable variations within furniture types are still more evident in tables. These, especially small tables, represent some of the most appealing products of French *ébénistes* of the eighteenth century.

The writing table is the basic and best-known type. The dimensions could be large, in which case it was termed a *bureau plat* (figs. 102, 103, 112, 118, 167). The top was first covered with velvet, then later with leather or sheepskin, and it was rimmed with a quarter-round section of copper that often had bronze mounts in the form of clips at the corners. In the Régence and later under Louis XVI the top was rectangular, but under Louis XV it was serpentine and occasionally slightly semicircular, curving around the user. The *bureau plat* sometimes had two drawers, but more often it had three large drawers which, in some of the beautiful pieces made in the first half of the eighteenth century, were separated by narrow drawers meant to hold scrolls. Writing slides concealed under the top were first located at each end of the table, then later another slide was added on one long side: sometimes they were on all four sides if the table was intended for a library. Drawers were not always present, and, under Louis XVI, they were restricted to a narrow apron around the table. The *bureau plat* passed through several stages before culminating its evolution. The three ample drawers of the Louis XV writing table were themselves a reduction from what was called a *bureau* (in the sense of writing table) in the century of Louis XIV. Until then it was actually only a piece of furniture with a table top below which drawers extended quite low to the ground on either side of a central panel; and it usually had eight feet rather than four. Around 1700 the central panel was replaced by a drawer that gave the piece a total of seven drawers. One of the Oebens made a piece of this type (now in the Musée de Tours) for Chanteloup. The format of a central opening flanked by two banks of drawers was in use into the Empire. The type continues to this day as the English library table, and also persists in France, notably Provence. The table-top pigeonhole units set facing the user on some *bureaux plats* were yet another carryover from the Louis XIV era. Usually the *bureau plat* was delivered with a file called a *serre-*

papiers, or *cartonnier* (figs. 6, 165). With a few exceptions it was an independent piece of furniture that was placed against the short end of a *bureau plat.* The file was composed of an armoire base and compartments for cardboard boxes above the level of the table top, and surmounted by a clock that could be an imposing decorative element.

On top of the writing table stood the inkstand (figs. 116, 130) which, in the most refined ensembles, had *ébénisterie,* lacquer, bronzes, and occasionally porcelain to match the furniture. The inkstand could be accompanied by a slant-top lap desk (fig. 167).

Superstructures like the table-top file were probably the origin of the slant-top desk now commonly called *dos d'ane* (back of an ass) (figs. 104, 111); other terms in use in the eighteenth century include *secrétaire à abbatant* (which led to confusion with the upright secretary), and, under Louis XVI, *secrétaire en tombeau* (in the shape of a tomb). The drawback of the *bureau plat* was that papers were exposed to prying eyes unless they were put away under lock and key in the drawers. *Ebénistes* and mechanics applied themselves to the problem of increasing the potential of privacy by enclosing the desk. The slant-top desk was the first step in this direction.

There are a few very rare double-sided slant-top desks (fig. 3), and the term *dos d'ane* should really be reserved for them. They were designed to allow two people to work at the same time, facing each other, but separated by two sets of compartments and drawers. The most extraordinary double slant-top desk is the one signed B.V.R.B. in the Getty Museum in Los Angeles. The Musée Magnin in Dijon has a very simple desk of this type designed for children and bearing the stamp Bon Durand.

The same desire to keep papers confidential was responsible for the development of the fall-front, or upright, secretary (figs. 27, 108, 145). Whereas the slant-top desk was free-standing in a room and therefore finished on all four sides, the upright secretary went against the wall. There was a long drawer at the top, and large drawers, or more often two doors enclosing shelves, drawers, or sometimes a coffer, in the lower section.

Further experiments based on the slant-top desk or the desk with a table-top unit led to the cylinder desk (figs. 106, 107), a semicircular shutter composed of horizontal slats rolled up around a cylinder housed between the compartments and drawers and the back wall of the piece. The great cylinder desk started by Oeben and completed in 1769 by Riesener was to have been the first of the type. When its top rolled up, it just missed the pendulum of the double-faced clock atop the desk. When it closed, it covered all the drawers: thus a single key was sufficient for the entire piece. When the rolltop opened, a writing slide was automatically advanced. The use of this rolltop, which may have come from Germany, quickly became a huge success. In 1768, before the completion of Oeben's great cylinder desk, Joubert delivered a rolltop file of ebonized pearwood to the Garde-Meuble. Roubo made note of an even simpler device in his 1772 book on *menuiserie:* a quarter-cylinder top formed by only two curved panels that divided and slid back to open (pl. 262 fig. 6). Following this principle, Parisian and provincial *ébénistes* around 1780 substituted the swinging rigid quarter-cylinder for the rolltop, and it is to be found on innumerable secretaries of the end of the eighteenth as well as the nineteenth centuries. Like the slant-top or upright secretaries, the cylinder desk could have a commode base and be topped off with a glazed showcase.

A multitude of small, elegant, ingenious, and easy-to-handle tables (figs. 8, 166) developed from the *bureau plat* and the secretary. The simplest, the small writing table (fig. 113), was a reduction of the large *bureau plat.* Its top could be of leather or velvet but also of veneered wood or marquetry. In the latter case there was a leather-covered writing slide on the longer side of the table. This slide itself could be converted into a lectern or be raised and reversed to reveal a mirror and small compartments for toiletries. Almost always a drawer in the side was equipped with three compartments for ink, sand, and sponge. *Ebénistes* in the circle of Oeben, Lacroix, and Riesener made little writing tables where the top slid back and simultaneously advanced the body of the piece, which contained a writing surface, lectern, and interior compartments (fig. 154). In the *secrétaire à capucin,* or *à la Bourgogne,* the top opened out one hundred eighty degrees allowing a set of drawers to pop up by means of springs. The mechanics of the *secrétaire à culbute* (fig. 105) were simpler: a graduated set of drawers and compartments contained in the rear of the table was hinged to swing up into position. Last, the *bureau en pupitre,* a lectern desk for use while standing, which had drawers, doors, or compartments in the lower section, should be mentioned. Should the *table à la Tronchin,* a rectangular writing table where the top could be raised for drawing, be grouped with these pieces? The form developed in the early years of the reign of Louis XVI, but the term only came into use toward the end of the century. There were also painters' tables with many shallow drawers for paints and brushes. The *bonheur-du-jour* (fig. 121) was a special kind of writing table with a built-in superstructure of drawers and closed compartments. It could have a shelf between the legs. As the name (literally "success of the day") indicates, it enjoyed tremendous popularity over the last third of the century.

It is difficult to formulate a precise definition for the genre of small pieces of furniture that could be used equally well as writing or dressing tables. The Victoria and Albert Museum, for example, has a cylinder desk whose lower section can be advanced and contains nothing but fittings for toiletries. Writing tables equipped with mirrors have already been mentioned. Conversely there are also pieces which are primarily dressing tables and which serve for writing only as a secondary function. In the eighteenth century the *toilette*, or dressing table, was not usually a piece of *ébénisterie* but rather a carpentry construction covered with laces and muslin on which a mirror, boxes, and trays of goldsmithswork, lacquer, or even Boullework marquetry were set out (figs. 15–17). The only dressing tables that survive, however, are those in *ébénisterie*, termed under Louis XV *toilettes de campagne*. They consisted of tables whose tops were divided into panels: the central panel could be raised from the back and was fitted with a mirror on the reverse, while two side panels opened out to reveal compartments for brushes and powder pots. Before the end of the eighteenth century they made dressing tables where the entire top raised to reveal a mirror (fig. 115). There were an infinite variety of hair-dressing or cosmetic tables: the rectangular dressing table became classic; the heart-shaped dressing table had an interior leather-covered writing surface and a small drawer in front for writing equipment. The type that developed at the end of the century, where a vertical mirror behind colonettes was set on a marble table top, was probably a man's dressing table, as it allowed the man to shave himself while standing.

The dressing table could be combined with a lady's table for use in bed (figs. 18, 19), but this was probably less common in the eighteenth century than one might believe today. It usually took the form of a rectangular or oval dressing table with a lectern, central mirror, and lateral compartments, and four short legs, which, when the bed table was not in use, rested on a base of matching *ébénisterie* designed for the purpose. The bedside mechanical table now in the Metropolitan Museum of Art, designed by Riesener with the aid of the court mechanic Mercklein for the lying-in of Marie-Antoinette at the birth of her first child in 1778, took a different form. The top was raised and lowered by means of a crank on the side to serve "different uses: 1. eating; 2. dressing; 3. writing, standing or seated."

Tables de chevet, or night tables (fig. 24), could be elegant and luxurious. They were hidden away in a dressing room during the day. Their two marble shelves were only rarely enclosed by doors or shutters. At the end of the Louis XVI era circular, or "snail-shaped," night tables appeared. *Tables d'encas* (snack), which were larger and higher and quite often oval with marquetry on all sides, were equipped with sliding doors that distinguish them from *demi-commodes*. Sometimes a wire fencing closed off the lower shelf, protecting the midnight snack from dogs. Like the dressing tables, *tables d'en-cas* were mounted on casters, and, at least under Louis XV, night tables were equipped with bronze carrying handles or open grips on the sides.

Tables à déjeuner (lunch) were also lightweight and easily transportable (figs. 26, 29). Some were ovoid with kidney-shaped top and slender legs as we see in the famous drawing by Hubert Robert (Musée de Valence) depicting Madame Geoffrin preparing to take a light meal. There were even smaller square versions with tops of marble or porcelain, and sometimes carrying handles. These were coffee tables, or *tables-cabarets* [the term *cabaret* was used at the Sèvres porcelain manufactory to designate a small tea or coffee set] (figs. 21, 23, 122).

Tables en chiffonnière were quite similar in appearance to the preceding type. References to them appear in the factory records at Sèvres and the name appears on a label still affixed to one example. The 1763 inventory of Mme de Pompadour, for instance, lists "one *vuide-poche* (catchall table) and small *chiffonnière* veneered in satiné," one "tambour *chiffonnière* with its two candle arms," and another "*chiffonnière* with veneered panels fitted with drawers." From the inventory drawn up on the death of the engraver Benoit Audran, we know that he had "a small *chiffonnière* with marble top, wood veneers and three drawers." The catalog of the sale of the duchesse de Mazarin (December 10, 1781) listed eight *chiffonnières* of different types: round, rotating, in the form of a coffer, night table, dressing table, with sliding doors, with Sèvres porcelain plaques, with lacquer panels. The 1790 inventory of Madame Elisabeth's little château at Montreuil further documents the popularity and diversity of *chiffonnières:* the one in her bedroom was "in the form of a bookcase," while that in her Turkish-style salon had "three drawers on the side." Most of these tables must have served as needlework tables (fig. 35). Some of them under Louis XVI were termed trough or spittoon tables. Their tops were designed as containers, and while for some years they were basket-shaped, they were later enclosed with raised sides, one of which could be lowered. Some of these tables had a drawer that could be fitted with writing equipment. There was still more specialized furniture for embroidery or needlepoint where the table top was replaced by a slanted frame for the canvas (fig. 34).

The introduction of dining and tea tables at the end of the reign of Louis XV was a result of English influence. Dining tables were treated as *ébénisterie* rather than simple carpentry as before, and could be extended to seat a variable number by a system of slides that was soon widely adopted. Tea tables (fig. 136) had tripod bases and tilt-tops of mahogany, occasionally decorated with porcelain plaques. There were similar tripod bases for small *guéridons* (fig. 32), tiny circular *ébénisterie* tables, as well as lecterns (fig. 120) and music stands: these small pieces could be veneered in precious woods, or lacquers, and Carlin signed a number of them that were decorated with Sèvres porcelain plaques. Migeon executed a sextet table around 1750 in solid mahogany. He seems to have had a disciple in the use of polished or varnished mahogany in the English manner in Canabas, who specialized in small serving tables with compartmentalized tops to accommodate table settings and bottles (fig. 31). There were precedents for this type of table as far back as 1735.

Gaming tables (figs. 30, 125, 126) can be subdivided into many varieties. They could be round for cavagnol or brelan (which was also played at five-sided tables), and they could have a central well for chips. Piquet and quadrelle tables were rectangular or square and often had pockets, cavities, or rounded projections at each angle. Tables for ombre and three-handed ombre were triangular. All these different types could be permanently covered with velvet or cloth, or they could be folding tables that displayed an *ébénisterie* surface when collapsed. Backgammon tables had removable tops and holes for candleholders on pegs: some had further elaboration with lotto and roulette on the removable top and various accessories in numerous drawers. The importance of gambling in the society of the eighteenth century must be recognized. The observation of a contemporary, Frénilly, is relevant to gaming tables: he describes a retired government official from Poitou as "such a gambler that he had practically no furniture other than backgammon tables."

Gaming tables were just as often executed in *ébénisterie* as in *menuiserie*. Bidets (fig. 123) and toilets, on the other hand, which are mentioned here for lack of an appropriate category in which to group them, were almost always *menuiserie*. Of course the pieces of very private furniture made at great expense for Mme de Pompadour, Louis XV, and Mme Du Barry, and the lacquer toilet of Marie-Antoinette can be cited as exceptions. Examples of *ébénisterie* armchairs and screens were equally rare (figs. 33, 36).

ARMOIRES

The commode and the desk were new items of furniture: their popularity was prodigious all through the eighteenth century and their ramifications were enormous. This was not the case with two traditional forms, the armoire and the cabinet, which fell out of favor in *ébénisterie* after 1700.

The armoire form remained vital in *menuiserie* in Paris as well as the provinces, but the taste for elaborate, costly *ébénisterie* armoires of the sort made by Boulle and Godron under Louis XIV disappeared. Cressent tried to keep up the tradition (figs. 1, 78), but such costly monumental furniture was no longer in demand for the new, smaller-scale apartments. Either the large armoire was a piece of *menuiserie* and was relegated to dressing rooms and secondary apartments; or it was decorated with precious woods and bronzes and it took on smaller proportions. In the latter case it was used to display collections, with the doors glazed or covered with wire screen and a drawer in the bottom. The bookcase was a variation which could be composed of several units and have many doors, but which was only occasionally treated as *ébénisterie*. Mention should also be made of the highly unusual pieces designed to hold card and stamp collections.

The relationship of some secretaries, corner cabinets, and commodes to the armoire has been discussed. The *bas d'armoire* (figs. 110, 114) was a piece that came to leaning or breast height, having single or double doors and a marble top. It was larger and higher and had a rectangular rather than a triangular plan, distinguishing it from the *encoignure*. In some cases the distinction was blurred: e.g., Louis XV commissioned Joubert to make four *bas d'armoire* for his bathroom at Versailles with rounded backs to conform to the wall paneling, and the resulting form was closely similar to an *encoignure*.

Cabinet doors in the superstructure of some secretaries have already been noted. This arrangement was common in the Netherlands, Germany, and England. It was unusual under Louis XV, even though the king commissioned a piece of this type that must have been made by B.V.R.B. (Musée du Mans): it has two glazed doors above a fall-front and two doors below it instead of the drawers that are found in the base of most non-French examples. The model was taken up again with more success around 1780, modified and reduced in scale, notably by Saunier, on cylinder desks that were surmounted by double-door vitrines. (This could also become a variation on a *bonheur-du-jour*.)

CABINETS

At the start the cabinet was no more than a deluxe coffer set on a stand. During the Louis XIV era it was the most sumptuous of all furniture. It reappeared in the eighteenth century in rather special circumstances in the form of great jewel cabinets like those created for Marie-Antoinette when she was dauphine and again when she became queen, and for the comtesse de Provence (the commissions were given to Evalde, Schwerdfeger, and Riesener,

78. Armoire with two doors. Veneered with tulipwood around lacquer panels on the front and marquetry of leaf sprays in violet wood on the sides. The inside of the doors veneered in tulipwood, with gilt bronze locks. A sumptuous example of the Louis XV style. Formerly in the collections of Mlle de Choiseul, Mme Burat, Baron Cassel, and Antenor Patiño. Stamped B.V.R.B. Circa 1750. (Patiño gift, 1956, Musée du Louvre)

81. Régence commode with two lar
drawers below two smaller ones. \
olet wood parquetry. Gilt bron
moldings framing the drawers, s
drawer pulls with their rosettes, tv
large hinged handles on the sid
elaborate escutcheons, corner moun
and double goat feet. Variegat
Campan marble top. Circa 172
(Jones Collection, Victoria and Alb
Museum, London) →

← 79. Commode with three drawe
one above the other, *à la Régence,* a
a projecting block front. Venee
with tulipwood and violet wood a
with gilt bronze mounts. Short ca
riole legs of the Transition style. (I
a simplified version in walnut in
same location, see fig. 91.) Stamp
by P. Garnier. Circa 1770. (Château
Montgeoffroy, Maine-et-Loire)

← 80. Detail of the corner of a comm
dating from the same period as tha
fig. 79 but more lavish and m
Louis XVI in style with more,
finer-quality, bronze mounts (see
view in fig. 155). Veneered with tu
wood and violet wood with marq
try filets. With two large drawers w
marquetry creating three vertical p
els on the facade; a third shall
drawer creating a frieze. For the ap
ment of the maréchal de Conta
Also stamped by P. Garnier and
ing circa 1770. (Château de M
geoffroy, Maine-et-Loire)

82. Early Louis XV commode v
two large drawers. Veneered in pu
wood with diamond shapes of tu
wood. Lavish gilt bronze mount
palm branches, flowers, festoons,
coco ornaments, scrolling feet, a c
standing on a platform with a tass
covering who seems to be bea
time at the center, and two infant
sicians at the corners "in relief, ha
the bodies visible, seeming to wa
come out." By Cressent. Circa 1
(Residenzmuseum, Munich) →

84. One of a pair of Louis XV commodes with two drawers. Veneered in tulipwood and violet wood with marquetry of leaf sprays in end-cut wood. Luxuriant gilt bronze mounts. The same model exists in lacquer at Windsor Castle and the Getty Museum. With the paper label of the dealer Darnault. Stamped by Joseph Baumhauer. Circa 1750. (National Gallery of Art, Washington, Widener Collection)

83a-b-c. Louis XV commode with two drawers. Veneered with tulipwood around lacquer panels, with filets of yellow and black wood. Gilt bronze mounts of a full-blown rococo style including swirling leaves forming drawer pulls. From the Festetics family and possibly the dukes of Hamilton. Stamped Delorme. Circa 1750. (Museum of Decorative Arts, Budapest)

85. Louis XV commode à la Régence with three ranks of drawers. Veneered with tulipwood and violet wood. Louis XV gilt bronze mounts of common quality. This type of commode is frequently found in France and throughout northern Europe unsigned or with the signature of a Parisian ébéniste. Stamped by Boudin. Mid-eighteenth century. (Nieborow castle, near Warsaw)

86. Louis XV commode à la Régence with three ranks of drawers. Veneered with tulipwood and violet wood. Louis XV gilt bronze mounts of common quality. There are similar commodes with the stamps of Hédouin and Mondon in the same castle (published by R. Stratmann). Stamped by M. Criaerd. Mid-eighteenth century. (Ludwigsburg castle, Baden)

87. Louis XV commode with two drawers and cabriole legs. Marquetry of leaf sprays. The gilt bronze mounts play an important role with corner mounts continuing in moldings down to the feet and frame element and drawer pulls worked into a central M-shaped motif. Stamped by J. Dubois. Circa 1750. (Musée Du Breuil, Langres)

89. Louis XV commode *à la Régence* but of unusual form with two large drawers with two narrower and shallower drawers above. Veneered in violet wood parquetry. Louis XV bronze mounts: the model of the mount on the front feet is the same as that of the commode in fig. 86. Stamped by Migeon. Circa 1750. (Mobilier National)

88. Louis XV commode with two drawers and cabriole legs. Marquetry of flower sprays within curvilinear panels defined by borders of crossbanded tulipwood edged with violet wood. The usual mounts, drawer pulls, escutcheons, apron mount, corner mounts, and feet. Stamped by Migeon. Circa 1750. (Paul Gillet gift, 1950, Musée des Arts Décoratifs, Lyon)

90. Medal cabinet commode with two drawers. Veneered in purple wood with marquetry panels of end-cut wood flower sprays on a satiné ground. The interior veneered in purple wood and fitted with two ranks of small drawers. The bronze mounts stamped with the Crowned C mark. Unsigned. Circa 1745. (Musée des Beaux-Arts, Lille)

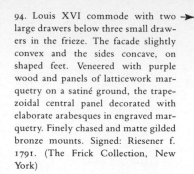

94. Louis XVI commode with two large drawers below three small drawers in the frieze. The facade slightly convex and the sides concave, on shaped feet. Veneered with purple wood and panels of latticework marquetry on a satiné ground, the trapezoidal central panel decorated with elaborate arabesques in engraved marquetry. Finely chased and matte gilded bronze mounts. Signed: Riesener f. 1791. (The Frick Collection, New York)

91. Transitional commode with three drawers. Straight uprights but short cabriole legs. Walnut with a mahogany stain. Louis XVI ring pulls, varnished rather than gilded. "Flanders" marble top. Similar commodes in less important rooms of the same château have wood tops (see figs. 79–80). Stamped by P. Garnier. Circa 1770. (Château de Montgeoffroy, Maine-et-Loire)

92. Transitional commode with three ranks of drawers à la Régence. Straight uprights but short cabriole legs. Marquetry of satiné, tulipwood, and violet wood in three vertical panels corresponding to the division of the upper ranks of drawers (cf. the Louis XV marquetry panels on the commode in fig. 88). Gilt bronze mounts almost entirely Louis XVI in style. Stamped Roussel. Circa 1770. (Rupert de Chièvres collection, Musée des Beaux-Arts, Poitiers)

93. Transitional demicommode in the form of a coffer with two doors opening onto drawers. Cabriole legs. Black japanned wood and lacquer panels. Fine gilt bronze moldings, corner mounts with rams' heads, and lion paw feet. Belonged to the comtesse de Boigne in the eighteenth century. Stamped by Montigny. Circa 1775. (Private collection)

95. Louis XVI commode with three doors opening onto two sliding shelves. Veneered with mahogany of milky figure. Bronze mounts cast by Forestier, chased by Thomire, and gilded by Chaudron "with the exception of the busts and tapering bases which are given an antique green patination like that produced over time." Stamped by Benneman. 1787. (Musée du Louvre)

96. One of a pair of corner cabinets with double doors. Veneered in tulipwood and violet wood with marquetry in end-cut wood of large flower sprays emerging from volutes. Sumptuous gilt bronze mounts. Belonged in the nineteenth century to the Orléans family and bear the marking the château d'Eu. Stamped by Latz. Circa 1745. (Ojjeh sale, Sotheby's, Monaco, June 25, 1979, no. 44, 2,600,000 f the pair)

97. One of a pair of corner cabinets (the second bearing the same signature) with a single door and an extra foot at the center. The central panel painted and varnished by the Martin brothers with a vignette in the manner of Boucher. Curvilinear rococo gilt bronze mounts. Published by A. Setterwall. Stamped by Boudin. Circa 1760. (Royal Palace, Stockholm)

98. Transitional demilune commode with two large
drawers and a cupboard on each side, on straight squared
legs. Black japanned wood and lacquer panels. The
bronze mounts still more Louis XV in style than neoclassical. Belonged to the fermier général J.-B. Roslin d'Ivry.
Stamped by C.-C. Saunier. Circa 1770. (Private collection)

99. Louis XVI demilune commode with a central door
opening onto four drawers, lateral corner shelves, and tapering fluted feet. Black japanned wood, ebony and lacquer panels. On the interior the door is veneered with
tulipwood with framing filets and the drawer fronts have
lacquer and japanning. Brocatelle marble top and shelves.
Lavish gilt bronze frieze, corner mounts, etc., and draperies on the apron. Stamped by C.-C. Saunier. Circa
1780. (Private collection)

respectively). Less imposing pieces (figs. 109, 119, 146), which were nonetheless highly embellished with bronzes, porcelain plaques, and lacquer panels, became the specialty of Carlin and Weisweiler, probably through the intermediary of Daguerre. It was the *marchands-merciers* who had B.V.R.B., Joseph, and Oeben make charming cabinets around 1750–60 that were small coffers with fall-fronts mounted on bases in the form of elegant tables. These pieces, which were used to hold jewelry, could also be used as medal cabinets (figs. 149, 151).

Such small pieces of furniture account for some of the most delightful expressions of eighteenth-century fantasy. They may have derived from the marriage coffer, which in Boulle's day could be treated in *ébénisterie,* just as there were caskets of fine *ébénisterie* that were not the simple products of *tabletiers* (specialists in small objects of wood, ivory, or tortoiseshell) (figs. 17, 117, 130). Some trunks instead of being common boxwork covered in leather were treated in the most perfect *ébénisterie* (figs. 25, 28). At the time of the Revolution Riesener appears to have made mahogany chests bordered in copper with stands of iron or wood that could be disassembled and stored in a compartment underneath. In outline they somewhat resembled night tables or *meubles d'en-cas.*

On the other hand, commodes, armoires, and large cabinets alike could be adapted to hold medal collections (figs. 1, 90) or shell collections: Gaudreaux, Cressent, B.V.R.B., and Oeben created extraordinary examples.

CLOCKS

The interest aroused by the technical advances of renowned horologists led to increasing extravagance in clock cases. Here again Boulle led the way, and the climax was reached at midcentury by masters like Cressent and Latz.

Clock cases tended to be gaudy rather than delicate, covered with applications of tortoiseshell and copper, japanning in red, green, or yellow decorated with little flowers, or marquetry or veneer of green-stained animal horn usually done by specialists like Goyer among others (fig. 13). The bronze mounts on these clock cases were usually of mediocre quality. The movement was surmounted by decorative cresting. A base supported the clock, either a flat base if it was to stand on a mantel or a console if it was to be on the wall.

The *régulateur,* or long-case clock (figs. 127–29), was provided with a far more refined *ébénisterie* case and with better-quality bronze mounts. The pendulum and weights necessitated a height of more that 2 meters (6 ft. 6¾ in.), making it an imposing piece, which, like the file cabinet, would be topped off by a large bronze. To house certain astronomical clocks with multiple dials, the case became enlarged and the bronzes enhanced in luxuriance and volume, as if to emphasize the mechanical wonders that lay inside. Under Louis XVI the form of the long-case clock became still more refined: sometimes it was provided with a barometer as a pendant. Although cartel clocks were usually bronze, some were done in veneered wood, just as certain scientific instruments were treated as *ébénisterie,* demonstrating the breadth of the field covered by *ébénisterie* in the eighteenth century and the hopelessness of trying to define its limits.

Chapter 12

SOME DISTINCTIVE CHARACTERISTICS

Without going into too much detail it is good at this point to call attention to some of the personal stylistic traits of the most famous Parisian *ébénistes* of the eighteenth century and to summarize what is known about provincial *ébénisterie*.

GREAT PARISIAN *EBENISTES*

André-Charles Boulle (fig. 15) was the link between the Louis XIV and the Louis XV periods, especially since his workshop in the Louvre continued and his sons worked there until the middle of the century. Boulle, probably influenced by Berain, was one of the innovators at the turn of the eighteenth century who introduced the lively contours, imaginative decoration, and systematic use of bronze mounts that would characterize French furniture for a long time to come. The technique for which he is best known is a marquetry of tortoiseshell and copper he used on the masterpieces he continued to create after 1700, like the commodes for the king's bedroom at the Trianon and the desk for the elector of Bavaria. He was one of the first to do geometric marquetry or parquetry in violet wood around 1715. Superb bronze mounts characterized the furniture made by this great *ébéniste* during the reign of Louis XIV, but their quality declined in works by his sons, which were often mediocre and gaudy, notably large, busy clocks that were a specialty of the Boulle sons and were imitated by others like Goyer and Langlois. The influence of Boulle (figs. 13, 17) was great throughout the century: it was transmitted through *ébénistes* who started in his workshop or that of his sons, like the Oebens, and masters like Levasseur, Montigny, and even Riesener who restored Boulle's fragile works and thus studied his style at close range.

Charles Cressent (figs. 1, 82) was the *ébéniste* of both ducs d'Orleans, the regent and especially his son Louis. In this role he succeeded Joseph Poitou, whose father was an *ébéniste* and rival of Boulle. The works of Cressent, which are never signed, are known to us through contemporary references and sale catalogs. His development is difficult to trace because we can date practically nothing of his between 1723 and 1748. He was as much a sculptor as an *ébéniste,* and he seems to have regarded exotic woods as glistening backgrounds against which to contrast and show off the beautiful bronze mounts which he certainly modeled himself. The shapes of his furniture were somewhat heavy. He used sober marquetry. His favorite woods were satiné and purple wood, which he used in large-scale lozenges and borders, then, probably a little later, in surrounds shadowing the design of his mounts. Bronze mounts constituted his main concern, and he had frequent conflicts on this score with members of the bronze casters' guild, who refused to allow him to cast them in his own workshop. Cressent's gilt-bronze furniture mounts range from picturesque motifs to the formal but pleasant style popularized after 1700 by Robert de Cotte and the duchesse de Bourgogne: female figures, *espagnolettes* (heads of women wearing ruffled collars) clearly influenced by Watteau, seasons, *singeries* (monkey caricatures), *rocailles,* and flowers. He used them as caryatids at the corners of furniture, or in pictorial compositions because he liked an emphatic central motif, or worked in among the *rocailles* of the borders. His palms, large flowers, vines, bronze dragons, and escutcheons decorated with chimeras are also found on furniture, which, being unsigned, is difficult to distinguish from that of his lesser-known contemporaries Doirat and Gaudreaux.

Antoine Gaudreaux was *ébéniste* to the Royal Garde-Meuble for a quarter century (1726–51), succeeding two forgotten masters, Hecquet and Guillemard. Like his predecessors, Gaudreaux did not sign his works, which are today all too little known: some of the most beautiful commodes and the most luxurious desks of the early Louis XV style, made for the king, came from his workshop. The archives of the Garde-Meuble, together with the surviving pieces of furniture that I have been able to locate, make it possible to trace his development from the compartmentalized veneers and filets of olive wood and palissander of the Louis XIV style to the "small squares and lozenges," "mosaics," and large reserves of violet wood covered with curvilinear bronze mounts inspired by the Slodtz brothers.

The *Migeon* dynasty (figs. 88, 89, 111) has been known from what appears to be its enormous production. On examining certain pieces more closely today, however, we see, in addition to the signature of Pierre Migeon II, who died in 1758, or Pierre III, who died in 1775, a second, less-obvious stamp of another *ébéniste*. In fact, the Migeons were not only furniture makers but also retailers who sold works by most of the good *ébénistes* of their day: Dautriche, Gerard Peridiez, Bon Durand, Mathieu Criaerd, Lacroix, Boudin, Macret, Dubois, and Bircklé. In consequence the style was somewhat heterodox. Through their orders the Migeons influenced an entire generation of *ébénistes* whose work they supervised to a greater or lesser extent. Their preference seems to have been for rather low, heavy, bombé forms. Bowed contours at the center or on drawer fronts, doors, and sometimes the bases of pieces indicate a predilection for curves shared by their associates. I believe the simple, almost austere, veneers of sheets of satiné or tulipwood, sometimes with borders of violet wood or purple wood, can be attributed to the Migeons. Multilobed veneers and, as with all their contemporaries, overall lozenge patterns forming parquetry can be found. They were among the first to make furniture of solid mahogany, perhaps initially for Mme de Pompadour, who was their client. Should their use of floral marquetry of polychromed or cross-cut wood be interpreted as purely personal, or influenced by other *ébénistes* like B.V.R.B., Roussel, and Boudin? Or might one suppose that it was rather the Migeons who influenced these *ébénistes?*

The importance of *Jean-Pierre Latz* (fig. 96) in French furniture of the mid-eighteenth century was recently brought to light by Henry Hawley. Close to B.V.R.B., this native of the Electorate of Cologne received royal protection in France as *ébéniste privilégié du Roy, suivant la cour.* Feulner and

Briganti published some of his very beautiful pieces. He worked either directly or through the intermediary of dealers for the courts of Berlin, Dresden, and Parma. He tried to cast the sumptuous bronze mounts of his furniture in his own workshop. His greatest success lay in the making of richly decorated cases for long-case clocks (which alone comprise twenty of the sixty-nine signed or attributed pieces that Hawley has cataloged). A clock in Belgium that is supposed to have been a gift of Louis XV may be added to the list.

Pierre Roussel (fig. 92) was an *ébéniste* who appears more important in the light of discoveries about some of the furniture in the Louvre, notably an elegant ebony desk with filets of copper and a tall ebony clock with blue-stained animal horn. Perhaps he was not one of the most original artists; admittedly, the leaders of the profession, Boulle, Cressent, Gaudreaux, and Migeon, had more personality. The influence of Migeon can be seen in his rather heavy bombé lines and his commodes, which extend very low to the floor. He used lacquer and japanning as well as floral marquetry. His personal taste seems to have led him to pursue color and fantasy and he rarely used parquetry or marquetry flowers or crosscut wood. He preferred flower sprays and large bouquets in variously colored woods; and he executed them with a solid technical mastery and a sense of tradition that earned him a respected place among his contemporaries. While others could be more brilliant, more audacious, or more appealing, Pierre Roussel, who came from a family of *ébénistes* and *menuisiers,* had all the seriousness of French *menuisiers.* He may have been a minor master in the Parisian context, but anywhere else he would have rated as a major *ébéniste*. It seems to me that he was particularly important in the transition from the Louis XV to the Louis XVI style. At the start the legs of his furniture were curved, but his forms became more and more rectilinear, especially in commodes, where quite early he adopted the three-part panel facade. He made regular and probably rather early use of motifs such as bouquets, trophies, utensils, landscapes, and ruins. He then went into more geometric decorations like lozenges, shaped panels, and checkered patterns.

B.V.R.B. (figs. 3, 20, 21, 22, 78, 100, 149, 151, 165, 166, 167) is famous and appealing in quite a different way. The *ébéniste* whose identity long remained a mystery was known by his initials. I believed him to be the "Bernard" mentioned in sales catalogs of the eighteenth century, and a thesis (which was never published but became widely known) by J.-P. Baroli at the Ecole du Louvre securely identified the initials as those of the Bernard Van

Risen Burghs. This family, which came from Holland, provided Paris with three generations of *ébénistes*. Their evolution from the purest Louis XV through the Transition style to Louis XVI is traced in pieces of furniture bearing the stamp B.V.R.B. The greatest and most prolific family member was Bernard Van Risen Burgh II, who can be considered the most charming and highly developed *ébéniste* of the Louis XV period. The contemporaries who mentioned furniture by Bernard already evidenced the admiration still felt today for his work. I believe that he may have been obliged to sign only with initials to maintain his anonymity by the one or two *marchands-merciers,* like Lazare Duvaux and Poirier, for whom he worked. He profited by their orders and benefited by their taste and inventive spirit. The forms of his furniture were almost always Louis XV and with rare exceptions they were light, thoroughbreds one might say, with fine joinery, tiny bronze shoes, and chamfered legs rounded on the exterior faces. Such delicate nuances demonstrate the sensitivity of this *ébéniste*. There are gentle contours to the panels of commodes and slant-top desks, for example, with gilt bronze accents to mark the culmination of the primary curves. He probably owed the idea of the violet wood branches that are typical of his marquetry to the dealers from whom he received his orders. He also used lacquers and japanning (on occasion boldly combined with wood veneers, as in the extraordinary armoire that was in the collections of Choiseul, Burat, and Patino, and is now in the Louvre; fig. 78). He also combined japanning with Sèvres porcelain plaques (used with the most extravagant fantasy, as in the superb commode of the prince de Condé, fig. 22). These decorations may have been prescribed by the commissions, as were the opulence of the bronze mounts and the beauty of the marbles he used. Although he was a little-known artist from a family of foreign origins, his work seems the embodiment of Parisian taste under Louis XV. He was, as if in spite of himself, the skilled instrument by which a product was made. His furniture, in any case, which was sought after in his lifetime by the dealers of the fashionable neighborhood of Saint-Honoré, remains today among the most highly prized of the eighteenth century. Furniture that can be attributed to Bernard Van Risen Burgh III continued the tradition into another style with pieces that are heavier but just as finely executed with beautiful panels of lacquer.

Joseph (figs. 84, 112, 151, 165), whose name was Joseph Baumhauer and whose stamp is decorated with a fleur-de-lys, probably also worked for the great dealers. He put his signature to superb pieces, ranging in style from the full Louis XV to the early Louis XVI, monumental architectonic pieces, commodes and *encoignures,* and beautiful writing tables that often have an unusual feature, a band of matted gilt bronze cut to exactly repeat the subtle curve of the legs.

Jacques Dubois (fig. 87) and his son René followed a similar course of development to B.V.R.B. and Joseph. Their talents were just as typical of the Louis XV style and yet one knows examples of their work in the Transitional and pure Louis XVI styles. In some cases they might show more forcefulness, vigor, and flair than B.V.R.B., but on the other hand less refinement. Their production was oriented toward large-scale *ébénisterie* furniture, commodes and *encoignures,* writing tables, slant-top or fall-front desks. Their specialty was imaginative luxury items and they worked under the *marchands-merciers*. Their style, which was occasionally somewhat heavy, perhaps because it was so opulent, always remained balanced. Like B.V.R.B. they used floral marquetry of end-cut wood, lacquer, and japanning. One also finds some polychrome marquetry like that used by Roussel. Their bronze mounts were full of imagination. They were perhaps more luxuriant and contained *rocailles* even more asymmetrical than those of B.V.R.B. There were heavy corner mounts as well as apron mounts with curvilear flourishes. At the end of the Louis XV era René Dubois seems to have introduced more grace and invention to the contouring of his furniture: secretaries of this period, while still bearing the father's stamp, I. Dubois, evidence great finesse and occasionally include picturesque chinoiserie elements. Larger pieces tend to be heavy and have classical motifs and bronze mounts that are massive but finely worked, e.g., the low cupboards in the Cleveland Museum and the Wallace Collection. The elegance of the bronze mermaids at the corners of the green lacquer commode and writing table also in the Wallace Collection cannot, however, be overlooked. A large number of rather mediocre small commodes, usually japanned, bear the stamp Dubois but they seem unworthy of great *ébénistes*. In contrast, two pieces of major importance must be given to Jacques Dubois: the so-called Choiseuil lacquer desk (which came from the château of Raincy) on which his stamp has been discovered, and the so-called Vergennes tulipwood desk on which his stamp has been discovered beside that of Migeon (whose stamp had been the only one previously known on the piece). How much of this piece can be credited to Dubois, and how much to Migeon, and also the bronze worker who made the extraordinary corner mounts? A payment of 1,809 livres occurs beside the name of Dubois in the employee ledgers of Pierre Migeon II, leading one to believe that Dubois was the author and Migeon the vendor of this masterpiece.

The Criaerds (figs. 18, 86) (also spelled Criard), Mathieu Criaerd and his sons Antoine-Mathieu and Sebastien-Mathieu, were of Flemish origin. They made many commodes and *encoignures* of good Louis XV contour, probably intended for sale through dealers, hence the japanning with which they are usually covered. The Criaerds supplied some beautiful tables to the Crown, but indirectly, through the intermediary of Joubert.

Gilles Joubert (figs. 4, 125), who was *ébéniste* to Louis XV during the entire second half of his reign, remains all too little known. His works are rarely signed. Among the considerable quantities of furniture that he supplied to the Garde-Meuble, some were products of his own workshop and others were purchased by him from colleagues such as Criaerd and Marchand. The royal archives reveal several aspects of his style. He is recorded up to a rather late date delivering commodes, desks, and tables (both signed and unsigned) that are in the most charming Louis XV style, but quite early he seems to have tried to react against curvilinear excess, e.g., his Versailles *encoignures* delivered in 1755, which already show straight tapering legs. Around 1770 he not only made frequent use of this type of leg but he also covered his most beautiful pieces of furniture with lozenge marquetry studded with tiny bronze rosettes. His bronze mounts themselves provide evidence of his desire for change in their bas-reliefs, acanthus leaves, and rosettes. Did Joubert precede or follow Oeben into neoclassicism?

Jean-François Oeben (fig. 154) died in 1763; nevertheless, he was the *ébéniste* who best characterized the transition from the Louis XV to the Louis XVI style. He was also the one who had the most profound influence on the Louis XVI period through the apprentices who worked in his establishment (like Leleu and Riesener) and through his family ties (his brother Simon Oeben and his brother-in-law Roger Lacroix were also *ébénistes*). His furniture shapes were full-bodied, almost massive, and just as often straight as curved. Sometimes he even used a Greek key ornament on the feet. He often used cube marquetry or, in his later years, lozenges and rosettes in marquetry compartments. A master of marquetry technique, he liked pictorial subjects of bouquets or baskets of flowers of polychrome woods on a fine-grained satiné ground. His complex interlaced borders became more rectilinear toward the end of his career but always retained the same technical characteristics: edging of a double filet of black and white and, at intervals, small plaques of sycamore rootwood. He was not only an admirable *ébéniste* trained in the Boulle workshop but also a bronze maker very much concerned with the quality and methods of attachment of his mounts. He soon abandoned rococo motifs for

long leaves derived from acanthus, laurel leaves, and goat heads. Oeben also used straight moldings whose attachment he attempted to conceal. On pieces of furniture that set standards of technical perfection for his day, Oeben developed ingenious mechanical works for the apparatus of doors and flaps or for the action of mobile parts that emerged or disappeared by means of springs or cranks. His mechanical talents seem to have been particularly appreciated by his contemporaries, and it was probably on this account that he won the commission for the great *bureau du Roi* (the cylinder desk of Louis XV belonging to the Louvre) which he designed and Riesener completed.

Roger Van der Cruse called *Lacroix* (figs. 114, 115, 146) signed a large number of good pieces of furniture either in the French form of his name R. Lacroix, or with his initials R.V.L.C. (Roger Vandercruse La Croix), and sometimes with both together. As there are a few pieces which bear the signature R. Lacroix together with that of Chevalier, Dubut, or Peridiez, it could be alleged that R. Lacroix and R.V.L.C. represent the stamps of two different *ébénistes*. However the pieces of furniture marked R. Lacroix and those marked R.V.L.C. are so similar in style that they must be attributed to a single *ébéniste* working for the *marchands-merciers* who may have at times required him to be anonymous. His production, although it included commodes, secretaries, and *encoignures,* emphasized small tables and *bonheurs-du-jour* (small writing tables with superstructures). This probably was the result of the orders he received from *marchands-merciers*. Lacroix's furniture is mostly typical of the end of the reign of Louis XV: often rather pronounced curves were retained and a given piece was more Louis XV or Louis XVI in style according to the date it was made. Lacroix's large oeuvre reveals him to have been a rather uneven *ébéniste*. He created a few perfect forms, but others were somewhat skimpy and inept, perhaps because he turned the work over to colleagues. The influence of J.-F. Oeben can be seen in Lacroix's bronze mounts and marquetry lozenges, rosettes, latticework, and baskets or vases of flowers. He also used flowering branches with the flower occasionally of end-cut wood in a pattern that does not vary from one piece to another, as well as motifs of Chinese utensils and neoclassical rosettes. Probably because of his contacts with dealers he made use of lacquers, japanning, and Sèvres porcelain. His bronze mounts were initially rococo but soon evolved toward neoclassicism: tapering legs with laurel leaves, volutes, goat heads, and, still influenced by Oeben, borders with rosettes, fretwork, or rings.

Pierre Garnier (figs. 26, 36, 79, 80, 91, 123, 155) played a role in the Transition period that was brought to light by the recent work of Svend Eriksen. Without achieving the renown of J.-F. Oeben, he had an excellent clien-

tele including the duchesse de Mazarin, the marechal de Contades, the marquis de Marigny, and probably some *marchands-merciers* as well. Much of his furniture is decorated with oriental lacquer. His somewhat heavy but powerful style shows him to have been a good *ébéniste* with originality.

—⟶ *Jean-François Leleu* (figs. 19, 23, 107) worked in the Transitional style for only a short time and as early as about 1770 became one of the leading exponents of the Louis XVI style. Like Riesener, he was a follower or disciple of Oeben. The straight lines that he used were almost always relieved at some point or other by a slight bulge or curve. Despite a tendency to heaviness, seen especially in his frequent deletion of feet in favor of a base directly on the floor, he well knew how to be distinguished and elegant. He did marquetry with lozenges, rosettes, and bouquets of flowers. Again one finds borders with a double filet of black and white. He also used solid mahogany to particularly good effect. His bronze mounts resemble those of Riesener, but Leleu used them more sparingly than his rival even on very opulent furniture for the prince de Condé. Classical motifs and borders in bronze that sometimes repeat the marquetry play a significant part in the architecture of some of his pieces.

—⟶*Jean-Henri Riesener* (figs. 94, 106, 113) is perhaps the most famous French *ébéniste* of the eighteenth century. Like his master Oeben and his colleague Leleu, he forthrightly adopted a style so personal that his furniture cannot be confused with that of anyone else. Thanks to numerous royal commissions that provide us with exact dates, we can follow step by step the development of his style in a way that is impossible for any other *ébéniste*. One sees a certain suppleness in Riesener's work over a period that extends from the completion of the *bureau du Roi* in 1769 until 1775, but one senses the advent of a new style which is already Louis XVI: a trapezoidal panel at the center of commodes, straight, chamfered, or fluted legs, frequent use of solid mahogany or walnut, marquetry which, although still influenced by Oeben, tends more toward the pictorial, and last, bronze mounts that are more deeply chased and more restrained in design than those of other *ébénistes* of the period. The personal style of Riesener really emerged in the years between 1775 and 1780: forms that were often heavier and had fewer curves, more frequent use of flowered lattice marquetry, mounts which continued to be classicizing but which made increasing use of flowers. Finally, the ultimate phase, from 1780 to the Revolution, where we witness the fully developed great Riesener style: forms that were almost totally rectilinear, latticework, which the *ébéniste* favored, with flower heads rather than full flowers in the compartments, lozenges of tulipwood, gray satiné, or, at the instigation of Marie-Antoinette, mother-of-pearl, and most especially solid mahogany used in a systematic way, the beautiful wood from Santo Domingo, or mahogany with chenille or speckled figure.

The *Sauniers* (figs. 98, 99) were a dynasty of *ébénistes* of whom the best known is Claude-Charles Saunier. This *ébéniste,* after having begun in a slightly toned-down Louis XV style, converted abruptly to the Louis XVI style. He made commodes, *encoignures,* tables, and desks, but apparently his real specialties were cylinder desks and console tables in *ébénisterie.* His style was refined and attenuated: his furniture forms were delicate without being frail. He veneered with contrasting tulipwood and ebony, lemonwood and purple wood, juxtaposing light and dark woods well before the nineteenth century. His bronze mounts were figured as fluted or scrolling friezes, inter-laced motifs, pendants, swags, and rosettes. Quite often he used simple bor-ders of bronze stringing. While he lacked the power of Dubois, Saunier seems to have been superior to Garnier and he played a considerable role in the Louis XVI era, ranking with Montigny and Carlin.

François-Gaspard Teuné (figs. 28, 31, 171) appears to have been an *ébéniste* of eminence from the evidence revealed by the study of the archives of the comte d'Artois. He supplied this prince with a number of great pieces of furniture that will win his talents due respect as they are little by little discov-ered and identified.

Martin Carlin (figs. 27, 32, 35, which is in the style of Carlin, 119, 120, 121, 122, 136) was a supplier to the dealers of the Saint-Honoré district, no-tably Poirier, Daguerre, and the Darnault brothers. This clientele explains both the quantity of small pieces of furniture that he made, especially tables, cabinets, and *bonheurs-du-jour,* and his frequent use of lacquer and porcelain plaques. His furniture shapes are typically Louis XVI: one could, however, point out the curve of the lower part of the legs on some of his small tables. He preferred legs of square section, mostly tapering. He used mahogany, tulipwood, and ebony as grounds for marquetry patterns composed primar-ily of wood filets. His bronze mounts varied according to the quality of the furniture that was ordered and the importance of the bronze maker from whom he obtained them. They ranged from banal rosettes and flowering branches, through the drapery swags and ribbons that one finds on a good number of pieces, to the magnificent foliation, flowers and fruit that can be seen on the famous pieces, now in the Louvre, ordered by Mesdames (the unmarried daughters of Louis XV) for their château of Bellevue.

Adam Weisweiler (figs. 109, 129), an *ébéniste* of German descent, had a style typical of the end of the reign of Louis XVI. He seems to have done a lot of work for the dealer Daguerre. Despite an occasionally extreme attenuation of the uprights, his furniture is often characterized by a certain heaviness, and there is an almost unpleasant disproportion between the different parts. One of the most peculiar pieces in this respect is Marie-Antoinette's little table in the Louvre, where Weisweiler created legs out of slender bronze caryatids mounted on ebony feet, supports too thin to provide stability to the body of the piece comprising drawers and lectern in bronze, steel, and lacquer. He was the author of numerous commodes, some signed and others unsigned, having three doors and top-shaped feet. The line of the apron is accentuated by wide bands of corrugated or striated bronze. Columns at the corners taper downward and are surmounted by curious spindle-shaped capitals with spiral fluting. Weisweiler often connected the legs of his little tables or cabinets with stretchers cut in complex and distinctive patterns. The woods he seems to have favored are ebony and mahogany, occasionally with a bramble figure. He made very little use of marquetry. However, the Japanese lacquer panels of the highest quality and the luxuriant bronze mounts with exquisite chasing demonstrate the importance of the orders he received from the *marchands-merciers,* as do the porcelain plaques featured in a number of his pieces.

Joseph Stockel (fig. 118) is an all-too-little-known *ébéniste* of the Louis XVI reign. He too worked for the *marchands-merciers* and directly or indirectly for the comte de Provence making furniture that was rather heavy but powerful. Weapons bundled together in *faisceaux* were a device he favored for the supports or corners of commodes or desks. He used mahogany or simple tulipwood veneer. Rectangular, circular, or semicircular compartments bordered with bronze strings of pearls or corrugated bronze plaques characterize the rather complicated architecture of his furniture. Very beautiful bronze lion paws, masks, trophies, and vases of flowers are silhouetted in sharp, bold relief.

Guillaume Benneman (figs. 95, 129) has usurped in large part the renown that to my mind rightfully belongs to Stockel. The great pieces in the Louvre that bear Benneman's stamp are the basis of his fame today, but he did no more than reveneer, enlarge, or copy furniture that should be attributed to Stockel. Moreover, during the years that he held the position of *ébéniste* to the Crown (1784–92) Benneman's role was more that of a subcontractor. He worked under the direction of the sculptor Hauré as chief cabinetmaker in a team that included the bronze workers Forestier, Galle, and Thomire. His royal furniture commissions entailed altering of existing furniture and, in frequent instances, copying pieces from earlier eras. The rather weighty architecture of his pieces and his regular use of mahogany were traits he shared with other *ébénistes* of his time. Among his best works are the pair of commodes (one now in the Louvre and the other in a private collection) that he made for the intendant to the Crown in 1787 (fig. 95). With assertive elegance these prefigure the Empire style in their patinated caryatids at their corners, upright form, and overall sobriety.

Charles Topino (figs. 24, 101) can be cited here as one of the minor masters who abounded during the reign of Louis XVI. He started his career during the reign of Louis XV and continued until the Revolution, maintaining a delightful mélange of the two eras in his furniture. The countless little tables and *bonheurs-du-jour* made by Topino possess great elegance of line. His furniture was always light, whether the legs were cabriole or colonettes prefiguring the Directoire and Empire styles. The marquetry was rather banal, but Topino avoided plain veneers, continuing to use flowers, rosettes, utensils, scrolls, and checkered patterns set off against light wood grounds. His bronze mounts, garlands, acanthus-type leaves, and rosettes were also rather ordinary.

The Jacob brothers (fig. 124), sons of the *menuisier* Georges Jacob, must be mentioned here among the most important *ébénistes* of the eighteenth century because of the role they played in *ébénisterie* during the Revolution. At that time they joined with their father to make chairs of mahogany as well as all sorts of other furniture in the latest style. In 1796 Georges Jacob ceded the direction of the business to his sons, but he continued as their artistic advisor. Working to the designs of the painter David and the young architects Percier and Fontaine, they created furniture more directly related to classical antiquity than any that had been made previously. Absolutely straight lines, caryatid or griffon supports, mahogany or lemonwood *ébénisterie* ornamented with classical palmettes in ebony or purple wood, such were the innovations of these *ébénistes* before they became exponents of the Empire style.

PROVINCIAL *EBENISTES*

The provinces differed from Paris in the frequent use of indigenous woods, especially for marquetry, which could have pearwood, cherrywood, holly, burled ash, burled walnut, or (in Southern France) olive wood elements. The lines between *ébénisterie* and *menuiserie* were often blurred: in several of the ports of western France solid mahogany was already in use under Louis XV. Paris style was disseminated through the provinces with a certain time lag, and true *ébénisterie* with veneers of costly woods remained long the exception because inlays were preferred.

Several provincial *ébénistes* can be identified: the *Haches* (fig. 132) of Grenoble whose marquetries continued the compartmentalization typical of the early eighteenth century well into the reign of Louis XV; the *Demoulins* (fig. 130) of Dijon, who had resided in Paris and retained a luxuriant style closely conforming to the latest creations of the capital in both Louis XV and Louis XVI periods; the *Coulerus* (fig. 133) of Montbéliard from a family of spinning-wheel makers, some of whom practiced marquetry and enjoyed the protection of the duke of Wurtemburg.

The distinction between French and German *menuisiers-ébénistes* in Strasbourg has been pointed out by Hans Haug. Only in 1780 were they brought together in a single corporation. The location of the city and its unusual religious politics made possible an accord between the two factions. The Rohan prince-bishops of Strasbourg had additional territories on the German side of the Rhine and they commissioned furniture locally. Strasbourg *ébénistes* of both factions, however, took their lead from Paris. *Bernard Kocke,* one of the German faction born in the bishopric of Paderborn, was sent to perfect his skills in Paris by Cardinal de Rohan, for whom he executed the beautiful French-style bookcases in the episcopal palace. A delight in marquetry on Louis XVI forms gives special character to some Alsatian furniture where *ébénistes* like *Jean-Georges Stern* (fig. 134) of Strasbourg and *Nicolas Camus* of Wissembourg made use of the contrast of yellow and black wood.

Regional styles are easier to recognize in *menuiserie* than in *ébénisterie.* Salverte wanted to make *Carel* a southwestern *ébéniste,* but the presence of the mark of the wardens of the Paris guild on some of Carel's pieces (fig. 104) and the documentation published by Vial indicate that this skilled *ébéniste* of the Louis XV era belonged to a Parisian family which retained its ties with the Dauphiné. Contacts with Paris became increasingly frequent. Parisian *ébénistes* and dealers who had spent some time in the capital then moved to the provinces, like *Grégoire* in Nantes, *Courte* (fig. 131) in Dijon, Oeben's brother in Tours, and Topino's brother in Marseilles, stimulated the development of style, at least in the big cities where *ébénisterie* began to be practiced in the second half of the century.

Chapter 13

LIST OF *EBENISTES*

T HE *ébénistes* listed in alphabetical order here were enrolled under the same conditions as the *menuisiers;* I have limited this listing to those names for whom our current state of knowledge provides some information. All, with the exception of a mere dozen, were established in Paris, and even among the exceptions, many moved to Paris.

I have deleted from this listing the names of the English, German, Swedish, and Italian furniture makers that Salverte included in his dictionary.

When the *ébéniste's* stamp (*st.*) is reproduced in the next chapter, its number there is given here.

Ancellet, Denis-Louis, *m.* 1766, *st.* 102

Angot, Jacques, *m.* 1743, *st.* 19

Armand, Henri (b. 1737), *m.* 1766

Armand, Jacques (1714–c. 1784), *m.* 1763

Artzt, Jean-André, *m.* 1785

Aubin, Jean-Julien (1734–1793), *m.* 1777, *st.* 4

Aubry, Louis, *m.* 1774, *st.* 6

Avril, Etienne (1748–1791), *m.* 1774, *st.* 5

Barrault, Joseph (c. 1730–1798), *m.* 1768

Barthélemy, Charles, *m.* 1777

Bary, Michel (c. 1690–1761)

Bayer, François, *m.* 1764, *st.* 24

Beauce, Louis-Laurent, *m.* 1787

Beauclair (Butte), Benoît (c. 1720–1803), *m.* 1767

Beaudret, Nicolas (1st third 18th c.)

Benneman, Guillaume, *m.* 1785, *st.* 56

Berluy, François (mid-18th c.)

Berluy, Pierre (1st half 18th c.)

Bernard, Jacques, *m.* 1760

Bernard, Nicolas (b.c. 1713), *m.* 1742

Bernard, Pierre (c. 1715–c. 1770)

Bernard, *see* Van Risen Burgh (B.V.R.B.)

Berthelmi, Nicolas (2d quarter 18th c.), *st.* 112

Bertrand, Jean-Pierre (b. 1737), *m.* 1775

Besson, Charles (1734–1808), *m.* 1758

Billiard, Claude (1688–c. 1760)

Birckel, Jean-Frédéric (1726–1809), *m.* 1786

Bircklé, Jacques (1734–1803), *m.* 1764, *st.* 114

Birclet, Laurent-Charles, called Birclé the younger (c. 1736–1776), *m.* 1766

Boichod, Pierre, *m.* 1769, *st.* 151

Bolten, Henri, *m.* 1774

Bonnemain, Pierre (1723–1800), *m.* 1751

Boudin, Leonard (1735–c. 1804), *m.* 1761, *st.* 106

Boulle, André-Charles (1642–1732)

Boulle, André-Charles, II, called Boulle de Sève (1685–1745)

Boulle, Charles-Joseph, called Boulle the younger (1688–1754)

Boulle, Jean-Philippe (c. 1680–1744)

Boulle, Pierre-Benoît (c. 1682–1741)

Brandt, Georges (c. 1746–1806), *m.* 1789

Brochet, Jean-Baptiste, *m.* 1741

Brullé, Jacques, *m.* 1776

Bruns, Jean-Antoine, *m.* 1782, *st.* 94

Buchette, François-Henri, *m.* 1770

Bunel, Pierre-Paul, *m.* 1778

Burgevin, Jean-Claude (c. 1667–1743)

Bury, Ferdinand, called Ferdinand (1740–1795), *m.* 1774, *st.* 21

Butte, *see* Beauclair

B.V.R.B., called Bernard, *see* Van Risen Burgh

Canabas, François-Antoine, *m.* 1779

Canabas, Joseph Gegenbach, called Canabas (1712–1797), *m.* 1766, *st.* 43

Carel (mid-18th c.), *st.* 142

Carlin, Etienne, *m.* 1753

Carlin, Martin (d. 1785), *m.* 1766, *st.* 7

Caumont, Jean (1736–after 1800), *m.* 1774, *st.* 38

Chapuis, in Paris(?) and in Brussels (end 18th, beginning 19th c.), *st.* 3

Charriere, P. (2d half 18th c.), *st.* 70

Chartier, Etienne-Louis, *m.* 1781

Chartier, Jacques-Charles, *m.* 1760

Chaumont, Bertrand-Alexis (1741–after 1790), *m.* 1767, *st.* 13

Chavigneau, Victor-Jean-Gabriel (1746–1806), *m.* 1787

Chevallier, Charles, called the younger (c. 1700–1771), *m.* before 1737

Chevallier, Jean-Mathieu, called the elder (1696–1768), *m.* 1743, *st.* 99

Chevallier, *see* Criaerd

Choquet, Claude-Julien (1696–1764), *m.* before 1737

Cléret, Pierre, *m.* before 1737

Cochois, Charles-Michel (d. 1764), *m.* before 1737, *st.* 12

Cochois, Jean-Baptiste (d. 1789), *m.* 1770

Coignard, Pascal (1748–after 1791), *m.* 1777, *st.* 44

Colbault, Pierre-Barthélemy, *m.* 1770, *st.* 88

Collet, Edmond (1781–c. 1755)

Cordie, Guillaume (c. 1725–c. 1786), *m.* 1766, *st.* 39

Cosson, Jacques-Laurent, *m.* 1765, *st.* 11

Coste, Charles-Louis, *m.* 1784

Couet, Louis-Jacques, *m.* 1774

Couleru, Abraham-Nicholas (1716–1812), *m.* in Montbeliard 1750, *st.* 162

Couleru, Pierre-Nicolas (1755–1824), in Montbeliard

Coulon, Balthazar (mid-18th c.)

Coulon, Gaspard (d. after 1774)

Coulon, Jean-François, *m.* 1732, *st.* 86

Courte, Jean-Baptiste (1749–1843), *m.* in Dijon 1777, *st.* 122

Couturier, Antoine, *m.* 1767

Cramer, Mathieu-Guillaume (d. 1794), *m.* 1771, *st.* 85

Crépi (Crespi), François, called le Romain (the Roman) (b. 1744), *m.* 1778

Cressent, Charles (1685–1768)

Cresson, Jacques-Louis (1743–1795), *m.* 1759

Criaerd (Criard), Antoine (2d quarter 18th c.), *st.* 134

Criaerd (Criard), Antoine-Mathieu, called Chevallier (c. 1724–1787), *m.* 1747, *sts.* 103 and 104

Criaerd (Criard), Mathieu (1689–1776), *m.* 1738, *st.* 147

Dautriche, Jacques Van Oostenryk, called Dautriche (d. 1778), *m.* 1765, *st.* 64

Defriche, Pierre, *m.* 1766, *st.* 63

Delacour, Jean-François, *m.* 1768, *st.* 100

Delaitre, Louis, *m.* 1738, *st.* 159

Deloose, Daniel (d. 1788), *m.* 1767, *st.* 57

Delorme, Adrien Faizelot-, *m.* 1748, *st.* 121

Delorme, Alexis Faizelot-, *m.* 1772

Delorme, François Faizelot- (1691–1768)

Delorme, Guillaume (1757–1795), *m.* 1786

Delorme, Jean-Louis Faizelot-, *m.* 1763

Demoulin, Bertrand (1755–1853), in Dijon

Demoulin, Jean (1715–1798), first in Paris, *m.* in Dijon 1780, *st.* 45

Demoulin, Jean-Baptiste (1750–1837), *m.* in Dijon 1783

Denizot, Jacques (c. 1684–1760)

Denizot, Pierre (c. 1715–1782), *m.* 1740, *st.* 51

Desforges, Jean (2d quarter 18th c.)

Desgodets, Claude-Joseph, *m.* 1749

Desjardins, Pierre, *m.* 1774

Dester, Godefroy, *m.* 1774, *st.* 34

Detroulleau, Jean-Baptiste (1737–c. 1780), *m.* 1767, *st.* 101

Doirat, E. (2d quarter 18th c.), *st.* 132

Domaille, Henri-Gilles, *m.* 1778

Dubois, Jacques (c. 1693–1763), *m.* 1742, *st.* 105

Dubois, Louis (b. 1734), *m.* 1754

Dubois, René (1737–1799), *m.* 1754, *st.* 105

Dubois, René, *m.* 1757

Dubuisson, Nicolas-René (b. 1728), in Paris and at Versailles

Dubut, Jean-François (d. 1778), *st.* 79

Ducourneaux, Jean, *m.* 1782

Duez, Nicolas-Joseph, *m.* 1788

Dufour, Charles-Joseph (1740–c. 1782), *m.* 1759

Duhamel, François (1723–1801), *m.* 1750, *st.* 15

Dupré, Pierre (1732–1799), *m.* 1766, *st.* 29

Durand, Bon, *m.* 1761, *st.* 30

Dusault, Nicolas-Philippe, *m.* 1774

Dusautoy, Jean-Pierre (1719–1800), *m.* 1779, *st.* 140

Ellaume (Alleaume), Jean-Charles, *m.* 1754, *st.* 89

Erstet, Jean-Ulric, *m.* 1763, *st.* 139

Evalde (Ewald), Maurice-Bernard, *m.* 1765

Evrard, Gaspard (2d quarter 18th c.)

Feilt, Gaspard (d. 1763), *st.* 28

Félix, Laurent, *m.* 1755, *st.* 107

Felizet, Edme-Jean (2d quarter 18th c.)

Ferdinand, *see* Bury

Fermet, Jean-Bénigne, *m.* 1759

Feuerstein, Jean-Philippe (b. 1749), *m.* 1785

Feuerstein, Joseph (1733–1809), *m.* 1767, *st.* 123

Filon, Gabriel-Cécile (1726–1798), *m.* 1750

Fléchy, Pierre (1715–after 1769), *m.* 1756, *st.* 31

Fleury, Adrien (1721–1775), *st.* 137

Fleury, François (mid-18th c.)

Fleury, René-Charles, *m.* 1755, *st.* 116

Fontaine, Jean-Michel, *m.* 1767

Forschmann, Augustin (b. 1727), *m.* 1773

Forster, Richard (d. 1794), *m.* 1788

Foullet, Antoine (d. 1775), *m.* 1749, *st.* 158
Foullet, Pierre-Antoine, *m.* 1765
Fromageau, Jacques-André (1735–1810),
  m. 1765
Fromageau, Jean-Baptiste, *m.* 1755, *st.* 84
Frost, Jean-Gotlieb (c. 1746–1814), *m.*
  1785

Galet, Jean-Baptiste (d. 1784), *m.* 1754, *st.*
  74
Galligné, Pierre-Antoine, *m.* 1767
Gamichon, Jean-Baptiste (d. 1832)
Garnier, Pierre (c. 1720–1800), *m.* 1742, *st.*
  42
Garré, Louis-Guillaume, *m.* 1741
Gaudreaux, Antoine-Robert (c. 1680–
  1751)
Gautié, Jean-Baptiste, *m.* 1761, *st.* 141
Genty, Denis, *m.* 1754, *st.* 108
Gigun, François Lébe-, *m.* 1786
Gilbert, André-Louis (1746–1809), *m.*
  1774
Gillet, Jean, *m.* before 1737
Gillet, Louis, *m.* 1766
Gosselin, Adrien-Antoine, *m.* 1772, *st.* 58
Gosselin, Antoine (1731–1794), *m.* 1752
Gosselin, Josse, called the younger, *m.*
  1768
Goyer, François, *m.* 1740, *st.* 25
Goyer, Jean, *m.* 1760
Grandjean, Jean-Louis (b. 1739), *m.* 1766,
  st. 10
Grevenich, Nicolas, *m.* 1768, *st.* 67
Griffet, Jean-François, *m.* 1779, *st.* 80
Guérard, Pierre, *m.* 1740
Guérin, Jean-Louis, *m.* 1778
Guignard (Queniard), Pierre-François
  (1740–1794), *m.* 1767, *st.* 98
Guillard, Pierre, *m.* 1777
Guillaume, Simon (3d quarter 18th c.)
Guillemain, Pierre (b. 1697)
Guillemart, François (d. 1724)
Guyot, Nicolas (1735–1812), *m.* 1775

Hache, Christophe-André (1748–1831), in
  Grenoble
Hache, Jean-François, called the elder or
  the son (1730–1796), in Grenoble, *st.*
  161
Hache, Pierre (1705–1776), in Grenoble

Hache, Thomas (1664–1747), in Grenoble
Haimard, Louis-Jacques, *m.* 1756
Hannot, Antoine-Simon, *m.* 1758
Hansen, Hubert, *m.* 1747, *st.* 133
Hecquet (1st third 18th c.)
Hédouin, Jean-Baptiste (d. 1783), *m.* 1738,
  st. 138
Henry, Jean (1747–1809), *m.* 1779
Henry, Jean-Baptiste, *m.* 1777, *st.* 77
Henry, Nicolas, *m.* 1773
Héricourt, Antoine (c. 1730–1792), *m.*
  1773
Héricourt, Nicolas (1729–1790)
Hertel, Georges, *m.* 1777
Hervieux, Antoine-Marie (d. 1793), *m.*
  1786
Hoffmann, Jean-Diebold, *m.* 1785
Holthausen, Jean, *m.* 1764, *st.* 66

Igou, Balthazar-André (d. before 1737)
Igou, Guillaume (2d quarter 18th c.)

Jacob *frères* (brothers), 1796–1803, *st.* 160
Jacot, Antoine-Pierre, *m.* 1766, *st.* 9
Jansen, Georges (b. 1726), *m.* 1767, *st.* 54
Javoy, Claude, *m.* 1779
Jollain, Adrien-Jérôme, *m.* 1763
Joseph, Joseph Baumhauer, called Joseph
  (d. 1772), *m. c.* 1767, *st.* 149
Joseph, Gaspard-Joseph Baumhauer, Jr. (b.
  1747)
Joubert, Gilles (1689–1775), *sts.* 127 and
  150

Kans, Jean, *m.* 1783
Kassel, Georges, *m.* 1779
Kemp, Guillaume, *m.* 1764, *st.* 131
Kintz, Georges, *m.* 1776, *st.* 32
Kirschenbach, Jean-Adam, called the
  younger, *m.* 1774
Kirschenbach, Jean-Jacques, *m.* 1778
Kobierscky, Jean-Georges (*fl. c.* 1790)
Kocke, Bernard, *m.* in Strasbourg 1741
Koechly, Joseph (d. 1798), *m.* 1783, *st.* 110
Koffler, Jean-Mathieu (1736–1796)
Kopp, Maurice, *m.* 1780
Krier, Charles (b. 1742), *m.* 1774

Lacroix, Pierre-Roger Vandercruse, called
  Lacroix (c. 1750–1789), *m.* 1771

Lacroix, Roger Vandercruse, called R. Lacroix or R.V.L.C. (1728–1799), *m.* 1755, *sts.* 48 and 153

Lafolie, Pierre, *m.* 1755

Lainé, Louis, *m.* 1740

Lancelin, Nicolas, *m.* 1766

Landrin, Germain, *m.* 1738, *st.* 146

Lannuier, Nicolas, *m.* 1783, *st.* 50

Lapie, Jean, called the younger, *m.* 1762

Lapie, Jean-François (1720–1797), *m.* 1763

Lapie, Nicolas-Alexandre, called the elder (d. 1775), *m.* 1764

Lardin, André-Antoine (1724–1790), *m.* 1750, *st.* 145

Lardin, André-Antoine, Jr., *m.* 1774

Lardin, Louis-François, *m.* 1774

Larzillière, Jean-Gérard (1st half 18th c.)

Latz, Jacques-Pierre (c. 1691–1754), *m.* before 1737, *st.* 72

Lebesgue, Claude, *m.* before 1737, *st.* 113

Lebesgue, Claude-Pierre (d. 1789), *m.* 1750, *st.* 113

Lebesgue, François (d. 1765)

Lebesgue, Robert-Claude (b. 1749), *m.* 1771

Leblond, Jean-François, *m.* 1751

Leclerc, Charles-Michel (1743–1805), *m.* 1786

Leclerc, Jacques-Antoine (1744–1792), *m.* 1779

Lefaivre, Charles (d. 1759), *m.* 1738, *st.* 148

Legry, Jean-Louis-François (1745–after 1792), *m.* 1779

Lehaene, Pierre-Joseph, *m.* 1789

Leleu, Jean-François (1729–1807), *m.* 1764, *st.* 152

Lemarchand, Charles-Joseph, *m.* 1789, *st.* 69

Lepage, Guillaume-Joseph, *m.* 1777

Lependu, Jean-Baptiste, *m.* 1782

Lesueur, François, *m.* 1757

Letellier, Jacques-Pierre, *m.* 1767

Levasseur, Etienne (1721–1798), *m.* 1766, *st.* 8

Levesque, Albert, *m.* 1749

Lhermite, Martin-Etienne, *m.* 1753, *st.* 157

Lidons, Louis, *m.* 1777

Lieutaud, Balthazar (d. 1780), *m.* 1749, *st.* 136

Limonne, Jean-Baptiste (d. 1761), *m.* 1737

Louasse, Nicolas, *m.* 1781

Loviat, Jean-François, *m.* 1779

Lucien, Jacques (1748–c. 1811), *m.* 1774

Lutz, Gérard-Henri (1736–1812), *m.* 1766

Maclard, Charles (d. 1775), *m.* 1742, *st.* 155

Macret, Pierre (1727–after 1796), *m. c.* 1758, *st.* 1

Magnien, Claude-Mathieu, *m.* 1771, *st.* 90

Maignan, Jean, *m.* 1786

Malbet, Pierre, *m.* 1765

Malle, Louis-Noel (1734–1782), *m.* 1765, *st.* 76

Mallerot, Michel (1675–after 1753)

Manser, Jacques (1727–c. 1780)

Mansion, Antoine-Simon, *m.* 1786

Mansion, Simon (1741–c. 1805), *m.* 1780

Mantel, Pierre (d. 1802), *m.* 1766, *st.* 125

Marchand, Nicolas-Jean, *m.* before 1737, *st.* 144

Martigny, Nicolas, *m.* 1738

Mathieu, Jean-Paul (d. 1745)

Maur, Jean-Georges, *m.* 1781

Mauter, Conrad (1742–1810), *m.* 1777, *st.* 49

Meunier, Pierre (b. 1735), *m.* 1767

Mewesen, Pierre-Harry, *m.* 1766, *st.* 117

Michaelis, Jean-Frédéric, *m.* 1787

Michaut, Jean-Louis, *m.* 1775

Migeon, Pierre, I (b.c. 1670)

Migeon, Pierre, II (1701–1758), *sts.* 120 and 143

Migeon, Pierre, III (1733–1775), *m.* 1761, see *sts.* 120 and 143

Milet, Pierre-François, *m.* 1767

Millet, Jean-Jacques, *m.* 1757

Molitor, Bernard, *m.* 1787, *st.* 59

Mondon, François (1694–1770), *m.* before 1737, *st.* 119

Mondon, François-Antoine, *m.* 1757

Mongenot, François (1732–1809), *m.* 1761

Montigny, Philippe-Claude (1734–1800), *m.* 1766, *st.* 129

Moreau, Louis (d. 1791), *m.* 1764, *st.* 46

Muller, Joseph-Adam, *m.* 1785

Nicolas, Antoine, *m.* 1765, *see also* list of *menuisiers*

Nicquet, Jean-Baptiste (d. 1781), *m.* 1775

Nocart, Jacques-Joseph (3d quarter 18th c.)

Oeben, Jean-François (1721–1763), *m.* 1759, *st.* 78
Oeben, Simon (d. 1786), *m.* 1764, *st.* 52
Ohneberg, Martin, *m.* 1773, *st.* 60
Ortalle, Charles, *m.* 1756

Pafrat, Jean-Jacques (d. 1793), *m.* 1785, *st.* 23
Paget, Dieudonné, *m.* 1786
Papst, François-Ignace, *m.* 1785, *st.* 73
Pasquier, Philippe (d. 1783), *m.* 1760, *st.* 62
Pêche, Guillaume (1752–1800), *m.* 1784
Pelletier, Denis-Louis, *m.* 1760
Péridiez, Brice, *m.* before 1737, *st.* 164
Péridiez, Gérard, *m.* 1761, *st.* 135
Péridiez, Louis (b. 1731), *m.* 1764
Petit, Jean, *m.* 1767
Petit, Jean-Marie (b. 1737), *m.* 1777
Petit, Nicolas (1732–1791), *m.* 1761
Petit, Nicolas (1730–1798), *m.* 1765, *st.* 22
Pierre, Louis-Claude, *m.* 1767
Pignit, Jean-Baptiste (1745–1791), *m.* 1777
Pionez, Pierre (d. 1790), *m.* 1765, *st.* 61
Plée, Pierre (1742–1810), *m.* 1767, *st.* 130
Poitou, Joseph (c. 1682–1718), *m.* 1710
Popsel, Jean (1720–after 1785), *m.* 1755, *st.* 2
Porquet, Jacques (1704–after 1788), *m.* 1767
Potarange, Jean Hoffenrichler, called Potarange, *m.* 1767, *st.* 65
Poussain, Marc-Antoine, *m.* 1772
Provost, Charles-Bernard (1706–1786), *m.* 1737
Przirembel, Godefroy, *m.* 1766

Quervelle, Jean-Claude (1731–1778), *m.* 1767

Raisin, Jean-Georges, *m.* 1755
Ratié, Jean Frédéric, *m.* 1783, *st.* 27
Reboul, Jean-Pierre, *m.* 1766
Rebour, Isaac-Simon (1735–after 1793), *m.* 1767
Reizell, François (d. 1788), *m.* 1764, *st.* 37

Revault, Claude (d. 1757), *m.* 1755, *st.* 124
Richter, Charles-Erdmann, *m.* 1784, *st.* 35
Riesener, Jean-Henri (1734–1806), *m.* 1768, *st.* 83
Rochette, Laurent (b. 1723), *st.* 126
Roentgen, David (1743–1807), *m.* 1780
Roger, Antoine-Symphorien, *m.* 1779
Roht, Michel-François, *m.* 1773, *st.* 75
Roussel, A. (d. before 1726)
Roussel, Jacques (d. 1726)
Roussel, Pierre, I (1723–1782), *m.* 1745, *st.* 36
Roussel, Pierre, II, *m.* 1771
Roussel, Pierre-Michel, *m.* 1766
Roux, Hubert, called Leroux, *m.* 1777, *st.* 26
Rübestuck, François, called Franz or France (c. 1722–1785), *m.* 1766, *st.* 71
R.V.L.C., *see* Lacroix
Ryssenberg, *see* Van Risen Burgh

Sadon, Mathieu (1730–1798)
Sageot, Nicolas (1st half 18th c.)
Saint-Germain, Joseph de, *m.* 1750, *st.* 17
Sar, Jean-Girard (b. 1724), *m.* 1766
Saunier, Charles, *m.* before 1737
Saunier, Claude-Charles (1735–1807), *m.* 1752, *st.* 91
Saunier, Jean-Baptiste, *m.* 1757, *st.* 156
Saunier, Jean-Charles, *m.* 1743, *st.* 115
Sauvage, André, *m.* 1752
Sauvage, André, *m.* 1769
Savard, Dieudonné, *m.* 1763
Scheffer, François, called Berger, *m.* 1782
Scheffer, Jean-Conrad, *m.* 1786
Schey, Fidelis, called Fidely (d. 1788), *m.* 1777, *st.* 109
Schiler (Schüler), Jean-Martin (1753–1812), *m.* 1781, *st.* 81
Schlichtig, Jean-Georges (d. 1782), *m.* 1765, *st.* 118
Schmidt, Antoine-Marie, *m.* 1784, *st.* 82
Schmitz, Joseph, *m.* 1761, *st.* 33
Schneider, Caspar, called Gaspard, *m.* 1786, *st.* 14
Schneider, Jean (d. 1769), *m.* 1757
Schüller, Jean-Philippe (b. 1734), *m.* 1767
Schumann, André, *m.* 1779, *st.* 55
Schwerdfeger, Jean-Ferdinand, *m.* 1786
Schwingkens, Guillaume (mid-18th c.), *st.* 163

Séverin, Nicolas-Pierre (1728–1798), *m.* 1757, *st.* 93

Séverin, Pierre-Charlemagne, *m.* 1787, *st.* 92

Simonot, Alexandre-Pierre, *m.* 1783

Sintz, Joseph, *m.* 1785

Stadler, Charles-Antoine, *m.* 1776

Stockel, Joseph (1743–1802), *m.* 1775, *st.* 53

Strach, Zacharie (beginning 18th c.)

Stumpff, Jean-Chrysostome (1731–1806), *m.* 1766, *st.* 111

Teuné, François-Gaspard (b. 1726), *m.* 1766, *st.* 87

Thibault, C. (2d quarter 18th c.)

Topino, Charles, *m.* 1773, *st.* 41

Toupillier, Denis, *m.* 1764

Tramey, Jacques, *m.* 1781, *st.* 16

Tricotel, Alexandre-Roch, *m.* 1767

Tuart, Jean-Baptiste, *m.* 1741, *st.* 20

Turcot, Jean-Baptiste-Charles, *m.* 1772

Turcot, Pierre-Claude, *m.* 1783

Turcot, Pierre-François, *m.* 1772

Vandernasse, Silvain-Lambert, *m.* 1771

Van Risen Burgh, called Bernard or B.V.R.B.: Bernard I (d. 1738); Bernard II (d. c. 1765), *m.* before 1737, *st.* 154; Bernard III (d. 1800), see *st.* 154

Vassou, Jean-Baptiste (b. 1739), *m.* 1767, *st.* 97

Vaudorme, Jean-Pierre, *m.* 1786

Veaux, Pierre-Antoine (1738–1784), *m.* 1766, *st.* 96

Vermunt, Gérard (d. 1764), *m.* before 1737

Vié, Sébastien, *m.* 1767

Viez, Joseph, *m.* 1786, *st.* 18

Virrig, Nicolas, called Nicolas, *m.* 1781

Vovis, Jean-Adelbert Wowitz, called Vovis (b. 1735), *m.* 1767, *st.* 95

Wackner, Valentin, called Valentin, *m.* 1781

Walter, Pierre (mid-18th c.), *st.* 128

Watteaux, Louis-Antoine, *m.* 1779

Wattelin, Pierre (b. 1719), *m.* 1757

Weber, Jean-Vendelin, *m.* 1786

Weisweiler, Adam (1744–1820), *m.* 1778, *st.* 68

Wirtz, Henri, *m.* 1767

Wolff, Christophe (1720–1795), *m.* 1755, *st.* 40

Chapter 14

EBENISTES' STAMPS

T HE COMMENTS on the subject of *menuisiers'* stamps are equally valid for *ébénistes.*

In the following pages the stamps are organized like those of the *menuisiers:* in six categories according to the height of their letters: less than 4 mm, 4 to 5, 5 to 6, 6 to 7, 7 to 8, and more than 8mm. It goes without saying that these dimensions are inevitably approximate. A seventh category is reserved for unusual kinds of stamps: with fleurs-de-lys, framed, circular, comprised only of initials, or arranged in two or three lines.

There are a few cases where the stamp of an *ébéniste* appears under two different numbers. This occurs when variants of his stamp have been re-corded.

Most of the stamps reproduced in this book were kindly transcribed by the inventory service of the Mobilier National, either recorded from the furniture belonging to this institution or based on the rubbings made by the author. Other stamps were communicated by generous colleagues, notably Messrs. Alcouffe, de Bellaigue, Jestaz, Landais, de Loye, Naudin, Quarré, and by experts such as Messrs. Dillée, Lefuel among others. My thanks to all for these contributions, many of which are published here for the first time.

EBENISTES' STAMPS

Stamps less than 4 mm high

MACRET 1	**E·LEVASSEUR** 8
J·POPSEL 2	**A◊P◊JACOT** 9
CHAPUIS 3	**J·A·GRANDJEAN** 10
AUBIN 4	**J·L·COSSON** 11
E·AVRIL 5	**C◦M·COCHOIS** 12
L·AUBRY 6	**B·A·CHAUMOND** 13
M·CARLIN 7	**CASPAR·SCHNEIDER** 14

DUHAMEL
15

TRAMEY
16

St GERMAIN
17

I • VIEZ
18

J ANGOT
19. ANGOT (J.)

J. TUART
20

F • BURY
21

N•PETIT
22

J•PAFRAT
23

F•BAYER
24

F•GOYER
25

H • ROUX
26

F•RATIE
27

G•FEILT
28

P•DUPRE
29

B•DURAND
30

P•FLECHY
31

G•KINTZ
32

J•SCHMITZ
33

G•DESTER
34

G•RICHTER
35

P•ROUSSEL
36

F•REIZELL
37

J • CAUMONT
38

G·CORDIE
39

C·WOLFF
40

C·TOPINO
41

P·GARNIER
42

J CANABAS
43

P·COIGNIARD
44

J DEMOULIN
45

L·M CREAU
46

L·FOUREAU
47

R·LACROIX
48

C·MAUTER
49

N·LANNUIER
50

P·DENIZOT
51

S·OEBEN
52

J·STOCKEL
53

G·JANSEN
54

A·SCHUMAN
55

G·BENEMAN
56

D·DE·LOOSE
57

A·GOSSELIN
58

B·MOLITOR
59

M·OHNEBERG
60

P·PIONIEZ
61

P H·PASQUIER
62

P·DEFRICHE
63

J·DAUTRICHE
64

J · POTARANGE [65]	J F · OEBEN [78]
J · HOLTHAUSEN [66]	J · F · DUBUT [79]
N · GREVENICH [67]	J · F · GRIFFET [80]
A · WEISWEILER [68]	J · M · SCHILER [81]
C · LEMARCHAND [69]	A · M · SCHMIDT [82]
P · CHARRIERRE [70]	J · H · RIESENER [83]
F - RUBESTUCK [71]	I.B FROMAGEAV [84]
I · P · LATZ [72]	M · C · CRAMER [85]
F · J · PAPST [73]	J F · COULON [86]
J · B · GALET [74]	F · G · TEUNE [87]
M - F · ROHT [75]	P · B · COLBAULT [88]
L · N · MALLE [76]	I · C · ELLAUME [89]
J · B · HENRY [77]	C · M · MAGNIEN [90]

C·C·SAUNIER
91

J·B·VASSOU
97

C·P·SEVERIN
92

P·F·GUIGNARD
98

N·P·SEVERIN
93

I·M·CHEVALLIER
99

J·A·BRUNS
94

J·F·DELACOUR
100

I·A·VOVIS
95

J·B·DETROULLEAU
101

P·A·VEAUX
96

D·L·ANCELLET
102

Stamps approximately 5 to 6 mm

CRIARD
103. CRIAERD (A.-M.)

L·FEL'IXC
107

M·CRIARD
104

D·GENTY
108

1DUBOIS
105. DUBOIS (J. et R.)

F·SCHEY
109

L·BOUDIN
106

J·KOCHLY
110

J ✦ STUMPFF
111

I·C·SAVNIER
115

N·BERTHELMI
112

R·C·FLEURY
116

C·LE BESGVE
113. LEBESGUE (Claude)

P·H·MEVVESEN
117

J·BIRCKLE
114

I·G ✦ SCHLICHTIG
118

Stamps approximately 6 to 7 mm

MONDON
119

FEURSTEIN
123

MIGEON
120

C·REVAULT
124

DELORME
121

P ✦ MANTEL
125

COURTE
122

L✦ROCHETTE
126

IOUBERT

127. JOUBERT

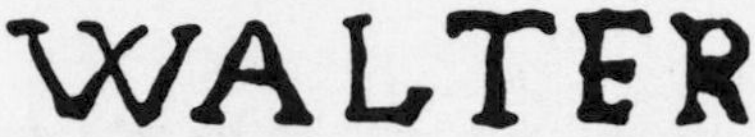

WALTER

128

MONTIGNY

129

J·PLEE

130. PLÉE (P.)

G·KEMP

131

E·DOIRAT

132

H·HANSEN

133

ACRIAERD

134. CRIAERD (A.)

G·PERIDIEZ

135

B·LIEUTAUD

136

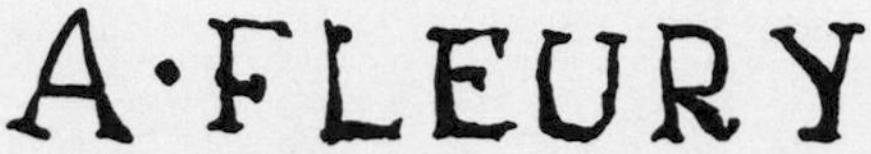

A·FLEURY

137

IBHEDOUIN

138. HÉDOUIN

J·U·ERSTET

139

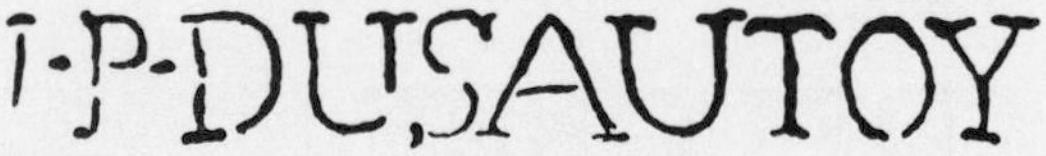

I·P·DUSAUTOY

140

I·B·GAUTIE

141

Stamps measuring more than 8 mm

CARF.L
142

G·LANDRIN
146

MIGEON
143

MCRIAERD
147. CRIAERD (M.)

MARCHAND
144

LARDIN
145

G·LEFAIURE
148

Unusual types of stamps

✤JOSEPH✤
149

U·F·LELEU
152

✤JOUBERT✤ ·
150

R·V·L·C
153. LACROIX (R.)

↵BOICHOD✿
151

B·V·R·B·
154. VAN RISEN BURGH (B.)

155. MACLARD

HACHE ·FILS—A·GRENOBLE

161

J · B
SAUNIER

156

M·E·
LHERMITE

157

ANT
FOVLLET

158

L·DE
LAITRE

159

JACOB FRERES
RUE MESLEE

160

+ANC+
MONTBELIARD

162. COULERU (A.-N.)

G
SCHWING
KENS

163

B
PERI
DIEZ

164

100. Commode console table with one drawer, something between a demicommode and a console table to go under a trumeau mirror (see fig. 12). Two cabriole legs. Japanned wood and lacquer panels. Beautiful rococo gilt bronze mounts. Duvaux sold several pieces of this type. Stamped B.V.R.B. Circa 1750. (Wrightsman Collection, Metropolitan Museum of Art, New York)

101. Louis XVI demilune console table with one drawer and four tapering legs. In this period console tables were done in *ébénisterie* as often as in *menuiserie*. Fine marquetry of flower swags and husk pendants on a *satiné* ground. Stamped Topino. Circa 1780. (Musée des Beaux-Arts, Rouen)

104. Slant-top secretary. A Louis XV model. Marquetry of delicate leaf sprays on a violet wood ground. The slant-top is fitted with a small ledge to serve as a lectern. Bronze mounts varnished rather than gilded. Stamped by Carel. Circa 1760. (Musée Carnavalet, Paris) →

←102. Large *bureau plat*. Veneered in tulipwood and violet wood. Beautiful bronze mounts, finely chased and gilded. A similar desk (see fig. 165 for its *cartonnier*), with mounts bearing the Crowned C, was published by Denise Roche as coming from the palace of Oranienbaum and having belonged to Catherine II. As part of the Dodge collection, Catherine II's desk was sold at Christie's London (June 24, 1971, no. 98), where it was bought by J. Paul Getty. I remember seeing that passionate collector on his knees examining the Louvre's desk (illustrated here), upset to find it superior to his own. Unsigned. Circa 1745. (Grog-Carven life interest gift, 1973, Musée du Louvre)

←103. *Bureau plat* of reduced size. An elegant model with two drawers and slender fluted legs with Ionic capitals. Veneered in yellow and green woods. A lady's desk, probably for a princess. Stamped by Montigny. Circa 1780. (Grog-Carven life interest gift, 1973, Musée du Louvre)

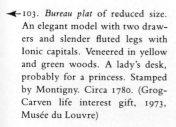

105. Desk *à culbute*. Roubo gives detailed plans for a piece of this type, which he also calls a *secretaire mobile*. Veneered with tulipwood. The top unfolds forward to form a writing surface, and a graduated set of drawers, contained beneath, swings up into position. There are fixed compartments for ink and pens on either side. Stamped by Rubestuck. Circa 1765. (National Museum, Helsinki) →

106. Cylinder desk with roll top. A generally Louis XV form repeated over and over by Riesener under Louis XVI. Veneered with tulipwood and violet wood in panels. Beautiful moldings. Only a few, but finely chased and gilded bronze mounts. Stamped by Riesener. Circa 1780. (Archives Nationales, Paris)

107. Cylinder desk with a solid curved top. A rigid form with straight tapering legs and two drawers in the apron. Latticework marquetry on a mahogany ground. The bronze mounts are few, but judiciously placed. Pierced gallery around the top. Stamped by Leleu. Circa 1780. (Rijksmuseum, Amsterdam)

108. Fall-front secretary *en armoire* with chamfered and curved corners on short shaped feet. Veneered in violet wood with bands of tulipwood between filets of yellow and black woods. A few bronze mounts. Stamped by Delorme and Durand. Circa 1770. (Private collection)

109. Fall-front secretary *en cabinet*. Rectilinear with stretchers between the legs. Veneered with ebony and lacquer panels. The fall front has a border of aventurine lacquer. Beautiful bronze mounts of models that appear to have belonged to the dealer Daguerre. Stamped by Weisweiler. Circa 1785. (Wrightsman Collection, Metropolitan Museum of Art, New York)

110. Short armoire. Drawers in two ranks three across above double doors. Veneered in violet wood with marquetry of flower sprays in end-cut wood. Gilt bronze mounts, notably framing elements with clasps at the corners that seem characteristic of this *ébéniste*. Stamped by Dubut. Circa 1760. (Fitzgerald sale, Christie's, London, Mar. 23, 1972, no. 87)

111. Desk with a slightly slanted top that seems to correspond to what Lazare Duvaux referred to as *petite table à abattant*. Marquetry in scalloped panels of satiné and purple wood. Gilt bronze mounts and bands. The top opens and is supported on two sliding iron bars. Stamped by Migeon. Circa 1750. (National Gallery of Art, Washington, Widener Collection)

112a-b. Small Louis XV writing table. Japanned wood and lacquer panels. Gilt bronze moldings framing the drawers, acanthus leaves at the center, corner mounts and feet. The elegant contour is emphasized by the molded gilt bronze rim surrounding the leather top, the thin gilt bronze moldings that edge legs and apron, and the flat matted gilt bronze panels (found frequently in the work of this *ébéniste*) that follow the curve of the legs. Stamped by Joseph Baumhauer. Circa 1760. (Grog-Carven life interest gift, 1973, Musée du Louvre)

113a-b. Small Louis XVI writing table. Smaller than the preceding table and rectilinear in form. A gallery surrounds the leather-covered top on three sides. A writing slide pulls out from the front. On the right there is a drawer fitted with writing equipment. Marquetry of satiné and sycamore partly stained green in rosettes and latticework bordered with filets of yellow and black woods. Very few bronze mounts, just pulls, escutcheons, and feet. Stamped Riesener. Circa 1775. (Private collection)

114. Low armoire with two doors of rectilinear form with chamfered corners and bracket feet. Veneered in violet wood with tulipwood or satiné and marquetry in end-cut wood of bouquets tied with ribbon. Gilt bronze mounts comprising rosettes, apron mount, escutcheons, and two diamond-faceted plaques. Stamped R.V.L.C. for Lacroix. Circa 1770. (Musée des Arts Décoratifs, Lyon)

115. Dressing table of slightly curvilinear form. The entire top raises to reveal compartments below. Tulipwood and violet wood marquetry in an overall pattern of lozenges within circles. Gilt bronze mounts comprising corner mounts, mounts on the knees, filets and feet, escutcheons, framing bands, and rim that is chased with a foliate motif found on furniture by Carlin as well as this *ébéniste*. Stamped R.V.L.C. for Lacroix. Circa 1770. (The Trustees of the Goodwood Collection, Goodwood House, Sussex)

116. Inkstand with panels of tole imitating Sèvres porcelain, mounted in gilt bronze. With the mark of the dealer Granchez, *Au Petit Dunkerque*. Circa 1770. (Doucet sale, Paris, June 7, 1912, no. 231)

117. Gaming box with the arms of the maréchal-comte du Muy, minister of war in 1774 (died 1775) and of his wife. Inscribed: Fait par Lepage 1776. (Jones Collection, Victoria and Albert Museum, London)

118. Writing table with two drawers in front and three compartments on the other sides whose lids are raised by pushing buttons hidden under the leather of the top. Still another compartment at the rear center contains a roll of green taffeta in an iron frame mounted on a spring to form a screen. Veneered in mahogany and with a raised bronze rim on three sides of the top. Escutcheons and feet of gilt bronze. Stamped by Stockel. Circa 1780. (Château de Bouges, Indre)

120. Reading table. Japanned wood, ebony and lacquer panels with *bleu turquin* marble on the shelf. Gilt bronze mounts and gallery. Drawer with leather-covered writing tablet. Stamped by Carlin. Circa 1780. (Grog-Carven life interest gift, 1973. Musée du Louvre)

119. Jewel cabinet in the form of a Louis XV table with Louis XVI ornaments. Veneered in tulipwood. Fine gilt bronze mounts, especially the fringe at the center (like the fringe Boulle used on his pedestals). Sèvres porcelain plaques. Decorated the bedroom of the czarina Maria Fedorovna at Pavlosk. Certainly from Daguerre's shop. Stamped by Martin Carlin. Circa 1780. (©The Detroit Institute of Arts, bequest of Mrs. Horace E. Dodge)

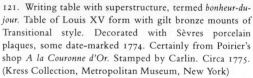

121. Writing table with superstructure, termed *bonheur-du-jour*. Table of Louis XV form with gilt bronze mounts of Transitional style. Decorated with Sèvres porcelain plaques, some date-marked 1774. Certainly from Poirier's shop *A la Couronne d'Or*. Stamped by Carlin. Circa 1775. (Kress Collection, Metropolitan Museum, New York)

122. Tea or coffee table. A severe form with a drawer fitted for writing. Veneered in tulipwood with a Sèvres porcelain top (date-marked 1784), and white marble shelf. Gilt bronze mounts including four plaques on the apron engraved with burnished palmettes on a matte ground. Certainly from the shop of Daguerre, Poirier's successor, and like him a purchaser of plaques from Sèvres for his furniture. Stamped by Carlin. Circa 1785. (Grog-Carven life interest gift, 1073, Musée du Louvre)

123. Bidet in the form of a stool. Walnut. Cursory Louis XV lines. The top upholstered in leather. Fitted with a blue and white faience bowl with the arms of the maréchal de Contades, made either at one of the manufactories at Rouen or Strasbourg, where the maréchal was governor. Stamped by Garnier. Circa 1770. (Château de Montgeoffroy, Maine-et-Loire)

124a-b. Library steps in the form of a stool extending to six steps (height 0.93m, 36⅝ in.). Mahogany. Simplfied Louis XVI lines. The top upholstered in leather and with gilt bronze hinges. Stamped by G. Jacob. Circa 1790. (Château de Bouges, Indre)

↓

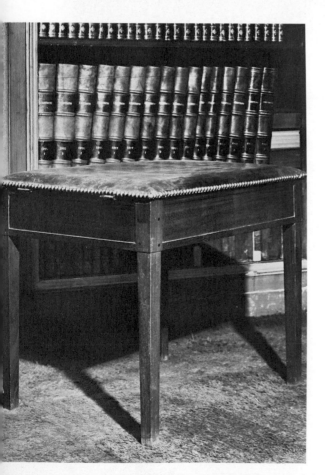

125. Game table. Square with Louis XV legs and apron. Cherrywood with filets of palissander. Tables like this one were delivered to royal residences by this same *ébéniste* in mid–eighteenth century. This one seems to have been part of the furniture of the fermier général Perrinet. Stamped by Joubert. Circa 1750. (Private collection)

126. Game table. Louis XV in form and gilt bronze mounts. Panels of marquetry in overall pattern of cubes within borders incorporating Greek key motifs. The top, which has a roulette game in marquetry, is removable and the inside is fitted for backgammon. Shallow drawers veneered in tulipwood containing a checkerboard and several games of goose or lotto, some of which are dated 1753. There is an identical table, with one of the games also dated 1753, at Longleat (Wiltshire). It bears the mark of Kemp, the son-in-law of Brice Péridiez. Stamped by B. Péridiez. Circa 1760. (Various properties sale, Ader, Gallieréra, Paris, Dec. 5, 1967, no. 90)

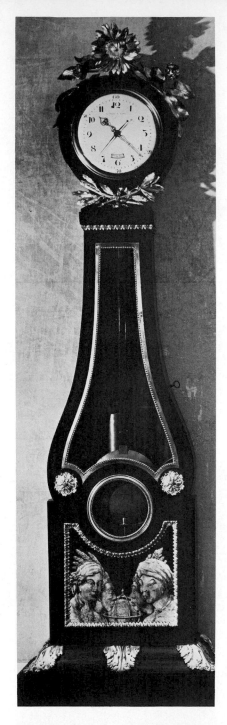

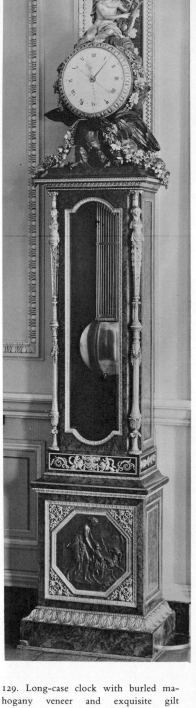

127. Astronomical long-case clock. Curvilinear case veneered in tulipwood with
lavish rococo gilt bronze mounts including a dragon on the lower section and a
figure of Venus at the top. The movement
with calendar and phases of the moon by
Antoine Saint-Martin, a clockmaker located on the Place Dauphine in Paris. The
case stamped by Rochette. Circa 1745.
(Oesterreichisches Museum, Vienna)

128. Long-case clock of a form that swells toward the base. Beautiful Louis XVI bronze
mounts including a sunflower at the top. A
large panel of glass below the pendulum reverse
painted in gold on a black background with the
faces of figures representing Asia and America
looking at a globe. There are clocks of the same
shape and with the same decoration at the top
in the Conservatoire National des Arts et Métiers and at Windsor Castle. Movement by Le-
paute. Case stamped by N. Petit. Circa 1770.
(Private collection)

129. Long-case clock with burled mahogany veneer and exquisite gilt
bronze mounts. Probably supplied by
Daguerre (cf. fig. 109). Surmounted by
figure of Apollo. Matching barometer-
thermometer has Urania. Both are described in Marie-Antoinette's clock inventory. Movement by Robin. Stamped
Benneman and Weisweiler. Circa 1785.
(Private collection)

130. Box with writing equipment with the arms of Jean Pérard, president of the Parlement of Burgundy. Marquetry on a tulipwood ground. Signed by Jean Demoulin of Dijon. Circa 1780. (Musée des Beaux-Arts, Dijon)

131. Louis XVI commode with two doors and a frieze drawer. Veneered in tulipwood with marquetry in yellow and black woods defining three panels on the facade, fluting, and twisted ribbon borders. Escutcheons, ring pulls, and feet varnished rather than gilded. Discovered by Pierre Quarré. Stamped by J.-B. Courte of Dijon. Circa 1780. (1975 acquisition, Musée des Beaux-Arts, Dijon)

132. Louis XV commode of extremely curvilinear form with two ranks of drawers. Floral marquetry and reserves of burled walnut. Bronze mounts varnished rather than gilded. Stamped by Pierre Hache of Grenoble. Circa 1750. (Musée Dauphinois, Grenoble)

133. Transitional commode with two large drawers and cabriole legs. Veneered in violet wood. Top and facade decorated in marquetry with three panels enclosed in frames incorporating Greek keys and having filets of yellow and black wood, and with bouquets of flowers in the center panels. Bronze mounts particular to the region: the escutcheons having the closed crowns of the dukes of Wurtemberg and princes of Montbéliard, and the drawer pulls cast with a fox and a stork. Stamped by Couleru of Montbéliard. Circa 1780. (Musée de l'Hôtel Beurnier, Montbéliard)

134. Louis XVI commode. Rectilinear form with three large drawers and a projecting block front, pilasters at the corners and squared legs. Veneered in burled walnut with marquetry in stained woods, pewter, and mother-of-pearl depicting urns and garlands on the facade and a pastoral scene in a flower wreath on the top. Signed by J.-G. Stern in Strasbourg on the occasion of his marriage in 1797. (Musée des Beaux-Arts, Strasbourg)

PART FOUR

Collections and
Collectors

Chapter 15

REPAIRS, COPIES, AND FAKES

J USQUE DANS les secrets que je crains de savoir" (To the secrets that I fear to know), Valéry's lyric verse (from *Charmes*) serves as an introduction to this delicate subject. Is it really necessary to know these secrets and repeat them? The subject, I admit, is occasionally irritating, sometimes disgusting, but quite often reassuring, considering what is normal and inevitable. I do not claim to encompass the unknown or disclose its formulas. I will leave many questions unanswered. Remaining objective seems to me the most sensible attitude: to know that furniture lives; to admire beautiful work, of whatever the period; to try, however, to understand what belongs to each century.

The uncertainty of many collectors is betrayed, when, confronted with a piece of furniture, they ask the question: Is it really old? This word *really*—is it meant to signify complete authenticity or sufficient age? Is the piece modern or has it remained in perfect condition since the eighteenth century? Has it undergone the repairs that would be normal given its supposed age? Must it be considered restored to an excessive degree, if not faked? The nuances are many and range all the way to the copy, which can itself date from the eighteenth century. The problem is serious, all the more so because it involves considerations of money.

The true connoisseur is content to favor this piece of furniture over that one, without questioning himself on the reasons for his choice. The expert feels, discusses, analyzes, compares, and tries to inform himself. The historian, for his part, observes the stylistic correspondences between the piece of furniture and what is known about its probable author; he makes note of the variations in taste and the reasons for possible changes or transformations; perhaps he will explain away certain doubts, mitigating them by seeking examples drawn from the recent or distant past that are encouraging on some points, troubling on others, and always used with discretion.

Fakes are difficult to demonstrate. They are sensed more often than proved, but a certain number of presumptions can be added to the first impression, which, provided that one has had some experience, must figure importantly in any judgment. Experience is gained by contact with objects. The best training lies in seeing a great deal and studying as closely as possible, at the same time being critical, comparing, developing an "eye" and an extensive, accurate visual memory.

Most connoisseurs and dealers have had this experience and will help the newcomer during his apprenticeship. The latter must, however, retain an independent critical sense and keep in mind that there is no authority, no matter how highly esteemed, who is not subject to error or oversight. Experts (in France an independent group of professionals who catalog works within their speciality for auctioneers) must by profession identify, authenticate, and guarantee. They are certainly authorized to do so by long-established practice, but they do take risks. A record unblemished by error may simply mean an opinion has never been challenged. Sufficient professionalism permits sound judgment in a field where scientific methodology scarcely exists. No one should be hesitant about having his own opinion, nor should he be modest about it. He should allow the more knowledgeable to talk but argue the points that he sees differently. He should also consult older craftsmen who are not influenced by current opinion, can judge the age of wood, and know more than one trick of the trade.

A sound attitude lies midway between the blithe confidence of the beginner making his first discoveries, perhaps soon to taste disappointment, and the skeptical point of view of one who having made a mistake never returns to the field. Experience is born of a critical eye, repeated errors, and lessons drawn if possible from each error. These simple truths must be kept in mind in a field where it is necessary to be prudent before being confident. I am adding this chapter to what I had written before in hopes that the effort will not prove useless. I am also responding to a criticism that led to an interesting and salutary experience—let me call it the lesson of the Left Bank Forger.

One morning around 1960 a letter arrived that was humble in appearance. Written in a trembling, untutored hand on cheap paper, it went roughly this way: polite compliments on my two little books (*Menuiserie* and *Ebénisterie*, parts 2 and 3 of this book); regrets that I had not covered the subject of forgeries in adequate depth (was this because of lack of information or did I reject the possibility of "good" fakes?); and at the close an invitation to come and see what could be done well in this area.

Two days later I found myself in the presence of a craftsman out of another age, proud of himself with good reason. In a poorly heated workshop at the back of a courtyard not far from Montparnasse stood two workbenches, the narrower of which was set near the window for delicate work. Amid the necessary disorder were quantities of models in wood and plaster, numerous packets of documents, and beautiful cleaned and polished tools. In sum, it could have been an illustration from Diderot's encyclopedia, and the man himself could have stepped from its pages.

He was about eighty years old and shriveled, but he had the penetrating gaze of an artisan enamored of his work, impassioned with a fervor that had led him to write the letter. He knew himself to be exploited by others who made no small amount of money off his talent. He insisted on demonstrating his knowledge to me. He wanted to name names to which I refused to listen. He seized his gouge as Menuhin would his violin, carved some small flowers and refined a molding. Perfection itself, the kind that vibrates from the hand of a master, art, warmth, craftsmanship.

He returned to the subject of his clients and his anger flared like a polemicist's. *They* were unworthy and dishonest. *He* was only an artist in chairs, and Louis XV more than Louis XVI. He also made a few beds. Signatures? *They* were certainly capable of adding them to his works, but *he* never did.

He was not a forger. I observed that a fake signature could be recognized especially if it was struck letter by letter. Smiling at my naïveté, he pulled from a drawer a stamp that he had made: M. Cresson. The cross-cut end of a piece of rather hard wood had been carved to leave the letters in relief, naturally in reverse. Secure in what I believed to be my knowledge, I remarked that eighteenth-century stamps were made of iron, not wood. Another triumpant smile. He did not argue but simply took a chair rail and a mallet and with the sure tap of the victor he impressed the mark of the "iron" that he had translated into wood. I believe in touching to judge the authenticity of a chair. I ran my fingers over the fresh signature. Then I understood. Metal would have broken the surface of the wood. This skilled artisan and connoisseur who denied being a forger had simulated the velvety surface imparted by age.

I asked for some statistics. These wood stamps did not last long. That did not matter because it was none of his business. His models were varied and well chosen, Tilliard, Foliot, and many others. He did not like the new clients, the children of those he had long worked for: they sent him, so he told me, mid-nineteenth-century beds bought at auction at Hotel Druout as material so that new chairs could be made of old wood: but he claimed to get his own back by leaving small pieces of mahogany under the seat rail, by which, according to him, his works could be recognized. He had worked since the age of thirteen. His production had been prolific, dependent on carved ornament, but surprising in its quality, consistency, and the "deformations" that could be induced.

I asked one final question: were there many like him still active in Paris? He was perhaps one of the last, and the rewards were too little to attract students. There was no lack of commercial outlets, but they needed to be more appreciative of the skilled craftsman, recognize his talent, and know how to use it well, to refurnish Versailles for example, or to restore antique furniture, and to prevent excesses, dishonesty, or inept work.

The line between restoring and copying is often very fine. Almost from the start there were borderline cases: extensive repairs could be necessary, and copies could become fakes. Techniques remain the same today as in the eighteenth century, and the division remains the same between *menuiserie* and *ébénisterie,* but the objectives are different, entailing an education for the connoisseur.

Tactile education figures importantly in the appreciation of eighteenth-century *menuiserie.* Fingertips are trained to play a large part in the comparative study of furniture whether heavily carved or with simple moldings. The hand, more than the eye, perceives the finish of a piece of wood and what can be called the polish of age: it should pick out the roughness of parts that have been remade, the abnormal unevenness resulting from artificial aging, carved ornaments that are too sharp, moldings that are too perfect, panels that are too rough, and supports too recently sawed. In a few exceptional cases, like the *mobilier des dieux* in the Camondo bequest at the Louvre signed N. Q. Foliot, differences which are noted by the eye only after they have been felt by the hand, are confirmed by the history (both remote and recent) of the furniture as far as it can be reconstructed.

Visual education is more important with *ébénisterie* furniture. To be sure, the hand as much as the eye can evaluate the craquelure of varnish or lacquer, and the quality, which should be neither too perfect nor too crude, of the carcass of a fine commode. It is, however, necessary to inspect closely the appearance of a varnish, the color of veneer woods, the chasing of bronze mounts, also the reverse side of the mounts and the marks they may have left on the veneer. The same is true for repaired or replaced parts whose date is difficult to determine without documentation. One would like to know everything. The bronze mounts on a Louis XV commode look regilded and one wonders when the regilding was done since it seems quite old. Under Louis XVI or Napoleon III?

The ideal way to develop experience and taste would be to compare two pieces that can be securely dated. This can be done in a few museums and historic houses. It would be best to have the answers in advance, to have read which was made in the nineteenth or twentieth century and which was old. Juxtaposing two pieces in this manner can furnish the best of exercises. At several places like Chantilly one sees side by side two chairs of similar appearance but suspects that one may be modern and the other old: the first is characterized by a more substantial chair back, a more solid placement on the four legs, clear-cut lines, and a cruder feel; the older chair, especially the eighteenth-century chair with a few rustic exceptions, will be more of a thoroughbred with finer joinery, a more slender and elegant frame, and tapering sections in the legs and armrests. It is also possible to study two large paired cabinets at the château of Menars that are identical at first glance: the one made for the Hotel de Greffuhle at the end of the nineteenth century has an icy perfection; while the other, which obviously served as its model, has a warmer feel and bears the stamp of J.-F. Leleu. These are excellent examples.

Grasping nuances, appreciating relative age, and attempting to reach certain knowledge constitute the hurdles surmounted by connoisseurs, dealers, and experts. It is also necessary to recognize that old repairs and replicas do exist. Where does forgery enter in? The process of looking through the eyes of a man of the eighteenth century and retracing the stages of the nineteenth century before arriving at the twentieth is recorded in the notes and reflections contained in the following pages.

EIGHTEENTH CENTURY

I made note at the start of this book that, apart from rather rare cases, Boulle furniture for example, the cult of antique furniture was not willingly practiced in the eighteenth century. Then they lived with furniture. The pieces of furniture themselves lived, evolved, and changed: they did not remain inert objects of indifference. In their dual role of function and display they were expected to please and, for that reason all the more, not to appear old; hence the minor repairs that helped reestablish their brilliance when accidents befell them. Adaptation to the changing context also entailed reworkings. They were regilded, reupholstered, and renewed. A modification could result from the desire to obtain a more modern effect by an updated detail. They went as far as making copies if that answered the need of the moment. This was true in *menuiserie* as well as *ébénisterie,* with certain differences which we know about thanks to the archives of the Royal Garde-Meuble.

Repairs were incessant. They could be more frequent in an important residence with its own upholsterer, where they did not hesitate to send for a *menuisier* or *ébéniste* and where they were more concerned with making an impression. In discussing the upkeep of furniture, we will see the concerns the eighteenth century encountered continuously, and even generated, on this point. It cannot be denied that the more magnificent a piece of furniture, the more one wants to retain its original attractiveness, and thus the greater the risk of denaturing or wearing it out by too frequent cleaning and restoration—and this has been true since the eighteenth century. One almost comes to the point of saying that the most beautiful pieces have probably had more restoration than the others. Without pushing this paradox too far, it is wise not to dodge the problem. The restoration of a piece of furniture can have less than salutary consequences.

Repainting or regilding a chair seems quite natural, but remember these words for future reference. The restoration can affect the wood itself. The woodcarver Charny, for example, restored for 3 livres the carving of "two old armchairs," and for 12 livres he "made for one an elaborate front leg." Alterations resulted from stylistic considerations, different use, changing taste, or simply caprice. In 1785 carved top-shaped feet were added to the legs of tables by Roumier and the Slodtz brothers in order to bring them to the right height for their new location at Compiègne, without any thought to the change in proportion. Hauré remade the armrests of Louis XVI's desk chair at Versailles, and, for the Cabinet du Conseil (Council Chamber) at Saint-Cloud he modified the armchairs and folding stools of an earlier model as well as the screen, which he simplified because it was found overornamented. The word *rhabillage* may surprise us, but we find it again and again especially in regard to a bed for the comte d'Artois, also in 1785, a bed for which Hauré used the expression *rhabillage de sculpture* in his bill, an expression that we might have thought coined by a modern forger. In 1787 Marie-Antoinette had the long crest rail of the settee in her bedroom at Versailles altered. The carving of this piece was seventeen years old and probably did not go with the room's recent redecoration involving the mantelpiece, bed, and hangings. The same year the corner seat at each end of two large settees supplied to Madame Elisabeth at Fontainebleau was removed in order to reduce the size of the pieces. This necessitated recarving the uprights, the side rails, and half of four legs in the rococo style of the settees. The result was a *retardataire* Louis XVI piece achieved by inauthentic Louis XV styling to create an effect more in tune with the taste of the day and perhaps better adapted to the paneling of the room.

Surprising alterations have taken place on very fine pieces, not the corrections requested at the time of the presentation of the model, which were made in the drawings or the maquette, but changes after the completion of the piece, demanded on various pretexts: an error that could have been made in the execution, an effect contrary to what was originally intended, or a capricious change of mind. Here are some examples. In 1784 François Foliot was asked to change the seat-rail, which was judged incorrect, on a settee among the furniture just completed for the use of the king of Sweden on his visit to Versailles. The furniture, including the revised settee, went on to be used by Queen Marie-Antoinette at the Tuileries, at which point additional armchairs were supplied by the same Foliot, Boulard, and Sené, all following the original model. Louis XVI's bed at Saint-Cloud, today at Fontainebleau, underwent too many misfortunes in the nineteenth century for one to notice the changes that were outlined under the eyes of the intendant of the Garde-Meuble: four bundles of axes that originally formed the uprights were transformed into pomegranates. Marie-Antoinette personally intervened to correct the carving of a fire screen that had just been delivered for her bedroom at Versailles in 1786. The case of the extraordinary bronze folding screen that came from the bedroom of Louis XVI at Compiègne and was acquired by the Louvre in 1944 is just as typical: the wood frame is by Boulard, but during the course of its execution it was decided not to have carved wood ornament but rather bronze plaques, which were ordered from Forestier and Thomire, in order to make the piece more lavish and durable.

Faced with these illustrious and documented examples, one begins to realize what prudence and caution should be the rule when dealing with more modest furniture where cutting down, adding, embellishing, and simplifying were of little consequence in a time when copies were easy to make, cost little, and required no effort, being relatively contemporary; but what difficulties they give us today when we try to track them down, and what skepticism they lead to!

Cleaning, restoration, transformation, adaptation—for *ébénisterie* all these are operations of the same order. Boulle furniture, being inherently fragile, poses one of these problems. Many pieces carry the stamps of eighteenth-century *ébénistes* like Leleu, Dubois, Montigny, Séverin, and Levasseur, whose exact role has not been made clear. Were these *ébénistes* only restorers who put their stamps on old pieces, or were they authors of fake Boulle furniture under Louis XVI? Montigny, for example, on his business card specified that he "made and restored to original condition all kinds of furniture in marquetry of copper and tortoiseshell . . . in the authentic style of the late Boulle."

In some cases sinful license was taken with the original piece of furniture. They spent money and more or less denatured an existing piece of furniture to make it fit their fancy. Lazare Duvaux did not confine himself to fine pieces. The daybook of the famed dealer takes us through all the steps, making us aware of the bizarre operations practiced on furniture which was still in use but which they wanted to modify. Odds and ends might have been done for poorer folk, but this was a question of a clientele drawn from the highest circles, suddenly concerned with small economies in the midst of enormous expenditures. Doubtless the work produced an attractive result; today, since it has aged along with the rest, it has become impossible to identify.

Not much at first, additions or modifications of drawers or panels sometimes made it necessary to go further. "Added to a table, veneered sides and a drawer" (no. 185 in Lazare Duvaux's daybook). "Removed the veneer from the sides of a writing table, changed the drawers and made two on the sides" (no. 512). "A shelf added to a table veneered in satiné wood" (no. 503). "A corner cupboard in solid mahogany, two doors added" (no. 1061). Were more significant changes wanted? "Had cut and veneered a commode in violet wood and sawn the marble" (no. 2075). "Had the bronze mounts redipped for a lacquer commode with several drawers, on which the holes left on the lower drawers were plugged, had relacquered by Martin, furnished with locks, ring pulls, and escutcheons" (no. 648). "Had Martin japan the sides of a lacquer commode, taken apart and put back together again" (no. 2273). Convenience and position turned on whim. "Had *cartonnier* veneered in violet wood lowered, reveneered, and put back together" (no. 1539). Here are two examples of the transplanting of a piece judged to be of secondary interest in order to create another more suitable object. For whom? For the "spend-thrift" Pompadour. "The fashioning of two writing tables of Chinese varnish whose tops come from a quadrille table" (no. 1683). "Repair of a folding fire screen, having cut down one of the panels to make another fire screen" (no. 1938). We are only as far as the middle of the eighteenth century!

The documents of the Garde-Meuble are rife with information of this sort. Just a few examples will suffice here. Riesener "adapted the carcass and the veneers" of a commode that he "varnished in old lacquer imitating that of the Chinese." He also added corner shelves to the sides of a lacquer chest for the Paris Garde-Meuble. Benneman removed the lacquer from a desk by Gaudreaux and gave it new wood veneers while altering the apron to incorporate drawers. He also installed two drawers in each of the two large commodes in the king's apartment at Saint-Cloud "which had been fitted with doors."

There is also the extraordinary story of the famous set of furniture usually attributed to Benneman (now in the Louvre and the châteaus of Fontainebleau and Compiègne) originally comprising four commodes made some months earlier for the comte de Provence, probably by the *ébéniste* Stockel, which subsequently became eight more or less new pieces through various operations of modification and reproduction. But how can we apply the words *originals* and *copies* in this case? Today we would think the removal of bronze mounts from one piece of furniture in order to decorate another to be scandalous. We would judge the transformation of a carcass to be vandalism. If we knew that pieces were made today to match antique pieces in order to create a set, we would be tempted to class them as *copies* or *fakes*. All of this, however, occurred in the eighteenth century with some of the most celebrated furniture in the world. Now that we are aware of its history, however, we may hesitate to attribute it to Benneman even though the pieces bear his authentic stamp, because he usurped authorship.

If judged by very stringent standards, the gilding of bronze mounts raises difficulties that sometimes go back to the eighteenth century. Gilding was more widespread under Louis XVI than under Louis XV. They were tired of varnished bronzes. Already under Louis XV bronze mounts were revarnished to restore their brilliance. Under Louis XVI we know from various documents that they gilded Louis XV mounts that had originally only been varnished. This is an old modification, but it is not an original gilding in the strictest sense.

The same is true of marbles. The marble top on a piece of furniture might not be that envisaged by its designer or *ébéniste* as it could have been changed even in the eighteenth century because of accidental damage, or, more commonly, changes in fashion, or the desire to match the color of the chimneypiece in a room to which the piece of furniture was moved. How many white marble tops were put on Louis XV commodes during Louis XVI's reign and since replaced by colored marbles that are now deemed, with justification, to conform better to the character of the furniture!

Copies done in the eighteenth century force us to compromise and make concessions in both vocabulary and chronology. Such copies usually served to complete an ensemble or to make up a pair at a later date within the same era. It was frequently a question of chairs (figs. 139, 140). If it occurred within the lifetime of the same style, there was little difference from the normal repetition that was routine in the trade over long periods as discussed above. On the other hand, when a copy in the Régence style was made under Louis XV (fig. 138), or a Louis XV copy under Louis XVI, there was an element of awkwardness and anachronism that should be perceptible. The most typical example known to us, or rather that we can document, is that of two armchairs today at the château of Fontainebleau. The two are similar in appearance. They have broad curves; their legs straighten and flatten slightly toward the top; their arms flirt with a scrolling form that is broken by a flat molding; their carved ornament of rods with ribbons, rosettes, oves, and floral crests with a mixture of *rocailles* and acanthus leaves seems to indicate a date of around 1770. We have proof that one of these armchairs was copied in 1791 by Sené and Laurent from an earlier model, preserved in the storerooms of the Garde-Meuble. As soon as one has this information it becomes easy to distinguish the original from the copy: it's carving is less precise, and the cross-pieces are square in section (while Sené lightened his frames by rounding off the undersides). Both have aged in the same way and been subjected to the same regildings in the course of the nineteenth century.

Many other copies are noted in the Garde-Meuble archives, leaving us rather doubtful as to the precise dating of a piece in the absence of documentation and as to the value that should be placed on a stamp. Two examples can be cited. In 1778 François Foliot II and Babel made a large set of beautiful

furniture for Fontainebleau, still Louis XV in shape but Louis XVI in decoration. In 1784 the same François Foliot added a settee to the set which this
time was carved by his brother Toussaint Foliot. One year later a chair with a
higher seat (called the king's chair) was ordered for the set. This was made by
J. B. Boulard and carved by Valois, but the shape and decoration were identical to that of the older pieces by Foliot and Babel. Another example: the
Elysée Palace had a large set of furniture in dire state of preservation but
whose original splendor cried for the salvation that the Louvre provided in
1943; the set, comprising a settee, two large *bergères* (easychairs) and six armchairs of a somewhat heavy opulence, was commissioned from Tilliard for
the visit of the king of Sweden to Versailles in 1784. There are four more
chairs that even at first sight are finer and more elegant and have great nobility; these chairs were copies, created the following year to enlarge the Tilliard
set when it was moved to Compiègne; the frames were ordered from Boulard
and carved by Guerin after models specially worked up by the designer Dugourc in the "genre of the furniture" that should be called the original but are
infinitely superior to it.

Ebénisterie furniture was also copied in the eighteenth century with the
same absence of scruples. In 1778, for example, Riesener made a cylinder
desk for Madame Victoire similar to the one he had made five years earlier
for the comtesse de Provence. And Benneman again, in 1786, created for
Louis XVI's use at Fontainebleau and at Compiègne two versions of the same
writing table, identical even to the rosettes, derived in turn from a model by
Joubert. No one would think of criticizing copies issuing from the same
workshop only a few years apart. The problem becomes somewhat more
vexing when the copies are by another *ébéniste*. Some time ago I published
the adventure of the two great pieces of furniture in the Ministère de la Ma-
rine (Navy Ministry) in Paris. One was a low bookcase with three doors
made by Gaudreaux in 1744 for Louis XV at Versailles. Riesener enlarged it
in 1784 making it into a five-door bookcase. The next year the same *ébéniste*
designed a piece similar to the first with three doors to form a buffet for the
ensemble. The Riesener piece is certainly closer to the original by Gaudreaux
than Gaudreaux's piece enlarged by Riesener. Which should today be considered original?

In order to create an ensemble for Compiègne in 1786, Benneman made
a secretary and a small commode in the same style as a commode made by
Joubert for Versailles in 1770. The later pieces appear to us at first to be furniture by Joubert. They bear the stamp of Benneman. They are "Jouberts,"

but fake ones; they are authentic "Bennemans," but not in his style. Moreover the gilding and chasing of the bronze mounts on Benneman's furniture betray the obsession with minutiae introduced in this field under Louis XVI.

More often than one might suppose, one should pause and debate the words *authentic* and *old*. The examples just cited are pieces of furniture with documentation to prove incontestably that they are eighteenth century, yet it is necessary to mention not one but several dates through the course of that century. One is obliged to add further considerations of *purity* and *sincerity*, notions that faded out little by little in the nineteenth century.

FIRST THIRD OF THE NINETEENTH CENTURY

One should be prudent and rather reticent in dealing with so-called eighteenth-century furniture that may have been made, completed, or restored in the nineteenth century, particularly in what is generally referred to as the first third of the nineteenth century. There were social and technical reasons for continuity in quality and workmanship. More than one ancien régime master was still living. Among those who lived on into the Consulat or Empire and have lately enjoyed considerable repute are J.-B. Lelarge, the widow Boulard, J.-B.-C. Sené, J.-H. Riesener, and G. Benneman. There were also some who remained active even later: J.-B. Demay (died 1848), who was the son-in-law of Sené; Michel-Jacques Boulard, who was the son of J.-B. Boulard; A. Weisweiler (died 1820), who may have worked for both Queen Marie-Antoinette and Empress Josephine; and B. Molitor (died 1833) a skillful courtier who worked from the Louis XVI period through that of Louis XVIII. In many cases, especially in *menuiserie* and bronzes, work continued without any interruption and although it was not strictly eighteenth century in the date, it was often the same hands. For some time the techniques and habits of the profession were carried on, although not necessarily in the same spirit.

The time-honored traditions and techniques of *menuiserie* remained almost unchanged until the introduction of mechanical methods in the middle of the century. They continued well beyond then in the countryside and even in Paris workshops of the Saint-Antoine quarter by craftsmen attached to the time-consuming manual techniques. The construction of a piece of furniture, the cutting and the working of the wood, sometimes even certain shapes and decorations did not vary. Many Art Nouveau chairs of 1900 retained eighteenth-century principles of construction, although their designers sought to be radically innovative. At the start of his career the noted Art Nouveau furniture maker Majorelle manufactured Louis XV style furniture. If at the middle of the nineteenth century, over and above the Empire style and its influence, the ties with older styles were reestablished with ease, it was because they had only been stretched thin, not cut.

The transition from the Louis XVI era to the start of the nineteenth century was often imperceptible, even in Paris. Precise dating is possible with the products of the Jacob family because of their successive use of different stamps. An armchair, now at Fontainebleau, executed between 1796 and 1803 and stamped *Jacob frères,* could be considered Louis XVI on the basis of its form and also the carved pearls and acanthus-leaf moldings. Only the presence of overstylized palmettes on the chair back and the exaggeratedly rectilinear armrests would be a little disconcerting. The Empire did not succeed in completely obliterating the eighteenth century, which continued to make itself felt in many details of decoration and shape, causing much doubt and confusion.

In the Grand Trianon there is a matching cabinet and desk published by Charles Mauricheau-Beaupré and Denise Ledoux-Lebard. I had thought they were stamped by Jacob-Desmalter, but it seems they are not. No matter, they remain pieces that intrigue me. They were delivered in 1809 by an *ébéniste* and dealer named Baudouin. There is such disparity between the cabinetwork and the bronze mounts that one wonders at first if there is a question of fraud. The pieces are peculiar: the carcass and mahogany veneer are clearly Empire. The cabinetwork is closely related to a great deal of other furniture of the period. With the exception of a few minor ornaments and moldings that are obviously Empire, the majority of the bronze mounts are Louis XVI: the male and female terms at the corners; the emblematic trophies that are silhouetted and treated with all the grace of the eighteenth century; the central plaque with its arabesques, cupids, and ribbons; the warm, bright gilding; all emanate from Riesener's workshop. Baudouin's bill does not contradict this: it documents only the delivery, not the manufacture. The following is a logical explanation: the mounts, while wrong for Empire, are authentic Louis XVI bronzes affixed to Empire furniture of hybrid character, destined for Napoleon himself. There are times when one cannot put blind faith in archival documents.

The best formula is to combine the historic text with the direct examination of the piece of furniture. Analyze and search out in the piece itself what is mentioned (or not mentioned) in the text. Then there are alterations so skillful that it is impossible to detect them today. Certainly the most successful are the earliest, those done in the late eighteenth and early nineteenth centuries.

If the secret had not been revealed in the Garde-Meuble archives and documents of the Revolution, we would never have suspected that the central panel of the cylinder on the *bureau du Roi* (belonging to the Louvre) or the large pictorial marquetry panel that decorates the commode made by Riesener for the bedroom of Louis XVI at Versailles (Musée Condé at Chantilly) was not original: the additions should be regarded with disdain by the scrupulous connoisseur, if not removed entirely from these two famous pieces. Yet it was Riesener himself who performed these modifications some twenty years after making the pieces. Similarly, the archives of the Musée Condé and a bill drafted by Leleu in 1772 reveal the *demi-lune* commode in the Wallace Collection to have been originally quite different from what we see today. Until recently this commode was universally admired as a perfect piece: it was reproduced in most furniture histories, and it had even been deduced from its mahogany veneer that Leleu, probably under the English influence, favored furniture with plain veneers to which he contrasted extremely rich bronze mounts. This commode, executed for the prince de Condé in 1772, was originally veneered with an elaborate marquetry replete with fleurs-de-lys and allegories of princely glory. Does its current veneer date from the Empire or is it more recent? It is still impossible to determine. It cannot be considered authentic, but it has aged sufficiently to appear normal to the greatest experts. The veneer is antique but less so than the piece by perhaps thirty years. It has the merit of being affixed to a piece whose carcass and bronze mount are of indisputable quality. The cautionary lesson it delivers is enveloped in beauty.

The first third of the nineteenth century encourages us to keep our eyes open and retain a critical attitude. There is as yet no question of fraud: imitation remains sincere (I was about to write "honest"). The work, the habit of reproducing an earlier piece, was only a continuation of eighteenth-century practice (fig. 74). The Restoration reinforced once again what had never been forgotten in matters of technique and ornament. We must have no delusions about the related risks that this presents to us.

Georges Jacob's models were reused in his sons' workshops and those of other *menuisiers*. There was a certain complacency regarding the old styles. Before the end of the Empire, flowers had reappeared in decoration. Already during the reign of Charles X, when conservative interests dominated, marquetry motifs and, on chairs, scrolling armrest supports, and legs like the consoles used by Jacob around 1770 had returned. Skillful copies, for which there had always been a market, replaced pieces in deteriorating condition or lost through dispersions, and completed sets that were considered too small for the new lifestyle. These enabled the artisans to keep up their skills and remain familiar with earlier styles.

The set of furniture by Foliot known as the *mobilier des dieux* that was discussed at the start of this chapter presents an excellent example: it appears to have been adapted and enlarged around 1820, probably for a man of the Old Order, the prince de Condé. In England, where the true passion for collecting French furniture was born, the practice of "redoing" and copying important eighteenth-century pieces was firmly established at an early date. At Windsor castle there are rather heavy armchairs in the Louis XVI style that bear the stamp of Morel and Seddon and the date 1829. In a well-documented study of Edward Holmes Baldock, Geoffrey de Bellaigue explained how this unusual London "gentleman" dealer (died 1845) sold Louis XV furniture to the English aristocracy. Some of his pieces were antiques that he imported from France, while others were restored, transformed, even reproduced to his order.

The phenomenon spread rapidly. Even in Paris specialists in reproductions became successful, among them the Beurdeley family, who will be discussed below. The mixtures of the two "antiques"—those of the eighteenth century and those of the nineteenth—become baffling. To the problem of honestly undertaken exact reproductions, such as were done during the first third of the nineteenth century, was soon added the problem of interpretive adaptations of older styles and finally that of outright forgery.

ADAPTATIONS AND COPIES IN THE NINETEENTH CENTURY

The simple acceptance that characterized the attitude toward earlier eras during the first third of the nineteenth century was to change rapidly and become more complicated. The intentions and viewpoint of the artisans and their clients changed as they copied antiques more than ever but with different objectives. Because antiques were lived with as much from necessity as preference: there were repairs, interpretations, and copies that ranged from faithful to fanciful. The casual but respectful familiarity with the past, based on solid education, was crumbling away. An almost glutonous appetite for relics of the past arose during the reign of Louis-Philippe. This did not always work to the benefit of antique furniture.

A growing segment of society, especially in France, enjoyed living with old things, a limited segment to be sure, but the richest one. Immediately we note that in their desire for comfort they often neglected eighteenth-century chairs in favor of seating made by the upholsterers currently in fashion, but in *ébénisterie* they were not put off by most lavish antiques. The example was set at the top: Louis-Philippe and his sons, as well as Empress Eugénie, scoured the Garde-Meuble for old pieces with which they surrounded themselves. Attics and storerooms took on new interest.

Disorder was part of this growing passion. In her Paris residences shown in the paintings of Giraud, Princess Mathilde had console tables that were old or in the old style, chairs such as those by Demay that are thought to have belonged to Marie-Antoinette (now at the Petit Trianon) were in among rows of Louis XV– and Louis XVI–style chairs. All told, she had more copies than antiques. In the early acquisitions of the Rothschilds, fakes were mixed in with eighteenth-century pieces. Three trends can be clearly discerned: living with adaptations of older styles; faithfully reproducing old pieces; and demanding authentic antiques. From these derive three consequences: "style" pieces, reproductions, and fakes.

Under the rubric "style" pieces fall imitative adaptations of earlier styles, varying in closeness to the originals. Market usage in Europe and America had been to label them correctly from the time of their manufacture and not to sell them as antiques. There is no error or fraud when the term *style* is used. The duc d'Aumale took his inspiration from Louis XV for the furniture of his small apartment at Chantilly. Fould, minister of state to Napoleon III, mixed Louis XIV and Louis XV "style" furniture in the sumptuous salons of the Louvre (offices of the Ministry of Finance). The empress Eugénie, who was a great admirer of Marie-Antoinette, had beautiful furniture carved for her by Cruchet in the Louis XVI style, notably for Saint-Cloud. The Rothschild and Pereire families took pleasure in such adaptations. The designer Prignot published two albums of designs for interiors where he proposed furniture in the "Louis XV genre" or the "Louis XVI genre." Let us consider one of these pieces, which came about in the following manner: the wealthy public took pride in the past, but it loved new and showy things and had no objection to a personal imaginative touch. Today we are obliged to admire the excellent workmanship, worthy of better cause, at the same time that we are shocked by the distortions. The proportions are never the same as those of the preceding century: they have been altered. The ornaments are offensive in their overabundance and confusion. The gilding is also distasteful whether on wood or bronze. The collector can rest assured that if he is looking for

Napoleon III, he will never confuse the eighteenth-century "style" pieces made in this era with true eighteenth-century furniture.

Exact copies were made frequently during this period. They are the most dangerous. They were made according to practices that remained unchanged. They have aged alongside the originals which at the same time were restored to look new. When a brilliant gilding has been applied to both the original and the copy and a patina has built up over time, then real difficulties of connoisseurship enter in, even though there was no fraudulent intent at the start. Chantilly and Compiègne have large sets of "Louis XVI" seat furniture with magnificent carving but of varying age. Many of the pieces were made for the duc d'Aumale or for the empress Eugénie, but there is no doubt that antique chairs served as the models, were copied faithfully, and were mixed in with the rest. Without being able to strip off the upholstery to make a thorough study, one is left to wonder—nineteenth century? And should one discover the stamp of Jacob or Sené, or see the mark of a royal inventory—then eighteenth century? Only some of them. The exercise is beneficial to those who want to learn to tell the difference between the two periods.

Adaptation or reproduction, the same artists (one must grant that such remarkable people are artists) enjoyed moving from one to another or found themselves obliged to by their clients. In both cases the same names recur: Jeanselme and Cruchet, Grohé, Dasson, and Beurdeley to mention the most famous. They were proud of themselves when they created variations on the themes of the great masters of the eighteenth century. They give us cause for concern when they copy faithfully Jacob, Cressent, or Riesener.

Fakes can result when reproductions have aged naturally or have been treated with fraudulent intent. It has become almost inevitable. It is the collector who creates the forger. The concern with age and the desire for authenticity developed with men of letters: Balzac and the Goncourts attached a sentimental value to antiques (or furniture that was believed to be old), to which historical value (real or imagined) was added. The mercenary value of antiques grew with the passion for collecting and the desire for perfect authenticity. A collector like Lord Hertford furnished Bagatelle with antiques, but a scientific catalog like that of Francis Watson shows that some fakes had already slipped into the collection. The richer and more exigent the collector, the more adept the forger became, since it was necessary to get around the nuances and susceptibilities that appeared in the collector. Along with famous eighteenth-century furniture, Prince Demidoff acquired many "style" pieces. However, we see in the sales catalog of his collection (San Donato, 1881) a new precise approach: Louis XVI consoles are stated to retain their original gilding; for *ébénisterie* pieces the name of the author is given, Riesener or Leleu. Baron Double owned, probably without knowing it, skillful copies, mixed in and lost among renowned sets of authentic chairs; through the donation of his collection some of the fakes went as far as the Louvre.

The artificial aging of wood and the clever reworking of furniture that was not necessarily fake to begin with can combine to lead us astray. We have distinguished the "style" piece from the copy, but if the latter faithfully reproduces a perfect eighteenth-century model, confusion is possible, especially if treatment of the wood or bronze has succeeded in giving this copy the appearance of the eighteenth century, and it has become a travesty of an antique.

The second half of the nineteenth century was not an unfavorable time for forgers even though it took them a while to realize it. The terrain was fertile, with collectors who were still novices, unversed in the history of furniture but rich and enthusiastic, and skilled craftsmanship still available and inexpensive. The great *ébénistes,* woodcarvers, and bronze workers who worked in period adaptations were not necessarily forgers when they made exact copies. The Beurdeley family headed an enterprise that prospered making "style" furniture and copies. They loved antiques, collected them, and copied the most famous examples in the Louvre and at Versailles. They organized numerous public auctions where authentic objects of art were mixed in with their own products: it seems thirty-five were held between 1839 and 1901. Still another can be added in May 1979, when their furniture attained very high prices reflecting its real merit. The sale of their holdings when they closed their workshops took up five catalogs, totaling more than 1,400 lots. It was of interest primarily for the bronze furnishings and the furniture where the eighteenth-century *ébéniste* who had made the original from which the piece was copied was sometimes named. The Beurdeleys declared that they stamped their bronzes, but it seems that they did little by way of marking their furniture. A question must be raised: Is it not possible that some of these pieces were later doctored by other people to make the copies into fakes? The danger exists.

Take a single chair from one of the great sets just mentioned and put it through the hands of a skillful gilder who will dilute the gold and give the piece the worn look of partial gilding that some dealers today go to lengths to produce on perfectly sound eighteenth-century pieces. Look at the fiber of the wood and you will find it sufficiently distended by time. None of the anticipated errors will appear in the ornament, which will seem stylistically homogenous, but perhaps a slightly clumsy or skimpy passage will all of a sudden bother you. The carving will seem sufficiently worn to the touch. If it is a question of the seat, it may have been upholstered with springs. There will be no trace of a stamp, unless one has been recently added. The undersides of the feet will be worn down with perhaps the traces of casters. The joinery may have loosened somewhat. The seat-rails will be painted yellow on the interior if the chair is gilded, white if it is painted, whereas they generally left the wood in its natural state in the eighteenth century. Certainly the chair could have been regilded or repainted, just as, whether it is eighteenth or nineteenth century, it could have been recently stripped.

Similar stumbling blocks are encountered in adaptations and copies in *ébénisterie*. Adaptations do not fool the forewarned connoisseur. The charming "Louis XVI" console tables made in 1860 by Poindrelle, *ébéniste* to the château of Fontainebleau, for the boudoir of the queen, do not deceive anyone. Nor do the fake Riesener pieces where there are even errors in the *ébéniste's* name in the signature. The furniture in the Louis XV or Louis XVI "style" manufactured by Sormani or Zwiener, who also made copies, is usually characterized by a particular style, *their* style, which does not lend itself to confusion.

There are still more delicate cases, such as the fake furniture of Cressent. It took a rigorous study by G. de Bellaigue to determine that only one of a pair of commodes with infants balancing a monkey on a swing could be dated to the eighteenth century (Waddesdon Manor, nos. 44–45). The question is even more ticklish when perfectly sound pieces bear stamps that are dubious or unknown: for example, the stamp of Millet (Pierre-François Milet? Jean-Jacques Millet? Or perhaps a Millet of the second half of the nineteenth century, who is noted by Mme Ledoux-Lebard?); a stamp that has been impressed one letter at a time on a superb Louis XV lacquer commode that came from the collection of the Esterházy princes and is now in the decorative arts museum of Budapest; or the stamp Portanier (whose name appears nowhere else but is here accompanied by the initials J.M.E.) on two fine Louis XV corner cabinets in the Hermitage Museum, Leningrad. The stamp alone is not sufficient reason to discredit the object. These pieces seem authentic. For the time being I prefer to acknowledge my uncertainty in these two cases and the lacunae in my information.

TWENTIETH CENTURY

In the course of the twentieth century the demand for French eighteenth-century furniture has increased amazingly the world over. Authentic pieces are subjected to more misfortunes and repairs than ever. The knowledge of collectors has increased, but so has the science and skill of the forgers. A race has been launched against time and men. Too much money and too much trickery are involved. Why shouldn't the connoisseur also bring to bear exigency and scholarship?

Veritable industries have been born, but there is hardly need for serious concern. A forger or manufacturer of antiques, Mailfert, published his memoires and his "recipes" in a book that made some stir on its publication in 1935. He boasted of having established a vast enterprise of fake furniture in Orleans, gave a number of examples of his practices, and named in a partly veiled fashion some of his clients. Two articles published by Hans Huth illustrate some of the pieces that have come from the Mailfert establishment. Unfortunately, I have not visited the Orleans workshops, but, judging from the illustrations given by Huth, the models are poor. A "Louis XV" commode for example resembles too closely a piece newly made in the Saint-Antoine quarter of Paris. Even if the wood were sufficiently doctored to appear old, few connoisseurs who frequent the museums would have been taken in. The stamps reproduced consist, on the one hand, of an *ébéniste* by the name of Crasson, who does not figure on any published list to this day, and on the other of the Parisian *ébéniste* Hédouin; for the latter, two different stamps are reproduced, which, instead of being made with a single branding iron, are ineptly composed letter by letter. Finally the so-called old labels affixed to the furniture to give it the cachet of authenticity are so childish that they would fool no one. This is not to say, however, that this industrialist of forgery did not make more ambitious pieces, taking greater pains than he did with those published in the two articles. The mediocrity of several pieces of *ébénisterie* in the Cognacq-Jay Museum seems to illustrate the truth of what he wrote on page 155 of his book. Mailfert had followers. Little workshops were established in the provinces to make "regional" furniture, i.e., copies of old pieces sold as copies, or fake antiques slightly doctored for the cityfolk desirous of rustic charm. Even when they are old, these pieces present little of interest. But all one has to do is see the way that some secondhand furniture dealers leave "style" armchairs exposed to the elements to realize that they will become "antique" and end up attractively presented in the windows of grand shops.

Another category of forgers is troublesome in a different way. Alongside the makers of ordinary products there are still excellent artisans capable of making fine "old" furniture. These are *menuisiers* and woodcarvers, *ébénistes* and bronze workers who work quietly, isolated, concerned with the quality of their work even though they do not earn enormous profits, intent on maintaining traditions that remain those of the eighteenth century. One can only admire and pity them. One such case was cited at the start of this chapter. They are few but formidable.

The total fake is rare. One is almost always faced with different degrees of age which are discussed above and which remain to my mind the essence of the debate. If the piece of furniture is fake down to its carcass, put together with old wood, beams, flooring, or elements of old paneling, the fraud is readily given away by too many dissimilarities between pieces of wood and by wormholes that run along the surface and are indicative of recent sawing. If, however, parts of an old piece of furniture have been utilized, the connoisseur must hesitate between what seems authentic and what troubles him.

We have seen how many nineteenth-century pieces could be confusing because, whether naturally or artificially aged, they have become *semiantique*. One should be alerted to a problem of date by overmeticulous workmanship, a perfectionism so extreme as to be icy, or the excessive neatness of unexposed parts.

The utilization of *true* eighteenth-century pieces is more subtle. Making two chairs out of one, embellishing carving that was originally simple, veneering an old commode of rustic character with knowingly patinated *ébénisterie,* upgrading the bronze mounts on a piece that had mediocre ones or adding mounts to a piece that has lost them: these are the procedures by which the authentic and the fake are mixed, and uncertainty becomes normal.

The alteration of an eighteenth-century piece is baffling. An old object is denatured by modifications that are often minor in order to make it better conform to today's taste and usage, and make it more saleable. The methods are many; a settee can be shortened into a two-seater, a toilet chair or a simple caned armchair can become a comfortable easychair, a bidet can become a *chaise ponteuse* or *voyeuse* for gaming. A country armoire can be made into two smaller wardrobes, an embroidery frame of precious woods can become a charming lying-in table, and a cylinder desk can be turned into a distinguished writing table. Inventiveness and commercial acumen combine to seduce. Can one speak of forgeries? It is a question of eighteenth-century pieces whose modification sometimes involves no more than a thorough restoration would, and the operation is sometimes one of reduction rather than addition. After all, didn't they do the same in the eighteenth century for greater utility or harmony? The decorator-cum-dealer who upholsters antique or "style" chairs with tapestry covers he has removed from chair frames that he thinks are too simple for them; or the upholsterer who adds a fake G. Jacob stamp

165

to an old chair he deems worthy of the master—are these men perfectly honest?

The repairs themselves, one after the other, could "modernize" a piece that is of value to the historian *dans son jus,* to use the dealers' expression—that is to say, not having been touched in principle since the eighteenth century. But in a state of disrepair is it pleasing in appearance? Isn't it a misrepresentation of how it originally looked? Moreover the question of price constantly enters into the quality and appreciation of a piece; it is a problem that must not be ignored.

In the meantime, to close this chapter, I will return to the advice I gave at the start. A great deal of seeing, handling, and comparing is the best education. It will form an intuition that must then be followed, with the realization that no one is infallible. One loves a piece or one doesn't. One buys it or one doesn't. Isn't this the wisdom of the matter?

Chapter 16

THE MARKET

SINCE THE EIGHTEENTH century the distinction between ordinary furniture and fine furniture has been reflected in the prices, the difference perhaps being even greater initially than today. The differential has remained through the price fluctuations of eighteenth-century French furniture. Sharing the common fate of decorative arts, pieces that were relatively expensive when new suffered a sharp decline in worth when they were deemed outdated. As they were gradually reclaimed from attics, their market value began a steady climb. The subject of changes in fashion and taste is most cogently presented by continuing to consider *menuiserie* and *ébénisterie* separately within the discussion of each major phase.

The eighteenth century was a period marked by prolific production and continuous design innovation to keep pace with the taste of the day. As we have seen, Europe, almost in its entirety, adopted the Louis XV and Louis XVI styles, purchasing the most sumptuous furniture as well as innumerable simple pieces that were easy to copy, such as armchairs, desks, and ordinary commodes. The century ended with the great dispersals of the Revolution, where sagacious purchasers in France and abroad demonstrated their appreciation of these beautiful pieces, even though they were out of date.

The nineteenth century started out as the century of the secondhand dealer. Some looked for cheap used furniture. Others, in rapidly growing numbers, sought antiques, and if possible ones with historic associations. There was a competitive aspect reinforcing this latter trend. Before the end of the century any French residence of importance had to have a set of "eighteenth-century" tapestry-covered seat furniture.

From the outset the twentieth century was one of collections. Great sales, great collections, great prices, and great dealers developed together. Paris became the focal point of the market, while England gave up many of its prizes, and America began to acquire treasures. Financial speculation entered into the picture: economic declines, depressions, and wars sometimes affected the market.

Several concluding paragraphs will be devoted to the period closest to us, the years 1960 through 1980. The antique has become an investment; security is sought in this investment, so it is bolstered by guarantees, expert opinions, documents, provenance from famous collections, and the identification of historic origins. Some collectors, true connoisseurs, still try to live surrounded by beautiful old furniture; others delegate the purchase and safekeeping to professionals. Today's financial instability and the demand for French furniture among oil millionaires has led to increased prices. I do not know whether these inflated prices will hold, but they can certainly be justified when the objects are authentic and beautiful.

It should be noted that in the following pages no attempt will be made to provide monetary equivalents. I leave it to economists to translate values into gold, silver, or some other standard: I am content to give prices in eighteenth-century French livres (livres, or ⤴), in old or current English pounds (£), in French francs, either those before the 1958 currency reform (francs, or fr.) or new francs (n. fr.), or in dollars ($), remembering how these currencies have changed in value over two centuries.

EIGHTEENTH CENTURY

We do not lack information on the eighteenth-century prices of newly made chairs in Paris. Under Louis XV a chair frame carved with a few little flowers cost 10 or so livres; a dozen livres under Louis XVI for a chair frame with four rosettes at the corners and sometimes acanthus ornaments on the top of each side rail of the back. Having it painted cost 2 or 3 livres, and basic upholstery work without the final fabric cost 5 or 6 livres. The fabric, when it was a nondescript velvet, an ordinary damask, or a print, came to about 6 livres per armchair. In total, an ordinary armchair completely upholstered cost 20 to 25 livres (fig. 45). A side chair, similarly decorated and upholstered, cost 4 to 5 livres less. A settee generally cost as much as three armchairs. Leather-covered chairs were only slightly more expensive: in 1760 the *menuisier* Clavery supplied armchairs with rounded backs covered in red leather to Migeon for 27 livres each.

There was a less expensive type, chairs with caning. A new caned armchair cost 10 livres in 1750 (fig. 42). But there were still more expensive chairs, especially those covered in tapestry.

Roland, the future member of the Revolutionary Convention, made note of the price of armchairs with Beauvais tapestry, which we also know from the sales records of the manufactory and the register of royal gifts. There was no special carving of the frames, but they were gilded. The tapestries were figured with people on the chair backs and animals on the seats. They cost 300 livres per chair. Beauvais took a good profit, but ordered the chair frames from Paris. It even appears that a first-class *menuisier*, Charpentier, together with a woodcarver whom I am unable to identify, made a specialty of chair frames intended for covering with tapestry, not only Beauvais, but also the still more valuable Gobelins tapestry (fig. 135).

Chairs covered with Aubusson tapestry were less expensive. In some cases the frames were made in the provinces, in others, Paris, because the Aubusson studios of the Marche region had outlets in several large cities. These chair frames, which, under Louis XV were left in the natural wood and varnished, and painted white under Louis XVI, are always extremely simple. They cost around 60 livres per armchair, tapestry included. The Cleveland Museum has a set of this type with the original upholstery for which the number of the order has been found along with the date 1781.

Luxuriance of carving, gilding or polychrome varnish, and costly brocaded or embroidered fabrics characterized luxury furniture. Of course pieces with little carved ornament could be gilded, but here we will address the category of exceptional pieces, often specially commissioned, with relatively outstanding carving, and sometimes with planned variations of ornament from one armchair to another. The basic frame, which was the work of the *menuisier* and was more carefully made and often more innovative, would cost very little less than a completely carved chair of the preceding category with moldings and ornaments; i.e., about 10 livres for an armchair. Naturally there were different price levels for carving. Under Louis XVI, when ornament took on greater importance, there was something of a hierarchy: for pieces with one, two, or three motifs one could in general peg the price at 15, 40, or 100 livres, respectively.

Curiously, it appears that, for royal furniture at least, carving was never more costly than at the end of the reign of Louis XV. Foliot and Babel submitted bills to the Royal Garde-Meuble between about 1765 and 1778 for chairs where the carving ran as high as 400 livres for an armchair. Prices came down again during the reign of Louis XVI, when the most sumptuous pieces hardly ever cost more than 200 livres. The table compiled for my first volume on French royal furniture based on the 1787 furniture of Marie-Antoinette's bedroom at Saint-Cloud can be used as a point of reference for the costs of joinery, carving, gilding, and upholstery.

The determining factor making some items of furniture infinitely more expensive than others during the eighteenth century, just as under Louis XIV, was the value of the silks used. This was especially true of beds where silk hangings were the essential component before 1750. Later, carving took on more and more importance, and it represented a considerable expense on the great beds of the Louis XVI period. The frame of the bed commissioned by Marie-Antoinette from Jacob for the Petit Trianon in 1783 cost 3,000 livres. The figure must be doubled for the large state beds created in the last days of the ancien régime.

Today we are amazed at the amount spent on fire screens and folding screens in the eighteenth century. These small items, fire screens especially, which were put near the fireplace and were meant to be seen at close range, were very refined and generally cost twice as much as an armchair. They have little market value today, even the most beautiful ones.

A great deal was also spent on console tables under Louis XV and Louis XVI. The average price was 50 to 80 livres, but it could run much higher according to the amount of carving, the quality of the gilding, and the marble.

As regards rustic furniture, the documentation we have covers primarily furniture made in the nineteenth century. Nonetheless it is possible to ascertain a few prices from references in inventories and archives. Thus a document in the Cote-d'Or archives gives us a price of 96 livres for a wardrobe with four doors, with a carcass of oak and pine interiors, delivered in 1781 by a Dijon *menuisier,* Potier, to the goldsmiths' guild of the same city.

In order to study the eighteenth-century market for furniture in a historic context, it is necessary to set apart the Revolutionary period. Social upheavals and the transfer of goods were such that there was more activity than at any other moment, not in the manufacture, but in the reselling of furniture. Many châteaus were emptied. The vast quantity of fabulous furniture amassed over the course of more than a century, especially in the royal châteaus, can be estimated from a few prices. The records of the auctions at Versailles are kept in the Yvelines archives, and the following remarks are drawn from them. Reading the auction records, one is tempted to assume that furniture was resold at the same prices that it commanded when new, but it is important not to forget the inflation that had begun. The examples selected are taken from October and November 1793: a *bergère* covered in printed cotton, 58 livres; a desk chair covered in red leather, 51 livres. In contrast to these ordinary items, here are some luxury pieces: Marie-Antoinette's so-called wheat furniture sold for 16,512 livres (the extraordinary polychromed ensemble was bought back fifty years ago by Versailles and is in almost mint condition and complete except for one important piece, the bed, which has not survived); and the queen's boudoir furniture, sold for 29,203 livres (it subsequently went to the Berlin museum). The poster announcing the sale published by Jean Cordey specified that this set was new, as it had never been used; curtains and *portières* (door curtains) were included with a settee, armchairs with cushions, two side chairs, and a fire screen. A passing note: this set, incomplete but still covered in the original fabric, was discovered in the possession of a hotelkeeper in the spa city of Hanover and purchased in 1896 by Lessing, director of the Decorative Arts Museum of Berlin. It seems that the set, which is of exceptional quality and was still in style in 1800, had been owned at one point by Queen Luisa of Prussia.

In the Versailles auctions, as in all others, there were price fluctuations from one day to another. It is unlikely that the usual consideration of condition was the explanation because, considering the source, one can assume that the pieces were generally in excellent condition. The successive sale of lots comprised of one armchair and six gilded side chairs covered with figured taffeta, forming a single ensemble for the Grand Trianon, provide a good example: they fetched 280, 265, 250 to 324 livres.

Beds generally brought high prices, on the one hand, because of the silk hangings, but also because of the bedding. In contrast some prices plummeted, principally those of furniture that seemed to have no further function.

Thus the *guéridons* (circular candlestands) from the Hall of Mirrors, which cost 5,000 livres in 1770, were sold for an average of 100 livres apiece.

If we return to the price of new furniture and examine eighteenth-century *ébénisterie,* we must take the commode for our first example. This piece could be very expensive in the early years of its production. We have already mentioned the 3,000 livres paid by Louis XIV to Boulle for his two Trianon commodes in 1709. Litigation published by G. Wildenstein in his *Rapports d'experts* between a bourgeois Parisian and the *ébéniste* Jean Coulon gives an evaluation of 80 livres for a walnut commode and of 650 livres for one veneered in violet wood. Later, when the commode became more common, prices dropped except for a few outstanding pieces. Let us examine the prices billed by Lazare Duvaux during the year 1755: 115, 144, and 250 livres for oak commodes veneered with violet wood, palissander, or purple wood (fig. 87), 360 or 470 livres for tulipwood commodes with gilt bronze mounts, each with Flemish marble tops. The lavishness of the bronze mounts went along with the quality of marble which, together with the size of the piece, influenced the price: a commode 4½ feet (1.46m) long, with floral marquetry and gilt bronze mounts and an Antin marble top cost 787 livres; and a large commode "veneered with tulipwood with flowers of violet wood decorated with much gilt bronze" probably the work of B.V.R.B., Joseph, Latz, or Dubois, cost 760 livres (fig. 84). Lacquer pieces brought high prices: a commode measuring 4½ feet, "Chinese varnish with cartouches and decorations of gilt bronze," Flemish marble, brought 630 livres; a commode measuring 5 feet (1.62m) also in lacquer, "Chinese heavily decorated with gilt bronze," brought 950 livres; and the wealthy Paris de Monmartel paid 2,700 livres for "a commode of antique lacquer heavily decorated with bronze," with a Portor marble top, measuring 5½ feet (1.78m). Under Louis XVI a price of 300 livres would buy no more than a simple mahogany commode. In 1775 Riesener asked 375 livres excluding the marble (a Sainte-Anne marble which cost 68 livres) for the speckled mahogany two-drawer commode, practically bare of bronze mounts, which he supplied for the king's study at Sèvres. Prices of 4,000 to 5,000 livres for a commode were not uncommon, and one made by Carlin (now in the Louvre) with beautiful lacquer panels and finely chased bronze mounts purchased from the dealer Darnault by Madame Victoire for her study at Bellevue cost 6,500 livres.

An explanation for the rise of prices can be found in the development of techniques. Bronze mounts reached a height of extravagance under Louis XVI, both in their chasing and gilding. Marquetry also became more complicated—on fine pieces simple parquetry gave way to latticework with flowers composed of hundreds of tiny pieces, and, further, literally pictures in marquetry imitating painting. More exotic woods were sought for veneers; speckled mahogany, yellow satiné, and amboyna. Since such furniture was more difficult to make and more had to be spent on the materials, it is understandable that the price increased (fig. 94). The trend was not limited to France, and we have noted the influence of the German *ébéniste* Roentgen on the development of pictorial marquetry and on the detailing of furniture which he brought to an unprecedented level. Certainly one cannot establish iron-clad rules because a full price range of furniture was made in all periods. It was during the reign of Louis XV that one of the most sumptuous pieces ever made was created: the cylinder desk traditionally called the *bureau du Roi*. Expensive in its mechanical works, pictorial marquetry, and its overabundance of beautifully chased and gilded bronze mounts, this piece took nine years to make and cost 62,985 livres, to which the payment of 7,644 livres to the bronzemaker Hervieux, and 2,000 livres to the clockmaker Lépine must be added. It could be argued, however, that the desk made for Louis XVI was even more expensive. This was the massive piece bought from Roentgen, where the bronze mounts were of only secondary importance and the bulk of the cost lay in the marquetry pictures and the complicated mechanics. Louis XVI payed 90,000 livres for this desk.

To get a clearer idea of the price difference between the two reigns, we will compare a few pieces by the greatest *ébénistes* of their respective periods: B.V.R.B. (Van Risen Burgh), on one hand, and Riesener, on the other. The results may suggest the superiority of Louis XV over Louis XVI furniture, but in fact the works of these two masters are equally fine, but collectors today prefer the earlier of the two. [The 1980s were marked by a rapidly escalating market for French eighteenth-century furniture in which Louis XVI furniture was much sought after and the best pieces achieved prices equal to those of the Louis XV period.] The difference in price between them reveals what might be called a more aristocratic style in furniture under Louis XV. When Mme de Pompadour bought one of the little slant-top desks by B.V.R.B. that are worth enormous amounts today, from Lazare Duvaux, she paid only 220 livres. The little blue lacquer desk that she chose for Bellevue (given by David Weill to the Paris Musée des Arts Décoratifs) must surely have been around that price. A luxury item like the tulipwood bidet with marquetry of violet wood flowers and very fine bronze mounts that Lazare Duvaux delivered for Bellevue (now in a private collection), which is almost certainly the work of B.V.R.B. although it bears the stamp of Simon Oeben, cost 360 livres. One has to find a truly extraordinary piece of furniture like the desk-bookcase ordered by Louis XV for the Grand Trianon (now the museum at Le Mans) to reach the figure of 2,500 livres.

Riesener's prices are completely different, and from the record of his earliest deliveries we are made aware of their high cost. He billed 3,000 livres for the little table (now in the Petit Trianon) in 1771 for the general intendant Fontanieu. The cylinder desks that he made over the following years for the royal family were 5,000 to 6,000 livres. At the same time, in 1774–75, he asked prices, especially for the king's bedroom at Versailles, far exceeding any seen previously: 7,180 livres for the commode that is today at Windsor Castle; 25,356 livres for the opulent piece that required a year's work (now in the Musée Condé at Chantilly). Riesener's prices rose as the lavishness of his furniture increased over the years; 3,500 and 5,600 livres, respectively, for a writing table and commode delivered for the Petit Trianon in 1777; and 5,600 livres for a corner cabinet, excluding the marble top. The furniture for Marie-Antoinette's boudoir at the Tuileries was costly: 4,600 livres for a small commode; 1,560 livres for a dressing table (now at the Petit Trianon); and 6,260 livres for a cylinder desk (now in the Louvre). Since most of the cost of these pieces lay in their marquetry and bronze mounts, the prices went down slightly when mahogany veneer replaced intricate marquetry. Thus each of the commodes delivered by Riesener in 1786 for the *Pièce des Nobles* of the queen at Versailles, large-scale pieces, veneered in a beautiful mahogany, with bronze mounts that were few but of a very high quality, cost a relatively modest 3,200 livres. Evidently Riesener's prices were viewed as excessive at the time because the Crown replaced him with Benneman after 1784. Prices, however, decreased very little; 1,600 livres for each of the commodes destined for Mme de Ville-d'Avray in 1787 (one now in the Louvre, fig. 95); and 3,000 livres the following year for the commode for Louis XVI's study at Saint-Cloud.

All the prices cited above applied to furniture when it was new. The purchase of secondhand furniture was common in the eighteenth century. It could be bought from *marchands-tapissiers* (dealers in upholstered furniture) or from *marchands-merciers,* and such prices are difficult to determine. It was also purchased at auction, and we do know from several annotated catalogs what some of the furniture bought in this manner cost. Ordinary mahogany furniture had scarcely any value, and as always there was a difference between the purchase price of new furniture and its resale value. At the time there was also a trend favoring lavish pieces, even out-of-date pieces, if they were attributed to respected *ébénistes* (which was particularly surprising because sometimes the *ébénistes* were still alive at the time of the sale). Thus at the de Selle sale in 1761 several pieces by Cressent exceeded 1,000 livres. Furniture by

135. Armchair with a flat back *à la reine,* from a set comprising two settees and eight armchairs with carved and gilded wood frames covered with Gobelins tapestries of the four continents. The model of the tapestries was created by Lenfant after cartoons by Eisen in 1748 for Bouret de Villaumont, treasurer general of the Maison du Roi. The chair frame stamped by Carpentier. Circa 1775. (Grog-Carven life interest gift, 1973, Musée du Louvre)

136. Mme Du Barry's tea table. A circular tilt top on a tripod base after the English model. Exotic woods and gilt bronze mounts with six Sèvres porcelain plaques surrounding a large circular plaque depicting *Le Concert du Grand Seigneur,* which alone cost 3,000 livres. Poirier directed the creation of this table, which was certainly meant to complete the Sèvres-porcelain–decorated furniture furnishing the salon of Mme Du Barry's apartment at Versailles. It was delivered after the death of Louis XV and sent to Louveciennes, where it was recorded in 1794. Subsequently it was in Empress Josephine's apartment at the Tuileries, and later at Malmaison, according to the inventory published by S. Grandjean. More recently it was in the Paris residence of a member of the Rothschild family (Sotheby's, Monaco, May 21, 1978, no. 21). Stamped by Carlin, 1773–1774. (1978 acquisition, Musée du Louvre)

137a-b-c. Walnut chair, part gilded on a white ground, from an ensemble created for Mme Du Barry at Louveciennes or Versailles. The fine carving probably by Guichard; frame, Delanois; gilding, Cagny. All three are mentioned in Mme Du Barry's bills. They worked under the architect Ledoux, perhaps to his designs. Several of these chairs retain the original covering in "white *gros de Tours* with trelliswork and bouquets," which cost 72 livres per chair. (Formerly Lopez-Willshaw Collection, Sotheby's, Monaco, May 26, 1980, no. 606)

138. Comfortable armchair with caned seat and back. Natural carved and polished wood. The high back and seat-rail carved with a shell. The arm supports are directly above the front legs. The seat is low (0.30m, 11¾ in.). A model that harks back to the Régence in its form and decoration. Undoubtedly a copy made to complete a set, it bears the stamp of P. Bara. After 1758. (Musée Jacquemart-André, Châalis Abbey, Ermenonville)

139–40. Two dining room chairs. Wood carved with moldings and painted white. Similar at first glance: the same chair back, the same rosettes on the rounded corners, the same seat-rail, even the same stretchers. Only a slight difference in the moldings. Part of the furnishings of Madame Elisabeth at Montreuil. One (139) stamped by J.-B. Séné; the other (140) by J.-B. Boulard, with the label of the painter Chatard. 1789. (Jean Robiquet gift, 1961, Musée Carnavalet, Paris)

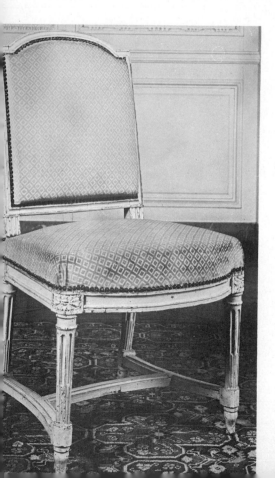

141. Armchair. Gilded wood. The pronounced backward scrolling of the chair back and the scrolling saber legs were termed *à la turque*. The carved moldings skillfully emphasize the form. Stamped by J.-R. Nadal, the elder. Circa 1770. (Private collection)

142. Armchair of the same design as the preceding but carved with cornucopias, crescents, strings of pearls, etc. by Rode for the Turkish Cabinet of the comte d'Artois at the château of the Temple. Now gilded but originally painted white by Ramier and covered with yellow and white damask. The frames made by Nadal's successor as *menuisier* to the comte d'Artois, G. Jacob. 1777. (Baronne Gourgaud gift, 1955, Musée du Louvre)

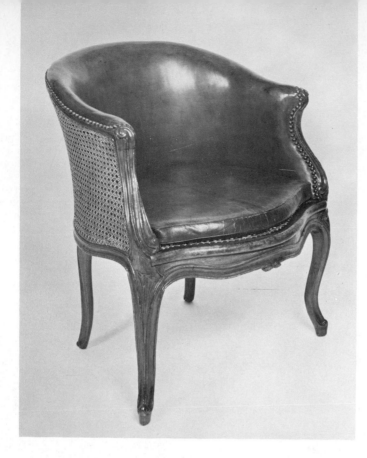

143. Desk chair. Wood carved with moldings and varnished. Pure, elegant lines. With the mark of the château of Chanteloup under the ownership of the duc de Penthièvre. Stamped by Michard. Circa 1765. (Ojjeh sale, Sotheby's, Monaco, June 25, 1979, no. 45, 45,000 f)

144. Desk chair. Carved and gilded wood. Of the same design as the preceding chair. The carved ornament illustrates the transition to neoclassicism. Probably used by the duc de Choiseul when he owned Chanteloup. Formerly in the collection of Jacques Doucet. Stamped by Michard. Circa 1770. (Musée Nissim de Camondo, Paris)

146. Secretary cabinet "with a corner cabinet on each side." Marquetry "of blue cornflowers and latticework on a white ground" (which has since turned green and yellow), "the marble white, and everything lavishly decorated and mounted in gilt bronze." With the exception of the Sèvres plaque (dated 1774) on the fall front, the secretary corresponds to the description of a piece delivered by Poirier for the comte d'Artois at the Temple in March of 1777 for a price of 768 livres. Several pieces of the type survive, notably one in a private collection in Paris, some with, and others without, Sèvres plaques. Stamped R.V.L.C. and R. Lacroix. Circa 1775. (Waddesdon Manor, Bucks)

145. Fall-front secretary. Veneered in mahogany with a flame figure with the finest quality of chased gilt bronze mounts. Made under the direction of the dealers Daguerre or Darnault. It decorated the Petit Cabinet of Madame Adélaïde at Bellevue. Owned by a descendant of Flahaut on the island of Guernsey (Digby sale, Sotheby's, London). Stamped by Levasseur. Circa 1785. (1950 acquisition, Musée du Louvre)

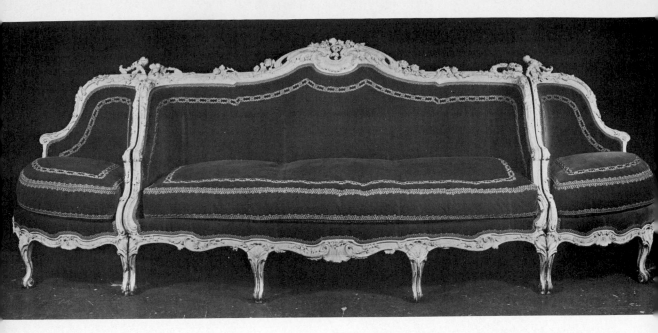

147. Louis XV settee with corner seats, termed *canapé à confidents*. In this case the corner seats are separate. Painted wood, richly carved with rococo ornaments and flowers. Part of a set comprising ten armchairs of two different models and this settee. Said to have belonged to Martial-Louis de Beaupoil de Saint-Aulaire, appointed bishop of Poitiers in 1759, and more recently to Antenor Patiño. Stamped by Heurtaut. Circa 1745. (Sale, Ader, Galliéra, Paris, Nov. 26, 1975, no. 96, 620,000 f. for the settee and six armchairs)

148a-b-c. Louis XVI *canapé à confidents* with attached corner seats. Gilded wood extremely finely carved, classical ornaments and flowers attributable to Antoine Rascalon. First-rate gesso-work and gilding by Dutems. It was originally covered in blue and white silk but recovered with Louis XVI Gobelins tapestry when Napoleon I used the settee at the Tuileries. Made for the Grand Salon of Mesdames at Bellevue. Formerly in the collection of the dukes of Hamilton. Stamped by J.-N. Blanchard. 1784–1785. (Gulbenkian Museum, Lisbon)

149. Coffer on a stand. Veneered in tulipwood and violet wood with gilt bronze mounts. A precious piece that prefigures the work of B.V.R.B. Comes from the château of Valençay (Talleyrand). There is a similar coffer in a private collection in Paris. Without *ébéniste's* stamp (but inscribed in ink B.V.R.B.). Circa 1730. (formerly Lopez-Willshaw collection, Sotheby's, Monaco, June 23, 1976, no. 93, 200,000 f)

150. Chair *à la reine*. Carved and gilded wood in a full-blown Louis XV style. Part of a set covered in Aubusson tapestry from an old home in Clermont, the hôtel de Chazerat. Stamped by Evrard. Circa 1750. (Musée Du Ranquet, Clermont-Ferrand)

151. Small fall-front cabinet, a jewel coffer or medal cabinet, on its stand. Veneered in tulipwood and violet wood with gilt bronze mounts. Similar pieces bear the stamps of B.V.R.B., Joseph or S. Oeben, and probably were the specialty of a single Paris dealer. Unsigned. Circa 1760. (Forsyth Wickes Collection, Museum of Fine Arts, Boston)

152. Chair *à la reine*. Carved and gilded wood. A fine example of the toned-down rococo style, it was part of the collection of a Paris antiques dealer. Stamped by N.-Q. Foliot. Circa 1770. (Mme Bouvier bequest, Musée Carnavalet, Paris)

153. Detail of the center of a demilune console table. *Bleu turquin* marble with matte, gilded bronze mounts attributed to Gouthière. A marvelous piece probably created for the residence of the duchesse de Mazarin on the Quai Malaquais in Paris, after the designs of the architect Belanger. Formerly in the collection of Boni de Castellane. Circa 1780. (The Frick Collection, New York)

154. Mechanical table with a top that slides back to reveal a writing surface and lectern. Sumptuous marquetry of flowers, rococo motifs, and latticework. There are related tables in museums in Munich, Malibu, and New York, as well as several in private collections. Stamped by J.-F. Oeben. Circa 1765. (Duchesse de Richelieu gift, 1970, Musée du Louvre)

155. Bedroom of the maréchal de Contades. The commode is stamped by Garnier as is all the *ébénisterie* in the château. The armchairs are by Michel Gourdin, whose stamp is found on almost all the chairs in the château, except the simplest, which are stamped by Porrot. There is nothing like this simple, tasteful ensemble that has remained untouched since 1771. (Château de Montgeoffroy, Maine-et-Loire)

"Bernard" (Van Risen Burgh) is mentioned in the sale catalogs of several noted collections; but one such piece, a small *vide-poche,* in the sale of the painter Boucher's collection in 1771, brought only 64 livres probably because of its outmoded Louis XV style.

During the Revolution the sale of used furniture took on massive proportions. Government auctions of the former furnishings of Versailles created trends that are interesting to follow. The value of Louis XV furniture collapsed with the most sumptuous commodes bringing only a few dozen livres. It appears that *ébénisterie* suffered more severe devaluation than *menuiserie,* which had fabrics in good condition or had been reupholstered. The toll that can be documented on certain pieces of Louis XVI *ébénisterie* in relation to its original cost was enormous. The *ébéniste* Riesener, incredulous at the market collapse and the reversal of taste that came with the fall of the ancien régime, bought back for laughable prices some of the pieces for which he had charged so dear. He appears to have brought financial ruin on himself in the process because he was unable to resell in the following years the pieces that he had reacquired for stock.

Some examples from Versailles sales of 1793–94 serve to illustrate the sudden loss of value. The 1774 commode discussed earlier and the corner cabinets that were made to go with it in 1780 cost, including the marble tops, 18,764 livres. In the Versailles auction they were sold as a lot with a writing desk, about which we have all the details of manufacture as it was made under the direction of Hauré in 1786 for the king's study and cost 5,716 livres. The sum paid for all these pieces at the time of their delivery was 24,480 livres. They were sold in the month of Messidor in the second year of the Revolutionary calendar for a price of only 5,000 livres!

To take prices of ordinary furniture, a writing table of mahogany with gilt bronze mounts was sold for 180 livres, and one of violet wood, probably Louis XV, brought only 20 livres; an upright secretary of palissander brought 125 livres; one veneered commode with a marble top brought 81 livres, another 28 livres; and a walnut commode with marble top brought 31 livres. A few astute secondhand dealers bought some of the most precious examples of eighteenth-century furniture for minimal prices. At that moment Paris and Versailles disgorged magnificent furniture that no longer had value.

NINETEENTH CENTURY

Eighteenth-century furniture was discredited in the first third of the nineteenth century, as demonstrated by the vitality of the Empire and Restoration styles. Even the most beautiful eighteenth-century pieces became secondary. Nonetheless the old traditions were carried on in the workshops, and many people continued to live with old pieces which they reworked.

Napoleon's often-quoted statement that he wanted "to create the new, not buy the old" was pronounced when he was offered a Riesener masterpiece made for the comtesse de Provence. It was said the original cost had been 80,000 livres, but it was offered to Napoleon for 33,000 francs. The furniture then passed to England and, according to Francis Watson's research, was resold in 1825 as part of the collection of Watson Taylor and purchased for £420 for George IV (Windsor Castle). The emperor did not turn up his nose at all old furniture. For a long time his bedroom at the Tuileries was furnished with pieces that had belonged to Louis XVI. He purposefully selected several Boulle commodes for his surroundings. Empress Josephine was too much a woman of the eighteenth century to give up the delicacy of the *ébénisterie* of the period. At one time she owned Mme Du Barry's Sèvres table (now in the Louvre). The Weisweiler three-tier table that came from her apartment at the Tuileries and is now in the Wallace Collection could have been, in spite of its style, not just a leftover from the royal furnishings but rather a personal acquisition of the empress. An album of the early years of the nineteenth century like La Mésangère's shows that among fashionable furnishings there continued to be small pieces, commodes, toilet tables, and *guéridons* or tea tables made of mahogany with filets of copper and having bronze handles, representing a simplified Louis XVI style.

If, in general, enthusiasm for eighteenth-century furniture was dampened by the interest in classical antiquity, it was not totally extinguished. It was in England rather than France that examples began to be collected. In a trend that rose to massive proportions draining France in the first quarter of the nineteenth century of an unheard-of quantity of eighteenth-century furniture, these pieces rapidly acquired a market value. Taylor and Beckford were interested in them; the English aristocracy sought them out; the regent and his friends, especially Lord Yarmouth, began to assemble collections featuring them. If we return to the case just cited of the Riesener commode of 1774 and his two corner cabinets of 1780, we can see the first signs of the change. According to the research of Francis Watson, these pieces were sold by Christie's in the 1825 Watson Taylor sale and were purchased for the account of George IV: the commode for 56 guineas, and the two corner cabinets for £48.

French eighteenth-century furniture was in general and widespread disfavor until the middle of the nineteenth century. There were, however, exceptions, including émigrés who bought back Louis XVI pieces during the

Restoration. It also seems that, from the Empire on, great aristocrats like Talleyrand would continue to surround themselves with eighteenth-century furniture. The Valençay and Sagan desks, beautiful tables made by the *ébéniste* Montigny, belonged to Talleyrand, and he had himself depicted next to a piece of this type in the portrait by Gerard. It is amazing to see in occasional sale catalogs or even in the novels of Balzac that a few names of great *ébénistes* surface: Boulle, Cressent, or Riesener.

All too long the province of junk and secondhand dealers, eighteenth-century French furniture reemerged little by little. The attraction first felt in England gradually spread. Great collections were assembled in the Napoleon III period, but until around 1900 new furniture and copies had a higher value than antiques.

Menuiserie furniture held less interest than *ébénisterie* unless the upholstery, especially tapestry coverings, gave it value. The Demidoff sale at the San Donato Palace in Florence in 1880 included many beautiful consoles, but the seat furniture was mainly copies where much was made of the beauty of the upholstery silks. In the following years important sales brought to light old chairs of the highest quality and soon their authors became known as their signatures were noted. The Double collection, sold with great success in 1881, contained several sets of furniture that brought high prices: the set called the *mobilier des dieux,* then covered in tapestry that was considered original to it and stated to have come from the king's bedroom at Versailles, was sold for 100,000 fr. The Hamilton Palace sale in 1882 also had beautiful gilded chairs and a bed with Beauvais tapestries (now in the Metropolitan Museum) that brought high prices. In the catalog of the sale of vicomte de Bondy in 1891 the name Delanois was noted in regard to chairs (fig. 137) that had been shown in the 1889 retrospective exhibition of French art where their exceptional quality had already been recognized.

Louis XVI *ébénisterie* furniture was more in demand than Louis XV, especially if it had historic or sentimental associations contributing to its value, like the furniture that passed for having belonged to Marie-Antoinette or Mme de Pompadour or coming from Versailles or the Trianon. In the catalog of the sale of the prince de Beauvau, on April 21, 1865, in the entry on a table which Empress Eugénie bought for 6,000 fr. (now in the Louvre), the names of Gouthière and Riesener were cited along with that of Marie-Antoinette. Little by little attention focused on certain *ébénistes:* Riesener was mentioned several times in the catalog of the sale of the collection of Prince Demidoff, and the name of Cressent was cited in connection with a slant-top desk (illustrated as lot no. 1538) that must be the work of B.V.R.B. and brought 12,500 fr. Attributions may have been erroneous and marks incorrectly transcribed (like Desier for Dester in lot 1781 of the same sale), but the trend was clear: not only was there an appreciation of the beauty of the pieces whose prices increased, but interest was growing in their authors. Two years later the sale organized by Christie's of the famous collections of the duke of Hamilton (fig. 148) (some of whose objects came from Beckford) was accompanied by a huge catalog illustrated with photographs, where the names of Riesener, Pasquier, and Montigny appear, and several pieces of eighteenth-century furniture brought more than £5,000. At the same time scholarly studies like that of Champeaux clarified the history of furniture and collectors became more attentive and demanding. In Paris the sale of the furnishings of the residence of Baron Double in 1881 was the occasion of a sensational auction. Eighteenth-century furniture had its avid collectors: outstanding among them, after the Rothschilds, was Isaac de Camondo, who tracked down the most beautiful specimens of French *ébénisterie* and was noticeable at the Double sale for the importance of his purchases. The same year at the Valanglart sale two pieces of furniture that had belonged to Machault, bearing the stamp of B.V.R.B. and decorated in blue lacquer with sixteen plaques of Vincennes porcelain, reached a record price of 115,000 fr. What a long way values had come from the start of the century!

THE TWENTIETH CENTURY

The trend of collecting eighteenth-century furniture grew stronger and went hand and hand with more serious study and an improved knowledge of marks. Collectors wanted authentic examples, and even if some, especially in the United States, continued to prefer expensive reproductions to the worn antiques, great collectors focused on original pieces. This is the period when collections were brought together that have remained famous: Castellane, Lelong, and Doucet in France, Vanderbilt and Morgan in the United States, and the Rothschild family in all its diverse branches. For the 1900 World's Fair in Paris, Molinier extracted the royal furniture owned by the French state from ministerial offices and the little-known museum warehouse of the Quai d'Orsay for an exhibition at the Petit Palais. After the exhibition most of the furniture found its way to the Louvre, where it was properly appreciated and studied. The cause of the original works was championed by the Société des Amis du Louvre, who supplied exact copies of the desks used by the various ministers of state in order that the originals might go to the museum.

Much of the furniture in private hands became part of collections so rich and important in their entirety that the proud collectors sought to maintain them intact after their deaths, like Wallace and Jones in London, Frick in New York, and the André family (Jacquemart-André) in Paris. The Camondos left remarkable collections: one of them, Isaac de Camondo, left his to the Louvre in 1911; the other, Moïse de Camondo, left his to the Union Centrale des Arts Décoratifs in 1936. In more recent times Mr. and Mrs. James A. de Rothschild with Waddesdon Manor, Mr. and Mrs. Charles B. Wrightsman with the Metropolitan Museum, M. and Mme René Grog-Carven with the Louvre, and Mr. J. Paul Getty with his museum in Malibu have acted in the same manner.

The acquisition by museums of an ever-increasing quantity of rare pieces could have resulted in a regrettable void on the market if dealers and auctioneers had not sought out the pieces that remained concealed in various châteaus. These otherwise unknown or disregarded pieces supplied the market and were offered to a growing number of collectors.

Because the châteaus were so important a source of supply, the center of interest in French furniture remained France and most particularly Paris. It is here that the greatest experts and connoisseurs were to be found, especially for seat furniture. This was already evident at the time of the San Donato sale, when the expert Mannheim was sent for from Paris. During the first quarter of the twentieth century, Mannheim, Lasquin, or Marius Paulme assisted the Paris auctioneers and brought the authority of their names to the principal furniture sales. England, however, with several great dealers and auction sales, particularly at Christie's and Sotheby's, presented serious competition to the Paris market, especially because the quantity of French furniture accumulated in the great houses of Britain over more than a century afforded a considerable source.

Auction sales, scarcely less famous than those of the end of the nineteenth century, brought increasingly sensational prices: the Lelong sale of 1903 and the Doucet sale (fig. 144) of 1912 for example. At the latter sale *menuiserie* brought outstanding prices: 36,000 fr. for a desk chair; 350,000 fr. for a large set of chairs by Lelarge covered with Beauvais tapestry; 225,000 fr. for six armchairs also covered in Beauvais of which, surprisingly, only one, that stamped Cresson, dated from the Louis XV period.

The period between 1920 and the Great Depression of 1930 was brilliant. A typical example is furnished by a caned chaise longue by Cresson sold for 27,000 fr. in the auction of Château de M. on May 31, 1923, with the note "regilded." This piece—at least it seems to be the same—was resold for 103,000 fr. at the Zambaux sale on March 20, 1929, described simply as "gilded wood." It was during this period that two famous sales took place in Paris with magnificent furniture, both *menuiserie* and *ébénisterie:* the Dutasta sale (1926) and the Polès sale (1927) (fig. 137). After 1930 the Great Depression caused a severe slump in the market. Paris remained at the head of the market and still had great auctions: Guérault and Founès in 1935, Burat (fig. 78) (where the B.V.R.B. armoire which would later be part of the Patiño donation to the Louvre reached a record price of 1,520,000 fr.) and the Coty sale in 1937.

World War II brought other changes; collectors in ever-increasing numbers wanted French eighteenth-century furniture, but the prices varied continuously. The three great centers remained nonetheless Paris, London, and New York.

RECENT YEARS

Before concluding this outline of great sales and prices, it is necessary to consider separately the years between 1970 and 1980. Economic changes have created buyers with new attitudes. Some of them are compelled to learn everything, and have the resources at their disposal. Others speculate or want to invest capital: these are sometimes corporations or investment groups. The old-time collector watches and waits, unable or not daring to buy in the face of rising prices. Sometimes the dealer himself withdraws from an active role to become an advisor. This is perhaps a passing phenomenon, and it would be a waste of time to dwell on it. It is, however, necessary to draw attention to certain facts.

The skillful publicity surrounding international auctions makes attendance a must for serious buyers, thus maximizing competition.

The extravagance of a piece of furniture matters more than its elegance. A sumptuous piece of *ébénisterie* loaded with bronze mounts will command a price rarely approximated by a set of chairs of much greater nobility.

A signature, or better yet a historic provenance, is taken as a guarantee of worth, and induces vertigo. On this point the French government and those who still call themselves collectors have done everything to insure the increase of prices. Folding stools, for example, whose prices have become ridiculous, are now available only to millionaires. A small armoire, sold at Monaco as dating from the early nineteenth century, comes back to Paris eighteen months later—it seems to be the same piece in that it is identical with the same fleur de lis at the top that appear to date from the Restoration—but it now is claimed to be of royal origin, dating from the Louis XVI period, and attributed to Riesener. The French museums purchase it for six times the Monaco price.

Prices that may seem crazy are not always unreasonable. Pieces of the highest quality are expensive: historic provenance raises the value further when it is noted in a catalog. A superb console by Riesener should have been acquired by those in charge of furnishing Versailles when it passed through the international art market on three different occasions: of course its origin was known to almost no one. When it was sold again with the Deane Johnson collection at Parke-Bernet in 1972 the provenance, the *Cabinet de la Méridienne* at Versailles, and the proof, its inventory number and the corresponding entry in the *Journal du Garde-Meuble,* were published, alas! Only then was there interest in the piece, and it brought $400,000. The quality had not changed but other factors intervened. While deploring past mistakes, one can still regret that, even at that price, the console was not acquired for Versailles, where it really belongs. It is said that the price rose still higher afterwards!

The value of a piece of furniture, especially at auction, varies according to the enthusiasm with which it is presented. The normal order of increase in value is upset when many good pieces are assembled in a single auction and a special atmosphere surrounds them. The name of the collector has its effect: Penard y Fernandez, Lopez, Patiño, Rothschild, Rosebery, Ford, Dodge, Wildenstein to cite some of the famous recent sales that took place in Paris, Monte Carlo, London, Mentmore, and New York. One may remember, for example, this observation made in an important French art magazine in 1970 on the subject of corner cabinets: these are pieces that are difficult to show properly and are out of fashion; in conclusion, a pair of corner cabinets is worth half the price of a single commode. Then came the Ojjeh (former Wildenstein collection) sale where a pair of corner cabinets by Latz which had been sold in 1933 and had been part of the furnishings of the château d'Eu in the nineteenth century, brought 2,600,000 new francs (fig. 96). Better yet, a single extraordinarily sumptuous corner cabinet by Dubois, long famous but whose historic origins remained unknown, was purchased for 7,600,000 new francs by the Getty Museum.

Examples of the Evolution of Prices from the Eighteenth Century to the Present

Menuiserie furniture

1 / 18th –19th century Large settee *à confidents* (with cornerseats at each end) said to have come from Versailles, but actually made for Bellevue by Rascalon and J.-N. Blanchard (fig. 148)	1784 2,600 # frame only	Hamilton Palace sale June 24–26, 1882 no. 1902 £ 1,176 covered in Gobelins tapestry	
2 / 18th–20th century Furniture for the cabinet of Mme Elizabeth at Fontainebleau: 1 settee, 2 *bergères*, 4 armchairs, 4 side chairs, and one higher chair for the king, by the Foliots, Boulard, Babel, and Valois	1778–1785 3,514 # frames only	Fleury-en-Bière sale December 5–6, 1927 no. 74 450,000 francs recovered in silk	
Furniture for the *cabinet du toilette* of Marie-Antoinette at Saint-Cloud by Sené	1788		
Daybed, *bergère*, and fire screen	1,370 # frames only	marquis de Casaux sale December 21, 1923 158,000 francs with original embroideries	
2 armchairs	480# frames only	Henry J. Horn sale, Christie's May 17–18, 1944 no. 35 £ 2,000	
Furniture for the king's Gaming Room at Saint-Cloud by Jacob Armchairs	1787 416# per armchair, gilded but not upholstered	Polès sale June 22–23, 1927 no. 233 18,000 francs per armchair	Lederlin sale March 22–23, 1933 no. 69 31,000 francs a pair
		Anonymous sale March 12, 1948 no. 45 200,000 francs a pair	MacManus sale Parke–Bernet October 29–31, 1952 no. 599 $280 a pair (modern copies?)

Menuiserie furniture (*cont.*)

Settees of the billiard room of the comte de Provence at Versailles by Jacob	1786 480# the pair	Demarsy sale December 1937 no. 79 11,000 francs the pair	
3 / 19th–20th century 12 Louis XV Gobelins tapestry–covered armchairs	Hamilton Palace sale June 24–26, 1882 no. 1905 £ 892	Leconfield sale, Christie's June 28, 1903 £ 9,450	Dutasta sale June 3–4, 1926 no. 134 1,220,000 francs
Chairs said to have belonged to Mme Du Barry at Louveciennes by Delanois (fig. 137)	Vte. de B... sale May 21–22, 1981 no. 176, 5,900 francs for 3 no. 177 4,000 francs	Polès sale June 22, 1927 no. 232 47,000 francs for 2	
4 / 20th century 2 Louis XV armchairs having the same upholstery of blue velvet and braid	Doucet sale June 7–8, 1912 no. 284 27,100 francs	Anonymous sale December 8, 1953 no. 79 800,000 francs	
Transitional Louis XV-Louis XVI daybed by P.-J. Pluvinet	Doucet sale June 7–8, 1912 no. 289 56,500 francs	A. Sussmann sale May 18–19, 1922 no. 116 56,000 francs	
6 armchairs and 4 chairs of mahogany covered in blue leather by Jacob	X sale February 29, 1928 no. 59 42,100 francs	Ernest Roux sale December 8, 1930 no. 84 38,000 francs	

Ebénisterie furniture

1 / 18th–19th century Secretary by Riesener	1777 8,120#	Hamilton Palace sale June 20, 1882, no. 518 £ 1,575
Writing table by Riesener	1777 3,500 #	Hamilton Palace sale June 20, 1882, no. 308 £ 6,000

Writing table with lectern by Weisweiler	1784 3,260 #	Berthon, dealer in collectibles, on the quai Voltaire circa 1840 3,000 francs	Prince de Beauvau sale April 21, 1865 6,000 francs	19th-century copy Parke-Bernet, New York April 4, 1952 no. 152 $130
2 / 18th–20th century Corner cabinets by Riesener	1786 3,200 # the pair	X sale, June 14, 1912, no. 72 170,000 francs the pair		
Writing table by Joubert	1770 496 #	Anonymous sale November 26, 1942 no. 81 242,000 francs		
Commode by Leleu	1772 2,460 #	Anonymous sale December 12, 1953, no. 123 1,150,000 francs		
3 / 18th–19th—20th century Slant-top desk by B.V.R.B.	1755 220 #	San Donato sale 1880 no. 1538 12,500 francs	J. Doucet sale June 7–8, 1912 no. 318 74,000 francs	Viel sale May 24, 1932 no. 98 91,000 francs
4 / 19th—20th century Lacquer wardrobe by B.V.R.B. (fig. 78)		Choiseul sale May 21, 1896, no. 4 39,000 francs	Burat sale June 18, 1937, no. 145 1,520,000 francs	
Lacquer chest with 10 drawers by B.V.R.B.		H. de C. sale May 7, 1897, no. 84 7,000 francs	marquise de Ganay sale May 8—10, 1922, no. 260 126,000 francs	
Pair of wardrobes with tulipwood and lacquer by B. Péridiez		Choiseul sale May 21, 1986 nos. 5–6 30,200 francs	Francis Guérault sale March 21–22, 1935, no. 87 270,500 francs	
5 / 20th century Commode by Leleu		Doucet sale June 7–8, 1912 no. 329 50,000 francs	Béhague sale December 5–6, 1927, no. 178 100,000 francs	

Ebénisterie furniture *(cont.)*

Small table by Boudin	Dutasta sale June 3–4, 1926, no. 153 132,000 francs		Blumenthal sale December 1–2, 1932 79,000 francs
Desk by Montigny	Bardac sale December 9, 1927, no. 112 270,000 francs		Blumenthal sale December 1—2, 1932, no. 173 135,000 francs
Cylinder desk by Boudin	X sale November 22, 1920 no. 88 50,000 francs	X sale June 8, 1922 no. 72 27,000 francs	Various properties sale June 25, 1937, no. 98 5,100 francs
Bas d'armoire cabinet by D. Gentry	Bickert sale December 3, 1934 no. 203 23,100 francs		Anonymous sale March 31, 1938, no. 78 15,000 francs
Desk by Topino	[Prat] sale December 20, 1932 no. 91 23,100 francs		X sale April 29, 1940, no. 93 27,500 francs
Cylinder desk, said to be that of the king of Sardinia by G. Cramer	Kraemer sale April 29, 1913, no. 162 127,000 francs		George Rasmussen sale Christie's February 24, 1938, no. 13 £ 514
Table with drawers, decorated with Sèvres plaques by Carlin	Mortimer Schiff sale Christie's June 22, 1938, no. 51 £ 1,050		Anonymous sale May 8, 1942, no. 72 300,000 francs

Recent prices		1960-1980
The so-called Saint-Aulaire furniture by Heurtaut comprising 1 settee *à confidents* (fig.147) 6 armchairs and 4 more armchairs of a different model	Paris sale December 8,1954 no. 202–3 15,500,000 francs	Patino sales, Paris June 6, 1975, no. 99 (4 armchairs) and November 26, 1975, no. 96 (settee and 6 armchairs) 1,135,000 new francs total
Two chairs by Delanois said to have belonged to Mme Du Barry at Louveciennes (fig. 137). In 1770 the gilding alone cost probably 84 # per chair	Polès sale Paris June 22, 1927 no. 232 47,000 francs	Lopez sale, Monaco Sotheby's May 26, 1980, no. 606 600,000 new francs

	For two "paired" folding stools	
2 folding stools from the queen's Gaming Room at Fontainebleau or Compiègne 1786-87 by Sené, Valois, and Chatard at a price of 191 # each (frame, carving, and painting and gilding, excluding the fabric and upholstering). The set totaled 64 folding stools, of which approximately 40 are accounted for today.	Paris sale December 14, 1937 no. 25 43,100 francs Home-Drummond sale Christie's, London June 27, 1946 no. 126 £ 472 (N. b. the provenance was not noted in those two sales, but was in subsequent sales)	Dodge sale, Christie's, London June 24, 1971 no. 69 £ 9,450 Redé-Rothschild sale Sotheby's, Monaco May 26, 1975, no. 277 120,000 new francs Ojjeh sale, Sotheby's, Monaco June 25, 1979, no. 40 500,000 new francs
Large writing table with removable legs by R.V.R.B.	Yale University sale New York November 14, 1959 no. 307 $37,000	Winston Guest sale New York December 2, 1967 no. 139, $50,000 Ojjeh sale, Sotheby's, Monaco June 25, 1979, no. 46 1,900,000 new francs
Commode with foliate scroll marquetry by Leleu	Henry Walters sale New York April 26, 1941 no. 729 $6,000	Ojjeh sale Sotheby's, Monaco June 25, 1979 no. 33 4,200,000 new francs
Commode from the queen's *Piè|ce des Nobles* at Saint-Cloud, a copy made by Benneman in 1788 for 1,144# of a commode by Riesener which cost 1,680 # in 1784	Burton sale Christie's, London April 29, 1954 no. 111 £ 1,785 (N.b. the provenance was not given here but would be in the following sale with the reference to the *French Royal Furniture*, no. 24)	Wharton sale Christie's, London March 19, 1970 no. 101 £ 12,000
Console table with Sèvres plaques by Carlin	Harewood sale Christie's, London June 28, 1951 no. 89 £ 2,310	Ojjeh sale, Sotheby's, Monaco June 26, 1979 no. 201 1,000,000 new francs

Chapter 17

DOCUMENTARY MARKS
AND HISTORICAL PROVENANCE

THE HISTORY of a piece of furniture can be written in many different ways to serve different purposes. It is of interest to those eager to learn about the past and helps the connoisseur who wants support for what he has learned from physical examination of the piece. The terrain to be covered, the inscriptions, stamps, signatures, labels, and numbers that one goes to such pains to record, as well as the archival documents, inventories, or catalogs that one tries to consult, must be considered as complementary and auxiliary to the furniture itself. The collector should be attentive to the marks and various different indications that are found on a piece. He should not fail to listen to what they tell him about its origins. He should try to assemble materials, both printed and unpublished, that help to trace the object's distant or recent history. He should first look into the author or authors of the piece, then who in the distant or recent past owned it or who might have played a part in its creation (fig. 155).

MAKERS' MARKS

The most important mark is that on the piece itself, which permits us to identify its author or one of its probable authors. In France in the eighteenth century the term for this mark was *estampille* (figs. 168, 170, 171).

The facsimile *estampilles* reproduced here (*menuisiers*, chap. 9, *ébénistes*, chap. 14) will have familiarized the reader with this sort of signature. It is pertinent to add some observations at this point on specific marks that in the main designate the maker. One can draw some conclusions from the presence or the absence of an *estampille*, but it is necessary to be aware of the limits.

The obligation of Parisian *menuisiers* and *ébénistes* to have their own *estampille* goes back to statutes of 1743 that were registered with the Paris Parlement in 1751. For the following half century every *menuisier* and *ébéniste* of the capital was obliged to stamp his pieces with an iron in the form of his name, and an impression of his iron had to be made on lead tablets kept at the guild headquarters. The obligation ceased to be enforced with the suppression of the guilds in 1789–90, but some masters continued the practice of stamping their products well into the nineteenth century, and newcomers from the Directoire period on seem to have adopted it. Essentially, from the middle of the reign of Louis XV until the Revolution, Parisian furniture generally bore the name of its author, whether *menuisier* or *ébéniste*. This gives collectors as well as scholars a distinct advantage in the study of Parisian furniture that does not exist for the rest of Europe with the exception of Sweden. The use of the *estampille* did extend from Paris into the provinces; but although generally prescribed by local rulings, it was not in regular usage outside of Paris except for a limited number of *menuisiers* and even fewer *ébénistes* in a few large cities.

In principle the *estampille* helps in naming the author or craftsman primarily responsible for a piece of furniture, but often it does more, providing the basis for other attributions, dating, and stylistic comparisons. The information is, however, neither foolproof nor complete. It is not proof of authenticity and must be evaluated objectively. Many problems exist deriving from ambiguities, lacunae, and exceptions that are sometimes difficult to explain.

Fake signatures became inevitable from the day that collectors began to attach almost as much importance to the *estampille* as to the piece of furniture itself. The publication of reproductions of *estampilles* furnishes easily accessible models, but even more frequently, a rubbing of the mark on an authentic eighteenth-century piece provides the outline to be reproduced in an iron (which can be made of iron or wood). An *estampille* that really appears to be eighteenth century enters in as an element to be appreciated in the examination of a piece of furniture. To suppose that a piece is old simply because it bears a signature is childish, but not to take the *estampille* into account would be to ignore a kind of hallmark. Certainly better knowledge of the style and practices of eighteenth-century *ébénistes* will lead forgers to avoid obvious errors in this eternal contest between connoisseurs and forgers. Some pieces could not be the work of certain *ébénistes* because of their date and style: a Louis XVI commode for example could not be the work of Mathieu Criaerd, who was not active after about 1767. But on the other hand, *ébénistes* of the Louis XVI period could very well make and sign furniture of the Louis XV style. We have already discussed the case of Riesener copying a commode by Gaudreaux, Boulle furniture signed by *ébénistes* of the Louis XVI era, and the *estampille* of Benneman that he affixed on pieces where little more than part of the carcass can be attributed to him.

The absence of an *estampille* can mean that furniture is provincial or, if it seems Parisian, that it dates before 1743, as with the furniture of Cressent and Gaudreaux. A Parisian *menuisier* or *ébéniste* might not mark his work because of resentment of this new rule, or simply by negligence. The lack of a mark could, however, also lead one to fear that the piece might date from the nineteenth century. Until the mid 1880s or even a little later, the study of signatures was unknown and imitations were poor. Thus the presence of an *estampille* that is known for a variety of reasons to date before this period offers real security: this is the case with sets of chairs where examination makes it simple to distinguish between the originals and copies, as only the eighteenth-century chairs are signed. Nonetheless, it would be senseless to take this as a rule.

An *estampille* can have been struck recently as well as in the distant past, or it may no longer be visible. It may escape even the most practiced eye, even in the moderate raking (oblique) light that reveals a mark that cannot be seen in bright light. A mark can be obliterated by the holes left by nails on a seat that has been upholstered with springs, by the rubbing of a marble top, or by repairs. It can be concealed under wedges, a thick coat of paint, or a label of eighteenth century or later date. Sometimes a signature has been intentionally obliterated. This occurred in the eighteenth century when some good colleague deemed it necessary to remove the mark with the stroke of his goudge when he sold or repaired the work of another; and today it happens when a forger removes a nineteenth-century mark or when a dealer decides it is useful to suppress a name that he thinks is not important enough.

An authentic *estampille* can pose other problems, in graphics, placement, or the manner in which it has been struck. The solution to such questions should come to light when monographs on the great furniture makers are written. There is a tendency today, in this fledgling science, to believe that there was only one *estampille* per master; but an iron could become dull, break, or be lost, and replaced. It is not impossible that an *ébéniste* or *menuisier* in the course of his career could have had two or three irons successively with minor variations between them. This point is sometimes taken too far, and repeated with too much assurance, without proof or examples, thus encouraging the imagination of forgers.

On a chair, the normal placement of an *estampille* is the rear seat-rail, either on the underside or the inner face. It is less frequently found under the side rail and only occasionally under the front rail. A few *menuisiers* like Cresson, Nogaret, and Lapierre usually stamped their unpainted walnut chairs on the exterior of the rear seat-rail. A few *ébénistes*, Riesener on occasion and Canabas often, also placed their stamps on the exterior of their solid mahogany pieces. The usual practice with *ébénisterie* was to stamp a commode, secretary, or *encoignure* at the top of the uprights under the marble, and a secretary or table under the apron. There are, however, exceptions. A few *ébénistes* signed writing tables as they did commodes, and their mark is only discovered in the course of restoration when the table top is removed: this may well have happened when *ébénistes* were working for retailers. The great so-called Vergennes writing table in the Louvre bears the mark of Migeon under the apron and was long assumed to be a work by him, but the stamp of the *ébéniste* who appears to have been its true author, J. Dubois, was struck on the uprights covered by the table top. Marchand signed, under the rear rail, commodes that were to be delivered by Joubert (one example is in the Wallace Collection). J.-F. Oeben, instead of stamping his secretary desks under the marble, often marked them on the back, a practice that Riesener continued in early works. Subsequently Riesener seems to have followed the practice of stamping his name several times on pieces coming from his workshop. Thus his commodes are usually marked four times, at the top of each of the uprights, and his corner cabinets twice, at the top of the two front uprights.

Last, the method of striking a mark should also be studied. Some irons struck deeply while with others the mark is almost flush. The *ébéniste* B.V.R.B. seems to have inked his iron for signing small tables so as not to drive it in as he did on large commodes, like the ones he made for the elector of Saxony.

Another problem is posed by multiple stamps. The *estampille* indicates, in principle, the author of the frame or carcass: the *menuisier,* not the sculptor of the ornament or the gilder; the *ébéniste,* not the bronze maker, or the lacquerer. When two *estampilles* are found on a piece of furniture, we must resort to hypotheses. With a chair there is the tendency to attribute one signature to a *menuisier* and the other to an ornament sculptor, but this explanation does not always work. The mark N.DLP.S., which is attributed to the woodcarver Nicolas-Martin Delaporte, is found together with the *estampille* D. Julienne on armchairs in the château of Azay-le-Ferron; but when the same stamp N.DLP. (granted, without the *S*) is found alone on chairs with no ornament other than simple moldings, should it be attributed to a *menuisier* of the same family, Martin-Nicolas Delaporte? The *estampille* H. Aguette accompanies that of the *menuisier* D. Julienne on two armchairs in the Arsenal library. The same two stamps appear on a settee with simple moldings in the château of Bouges. This Aguette, who is otherwise unknown, could hardly have been the woodcarver in the latter case. By the same token the *estampilles* N.-S. Courtois and P. Bernard on an armchair formerly in the Jules Straus Collection seem to correspond to the names of *menuisiers.* On the contrary one tends to interpret as woodcarvers' marks the letters C. JV. M. found together with the *estampille* P. Forget on two chairs in the Musée Magnin in Dijon, and the initials M.P. on a Louis XVI armchair in the Strasbourg museum that bears the *estampille* L.-C. Carpentier. Finally, the letter *S,* which figures in the stamp of Canot, brother-in-law of Nogaret, could stand for sculptor or *sculpsit.* As can be seen, there is a great deal of uncertainty on this subject.

In *ébénisterie* the usual interpretation of two marks is that one represents the *ébéniste* who made the piece, and the other, the *ébéniste* who repaired it. There are a few pieces bearing three stamps, like a secretary in the Musée Lambinet at Versailles, which bears the *estampilles* of R.V.L.C., Peridiez, and Dubut. A double *estampille* may also indicate that the piece went to a second *ébéniste* who retailed it. Migeon and Boudin were as much dealers as furniture makers; thus one quite often finds their signatures in a noticeable place on a piece that bears the mark of another *ébéniste,* and the first mark is taken as a record of sale while the second to denote authorship. Finally the suggestion of F. de Salverte seems plausible for several cases of double *estampilles:* one stamp could indicate the author of the carcass and the other the author of the veneering. This hypothesis was offered in the case of Provost and Krier, and Petit and Gosselin. Lists should be compiled of both names, whether co-authors or maker and vendor, so that they can be studied for repeated combinations and correlations. Such statistics would help to shed light on the problem.

Beyond the *estampilles* there are signatures engraved in wood or written in pen or pencil that must be mentioned in the context of authors' marks. An inscription that was brought to light by Henry Hawley, engraved on the case of a clock in the Cleveland Museum, yields the name Latz. The signature Foulet (not necessarily that of the *ébéniste* Foullet who used a double *l* in his *estampille*) is engraved in the marquetry of the fall-front of an otherwise anonymous secretary in the Wallace Collection. More than one *menuisier*-sculptor, proud of his work, inscribed his name on the front of a provincial armoire. Last, a handwritten signature is sometimes found on a drawer or carcass: one of the Migeons signed in ink a dressing table in the château of Champs, as well as a slant-top desk in Frederiksborg castle in Denmark; the signature *Stadtler et beniste rue Royalle a Paris* appears in this form on the cylinder desk belonging to Stadtler's father-in-law, the great *ébéniste* Leleu, which is now in the Oesterreichischesmuseum, Vienna.

The pen-and-ink signature of the *marchand-mercier* Poirier can be read inside several pieces bearing the stamp of B.V.R.B. or Carlin. Quite often, too, an upholsterer wrote his name in pencil on the frame of a chair when he upholstered or recovered it. A systematic study of these signatures should be undertaken as it would help to complete the history of some pieces.

The systematic recording and study of the labels that are still present on quite a number of pieces would be worthwhile. Of course it is not imperative as it is for historians of English furniture, but it would uncover new information. Printed labels often have beautiful typography and a pictorial subject or vignette accompanied by a fascinating text. There are *ébénistes'* labels (Montigny, Severin, Koffler, Hache, Demoulin), also those of *tabletiers* (Auxerre, Biennais), and especially dealers (Bertin, Daguerre, Darnault, Duvaux, Granchez, Poirier, Tuart).

KOFFLER

Dealer, Artisan, *Ebéniste,* Mechanic, and Designer Residing at Enclos Saint-Jean-de-Latran, IN PARIS Makes all sorts of objects in the French, English and German style, Furniture in mahogany, tulipwood, & marquetry woods; sweet-smelling woods of all varieties. Mechanical Secretaries, Desks, Commodes, Bookcases & other Domestic Furniture; all sorts of mechanical Tables with lecterns. Portable Coffers, very practical for ladies' toilet and needlework, & other Coffers with fittings for travel; all kinds of small Tables with drawers; all sorts of Spinning Wheels and Spindles; needlework Frames and tapestry Looms; Shuttles & in general everything needed for Women's Work.

Butter churns of different sizes, in mahogany and other woods, very good for the country, with which butter can be made in very little time.

Room scents with their globes, of different sizes, serving to eliminate bad air from apartments, in which any odor desired can be placed.

Retail and Manufacture of any Game imaginable, for the city or country, such as Games of practice & of skill; Checker-boards in solid cases, with contrasting ivory & ebony.

Also designs are made, for Furniture as well as Games of practice and skill. All sorts of models are made for Textiles and other Manufactures, & for Machines of all kinds. Commissions are accepted from the Provinces and foreign Countries.

There are two other types of labels to add. One concerns mainly the *menuisier* Georges Jacob; some chairs and even beds bearing his *estampille* still have a glued white paper label, measuring about 10 × 3.5cm, with no printed heading or date or maker's name, only an indication of the client to whom the piece was to go (fig. 170). It can be surmised that Jacob adopted this practice in order to avoid errors in his immense production. A second type relates closely to the marks of royal furniture: it comprises labels, which in the last years of the reign of Louis XVI, the painter and gilder Chatard systematically glued on frames that passed through his hands. These little pieces of paper outline part of the manufacture of the furniture, bearing, in addition to Chatard's name and the heading of the Garde-Meuble, the number of the order or commission, and the destination. Documentation of this type, if it is still where it was originally affixed, provides as much if not more information than an *estampille*. I do not believe that such labels have yet been forged. They provide an interesting means of verification and can be used to good end.

All other marks which can help in tracing the manufacture of a piece should be observed, even though interpretation sometimes remains vague. The marks of *gainiers* (makers of sheaths and cases usually covered in leather) can be cited. I know currently of two examples, both in the form of circular stamps, but I do not know which master to attribute them to.

The mark of the crowned *C* which is found on bronzes of the middle of the eighteenth century (figs. 90, 102) and was long thought to be a maker's mark was attributed to Cressent or Caffieri. It is now taken as an indication of the date of manufacture or, more precisely, sale, since the discovery made by Henry Nocq in 1933 that the mark represented payment of a tax imposed between 1745 and 1749. There are, however, forgeries.

By the same token, the marks, whether roman numerals, arabic numbers, or simply notches, which the *menuisiers* wrote or incised on the rails of their chairs, must not be confused with signatures. Studying them should lead to a better idea of the practices of certain workshops. The marks are of two types: the first were to retain the order necessary in a large set and were probably for the use of the upholsterer; other marks were references to facilitate assembly, either in the *menuisier*'s workshop or in the ornament sculptor's, or, reassembly of chairs which had been dismantled for shipment (fig. 169).

Nothing that brings us closer to the authors of the furniture should be neglected, even nineteenth-century marks, which are far from useless where they exist. The Beurdeleys have already been discussed and the mark E.H.B., which I had thought to be that of a skilled forger or a restorer working in England at the end of the nineteenth century. If one accepts the well-documented identification offered by Geoffrey de Bellaigue, this must be taken to be the mark of E. H. Baldock, who stamped his initials in the second quarter of the century on good and bad pieces alike. In addition, in his catalog of the furniture at Waddesdon Manor, Bellaigue has not hesitated to make use of the marks of nineteenth-century Paris locksmiths to further his arguments and datings.

GUILD MARKS

The hallmark composed of the three letters JME joined in a monogram, standing for *Jurande des Menuisiers Ebénistes* (fig. 171), provides, in principle, proof that a piece of furniture was made in Paris between 1743 and the Revolution. It has been stated above that this mark of the guild wardens, affixed during their inspection visits to the workshops, is found more frequently on *ébénisterie* furniture than on *menuiserie*. Its application was therefore not systematic. It is not proof of authenticity since it can be forged easily. The stamp was probably not limited to a single iron in the eighteenth century. It almost always measures about 6 × 8 mm, but the same monogram is found slightly larger and more attenuated in outline on pieces whose authenticity it would be foolhardy to doubt.

The vagueness and uncertainty are still greater with provincial furniture, where the guild mark seems to have been the exception. In their *estampilles* the *menuisiers* and *ébénistes* often followed their name with that of their home town, Lyons, Montbéliard, or Grenoble, but that was by way of a personal signature. There were probably some guild marks, possibly a fleur-de-lys for Lille and an ermine for Nantes, but this is only guesswork in a little-known domain.

MARKS OF OWNERSHIP

Where was a piece of furniture made and by whom? The marks discussed above help to provide the answer. For whom and when? Marks of ownership occasionally put us on the right track. Branded or stenciled marks are found with or without accompanying inventory numbers. They usually indicate a collection or château where the piece was located in the eighteenth or nineteenth century. Thus, for the Restoration period L.B. seems to have been the mark of the prince de Condé, and under Louis XVI a stamp decorated with an anchor and various initials was that of the duc de Penthièvre, AB for Amboise, AT for Anet, B for Bizy, CP for Chanteloup, C9 for Châteauneuf-sur-Loire. Similarly the letters BV under a closed crown formed the mark of Mesdames at Bellevue (a château that had belonged previously to Mme de Pompadour and Louis XV). There are descriptions of the several stamps used for the garde-meuble of the comte d'Artois and the marks are found on a number of pieces: a cursive interlaced AT under a closed crown for Artois; CDT for the château and the priory palace of the Temple, B for the pavilion of Bagatelle, M for the château of Maisons (Maisons-Laffite). The mark of the Garde-Meuble of Marie-Antoinette is circular and accompanied by the initials GR with the initials of a château, CT for the Petit Trianon, or letters designating the principal royal châteaux.

Furniture belonging to the Crown bears marks that are easy to recognize. The initials designate a residence: CH, CP, F, LM, M, ML, R, St C, TH, W signify Choisy, Compiègne, Fontainebleau, La Muette, Meudon, Marly, Rambouillet, Saint-Cloud, the Tuileries, and Versailles. Two letter G's, interlaced and surmounted by a crown, seem to have been the mark of the Tuileries just before the Revolution. Some of these initials were taken up again, with minor changes, in the nineteenth century to designate the various national palaces. Limiting the discussion to the essentials, it is still necessary to cite the letters GM, MP, and BT for the Garde-Meuble, Menus-Plaisirs, and Batiments du Roi; and ASS. NAT. for the Assemblée Nationale during the Revolution; and RF, GM, or a Phrygian cap for the Mobilier National during the twentieth century: an oval shield with three fleurs-de-lys surmounted by a crown was used to mark royal furniture during the Restoration, etc.

The marks of the royal châteaus of France are usually accompanied by painted numbers that can be either the registry number in the *Journal du Garde-Meuble,* or the number in the inventory of a specific residence. Occasionally, toward the end of the reign of Louis XVI, the inventory number and the crowned initials designating the château were put on small paper labels glued underneath the furniture.

Marks of this nature, identified in archival documents, afford the collector and scholar great satisfaction, but also alas, provide forgers with models to imitate. The study of such marks is beginning to be taken up beyond France; other royal garde-meubles, in England, the Scandinavian countries, Italy (here especially the marks CR, C, and DC), and Greece offer many a new perspective. Last, private collection marks existed about which we know nothing. To whom, for example, did the mark of the initials BR under a baron's coronet belong? It was struck on a Louis XVI stool at Bouges that bears the *estampille* C.F. Normand. There is so much to be done on this subject! The publications of Theunissen and Nicolay were not written very long ago, yet almost everything they contain on this subject of marks is erroneous. I have directed my efforts to French royal furniture and to certain princely residences, but there is much to be discovered in related fields for young scholars who want to undertake original and valuable research. The field of the historic origins of furniture is vast and many areas are unexplored. Data are not lacking, but it is necessary to assemble, verify, and work on them. The resource offered by unpublished marks and the explanation they require should attract courageous scholars.

HISTORIC ORIGINS

The history and authenticity of a piece of furniture can be demonstrated in the few cases where all or part of its provenance, from its creation in the eighteenth century through something of its history in the nineteenth and twentieth centuries, can be traced. This is true of a good number of royal and princely pieces. One must, however, beware legends and unsupported traditions and reaffirm that, from beginning to end, it is the piece itself that must "speak."

When the piece comes from an important residence that is not necessarily princely or royal, what remains of old archives can quite often be combined with marks of ownership still inscribed on the furniture. Inventories, which were accompanied by the numbering of the furniture itself, or where, in the case of an estate, the notary drew up a sufficiently detailed description, form a basis for research and identification. Accounts, bills, and registers that document commissions, as well as records of delivery and transfer, complete, sometimes in detail, the description of a piece, add information concerning its creation, and explain some of its special features. Therein lie special rewards for the scholar and collector. But tread cautiously!

French royal furniture has furnished information that I believe can cast new light on the identification and history of a large number of pieces of primary importance. I also see the drawbacks. I have enjoyed rediscovering the mechanisms of the Royal Garde-Meuble, breaking down the works of this bureaucracy, showing what it is possible to extract from such a source. Was that an error? I don't believe so from the point of view of scholarship, which takes priority to my way of thinking. But publishing the results draws the attention of unscrupulous people to this subject, giving forgers the opportunity to exercise their skills. The archives of the Garde-Meuble are in the public domain. The *Journal du Garde-Meuble* is at everyone's disposition. There are even microfilm copies in circulation. Even the most ignorant talk about it with conviction. People who have never set foot in the Archives Nationales declare, "It's in the archives!" What extra value a "rediscovered" would-be history adds to a piece! What false security too! At the same time people are talking so much about refurnishing Versailles, prices are rising proportionally to their often rash declarations. Faking or at least transforming pieces has become tempting. The catalogs of the great international auctions nonetheless furnish documents to those who feel more secure in purchasing on the basis of "an eighteenth century bill." I am convinced these observations are almost totally accurate, at least for the present. I do not believe that forgeries are yet being made from scratch, but "adjustments" will quite naturally appear. It is easier to imitate an inventory number corresponding to the information in a document than it is to forge a bank note. One must be on guard. Recently a widely circulated story, right or wrongly, gave me qualms. I will call it the "Kitchen Cupboard of a Great English Manor."

A short time after the sale of the furniture of Mentmore, a prominent Paris antiques dealer, a very courtly gentleman of exemplary prudence and a member of a family specialized in eighteenth-century furniture for three generations, approached me in a bantering tone: "I see the museums of France are now buying kitchen cupboards!" I investigated. It was an upright secretary, said to be by Riesener that was sold as having come from Versailles with the supporting document, inventory numbers, and illustrations. The piece brought a high price, and now it was being called a fake! I have not seen the piece nor do I intend to. I had, however, been several times to Mentmore; I saw and studied most of the great furniture in the house. They were kind enough not to show me either the "kitchen cupboards" or the furniture in secondary rooms. The current craze for and the dangers of royal furniture are summed up in this story: on one hand, no piece is overlooked, but on the other, people seem to lose their heads. To what error of vision can one attribute the purchase of this piece? I find it even more difficult to understand since the place that it is said to have come from in the eighteenth century no longer exists. Some say the secretary is a complete fake, others that it is in part old. I tend rather toward the second opinion by virtue of the principle that I just set forth: total fakes are rare. Perhaps it is an old carcass, more or less reveneered, and the bronze mounts applied or added to some time ago. Why shouldn't one of the numbers that the piece bears be old, in this mix-up for shrewd connoisseurs to try to unscramble? Enthusiasm can be a poor guide if it did not originate in the splendor of the piece itself. "Historic" furniture, especially that of Versailles, can have a seductive effect on those who are susceptible.

I will cite three more examples of the uncertainty that can develop around royal furniture. The admirable *mobilier des dieux* includes a large settee that may be, in my opinion, a sufficiently aged modern copy. This settee has the inscription *Chambre du Roy* which some have read as the bedroom of Louis XV at Versailles. A great collector like Isaac de Camondo was not fooled. It was to the Louvre, not Versailles, that he left the set of furniture. False inscriptions and fake inventory numbers can have a certain age. I have copied down a forged number inscribed on a piece of furniture that was also fake, and well done. It was a skillfully patinated reproduction of quite recent date of the commode delivered by Gaudreaux in 1738 for the bedroom of Louis XV at La Muette. The forger faithfully copied the number 1131 on the back of the piece without any idea of its significance. I do not know the whereabouts of the original, but I can say I almost saw it, by way of the reproduction, in 1942. My last example is one of an "improvement" wrought on a dressing table whose Garde-Meuble number is authentic but whose original walnut was veneered with mahogany in order to make it a more distinguished piece.

I will summarize this observation on the marks of furniture from the royal châteaus of France with three points: evaluation of the piece of furniture itself must have priority; archival documents must be read with an understanding of how they were written; irregularities of whatever degree should be suspect. Aside from these caveats, which encourage caution, it cannot be denied that such pieces of furniture offer both historical and aesthetic interest (fig. 162), if they are still in sound condition, of course.

Marie-Antoinette's private garde-meuble (fig. 159) poses a special problem. The marks have been known for a long time, and I am afraid that there are apocryphal versions. The queen's inventories have not yet been found, and although I am reconstituting them little by little, verifications are still very difficult.

The princely residences of France offer a fascinating aspect of the history of furniture, one that is more complex, difficult of access, and less well published than royal furniture. There seems to have been no identifying mark for the furniture of the house of Condé in the eighteenth century, but it may be possible to trace the history of the most important pieces. When the superb commode by Leleu came up for auction in 1953, I was certainly the only person who could identify it as made for the prince de Condé at the Palais Bourbon in 1772 because I had copied out this *ébéniste*'s bills in the archives at Chantilly and I had not yet published the 1779 inventory of the palace. With luck and the advantage of surprise I was able to acquire the commode for the Louvre.

We have just noted the marks placed on furniture having belonged to the comte d'Artois and the duc de Penthièvre in the Louis XVI period. Major portions of the comte d'Artois's accounts survive, as do inventories of several of the duc de Penthièvre's residences, but neither has been published. On this score one can hope to learn the history of a certain number of pieces (figs. 25, 142) before these inventories and marks fall to the use of copyists, both of documents and of furniture.

One last thought before leaving the subject of royal and princely furniture: the residences from which these pieces came were immense, and everything from the most sumptuous to the simplest furniture could be found in them. Vast numbers of all kinds of things coming from these residences have been dispersed. Enough exists that there is no need for copies to be made.

The furniture is almost always beautiful. The effort must be made to find and study them.

Family traditions constitute a more modest source of information that should not be neglected, especially when there are papers to give weight to what could otherwise be no more than pious legends. Here again it is necessary to disentangle truth from fiction. Furniture that has remained in situ since the eighteenth century, with old bills, wills, or bequests that provide documentation, does exist (figs. 98, 155, 156, 157, 160): it is rare but comforting. Misunderstandings involving bad faith, recent installations that are claimed to be old, labels concerning spurious divisions of inherited property, so-called gifts of the "martyred queen" that impressionable, and not always disinterested, souls invented in the time of Louis XVIII and the duchesse d' Angoulême, do these present serious danger? All that is necessary is to maintain objectivity.

This note of warning points out the difference between two attitudes: a spirit of finesse and one of conceit. Those with the former may not be familiar with the documents or the books, but they possess, whether by instinct or education, something that can only be called flair or taste. The others try to appear to be scholars even if they are short on methodology and training. They repeat and assert with authority, and make mistakes with brio. I prefer the former. A piece of furniture contains its own explanation. The sincere connoisseur builds up his expertise through everything he sees. He must then have confidence in his judgment, follow his star, and not always listen to others. It is not forbidden for him to have a passion for history, to be interested in marks and old catalogs and papers; he should regard them as aids and amusements. He should look first at the qualities of the piece of furniture itself.

Chapter 18

UPKEEP AND RESTORATION

U PKEEP AND RESTORATION are two steps that, if they have always been carried out wisely, should not pose any problems. Antiques are fragile, however, like very old people. Their appearance has changed and it is necessary in most cases to undertake restoration.

I will devote less space to the problems of restoration than to the favorable conditions that are the means of avoiding it. I recommend the excellent book by Daniel Alcouffe, *Restauration du mobilier* from which I quote the following judicious statements: "On a technical level restoration requires more skill than manufacture does." "It is regrettable that people decide for reasons of economy to repair their furniture themselves since this usually only makes the condition worse" (p. 273).

MENUISERIE FURNITURE

Frames

As we have stressed, the techniques used in France in the eighteenth century guaranteed solidity. Made with well-dried wood, pieces rarely warp. Joined with dowels or in some cases screws, without any glued parts, they stand up well to dryness, which only becomes dangerous when it is so extreme that the wood splits. Only with mahogany chairs is there a real problem with dryness, because, when too dry, any minor impact can cause a mahogany chair back or leg to break.

The main danger is dampness, which causes mildew and rot from wormholes. As the problem always begins in the legs, many a wardrobe, commode, or chair has had the legs turn to the consistency of sponge. Subsequently eaten away by worms, they disintegrate, break, and have to be replaced. For the same reason beautiful chairs are sometimes marred by cut-down legs, unless their normal height has been restored by a tricky repair. As wood rots, worms get in and eat out their holes, weakening the wood further. The best remedy is first of all to move the piece to a more salubrious spot. Before thinking about replacing the affected leg, one must try to treat it so that the integrity of the eighteenth-century piece of furniture can be retained as much as possible. The Institut Pasteur has perfected a product that can be injected into the wormholes to destroy parasites.

Another cause of destruction in *menuiserie* is disjointing. The method of assembly is such that if the joints come loose, the piece quickly falls apart. A certain play is evidenced in many old chairs due to the enlargement of the holes for the dowels. If the dowels are lost, the tenon will come out of its mortice, the leg will become detached from the seat-rail, and the chair back from its uprights. On large pieces one sees frames or panels sprung at the joints and doors of armoires coming off; sometimes drawers are lost. The solution, especially for chairs, is to watch the dowels and replace them when they no longer fit snugly in their holes. Many chairs have been reinforced underneath with the aid of wooden angle blocks, which are only bothersome to someone turning the chair over to study it. Wooden angle blocks are either glued or screwed to the seat-rails in the corners, and they make the seat really solid. The crude method of consolidating chairs as well as larger pieces with angle irons or metal plaques should be rejected, especially for chairs. Seats are sometimes reinforced by the addition of facing to the wood inside the seat-rail in a way that can be relatively discreet.

Vandalism has been responsible for innumerable disasters in furniture. Unintentional damage, like broken legs, can result from excessively rough use; but people have also, for their own reasons, raised or cut down the legs of chairs. The chair reserved for the king in royal residences was made higher than the rest of a set. Ignorant of the custom and upset by the difference in height, egalitarian souls often cut this chair down to the size of the others. Beds have been enlarged, cut down, and recarved: a prime example is Louis XVI's bed at Saint-Cloud, a masterpiece by Sené, which was transformed into a double bed, with head and foot of different heights and, further, horrendously regilded for use in the duc d'Orleans's apartments at Fontainebleau under Louis-Philippe. Peasant furniture was also subjected to this kind of transformation which, far from being fraudulent in intent, was just part of the life of furniture: some of the buffets from the region of Bresse have had clocks added to them. The ideal remedy for such evils would be restoration to their original state. Even when possible, which is rare, this is expensive. The matter also requires prudence, because it is difficult to ascertain in some cases whether the transformation was not conceived early on, and should therefore be respected.

Painting and Gilding

Care of waxed wood furniture is simple. A small amount of pure wax applied with a dry cloth gives a magnificent shine. It is quite the opposite for painted furniture. Even supposing the piece has kept its original painted surface, dust and dirt make it unattractive. After taking off the mounts the piece should be freshened up and brightened by washing with mild soap and water. There is reason to be prudent and perform such cleaning rarely, in order to avoid damaging the original coat of paint. If one is lucky enough to have a piece with the original varnish protecting the paint, the problem is simplified: the original paint can be uncovered by dissolving the varnish, which may have darkened and thickened. It is advisable, then, to protect the paint with a new coat of varnish. A well-known Parisian upholsterer was able to remove the varnish that gave a dead white color to a set of armchairs by Jacob and blurred the definition of the carving to such a degree that it looked as if the chairs had been painted in the late nineteenth century. Once the varnish was off, a subtle water-based painting in lilac and white was revealed.

A delicate problem is raised when one tries to find the original paint under several successive layers, especially when one has to try to remove the thick black paint often used on eighteenth-century pieces during the reign of Napoleon III. The work, which must be done with a scraper or a light tool of wood for the most delicate parts of the carvings, is long and costly. It seems to be the only alternative, however, since one must avoid stripping, a brutal and simplistic solution which returns a piece to the raw state for which neither the carvings nor the frame were intended. Do not get carried away if it is necessary to do some in-painting, because an entirely repainted piece of furniture will look too cold and will be especially disagreeable if it has been patinated or its recesses have been given the semblance of accretions of dirt.

Gilding poses still more complicated problems. Too many collectors are content with a poor gilding, or they simply do not care. It has become the norm in auction catalogs to state that an eighteenth-century chair is regilded even when it is not. Gilding gets dirty and darkens, but what can be done? The problem would never come about if the eighteenth-century practice had been continued of covering painted or gilded chairs with dust sheets when they were not in use. There is an even worse problem with gilding: it chips off. Dryness can be the cause: the gesso ground hardens; the wood dries out and shrinks; the gold comes off in flakes, exposing the white undercoat or the wood itself in spots, giving a leprous effect. Transport, knocks, even the pressure of warm, damp fingers result in damage; therefore, great care must be taken in handling gilded furniture. Touch-ups can remedy small losses of gilding. There is as yet no effective remedy when the entire gilded surface lifts. One moistens, consolidates, and reaffixes the gold to the gesso and wood as much as possible. Regilding is very costly and almost always crude and unattractive. Above all, beware the reddish gilding with patches and streaks of bright gold to which today's decorators have accustomed us. This currently fashionable sort of gilding is done for reasons of economy and easy effect. The fragility of gilding has been the cause of repairs and restorations of greater or lesser degree during the course of the nineteenth century on almost all gilded furniture. Sometimes it is only skillful retouching with gold leaf on an otherwise solid gilding. Then it is barely visible and of little consequence. Alternatively, especially in England, or in France at the Garde-Meuble, a liquid gold in solution has been used. Then the gold looks dull and grainy but the situation is not hopeless. After making a few discreet tests, one can try to uncover the original gilding. I will cite one example: at the Louvre on a pair of armchairs purchased at auction which appeared to be regilded, a simple cleaning, without any addition of gold, allowed us to recover the original gilding. It must be admitted that these chairs had received the finest attentions of the workshop of Georges Jacob. Even if it is more expensive, as is usually the case, a fine eighteenth-century piece deserves to be treated with respect and have the effort made to uncover its original paint or gilding where possible. Above all, the matter should not be taken lightly, as there is no knowing what will be found. The *mobilier des dieux* was cleaned, a laudable idea in itself, but a tricky operation on such famed furniture, and one which would have only a short time previously been considered vandalism. No great erudition was needed to see that the old gilding was worn, that the undercoat of red clay was showing through, and that cleaning was going to necessitate regilding. The way was laid open, and in our time this celebrated set of furniture whose gilding was somewhat dull but not damaged was "rejuvenated" in a strange fashion indeed.

Upholstery

The rule should be the same, preserving and restoring the original upholstery as much as possible, not just the foundation, but especially the covering fabric, even when it shows wear. If not, the most lamentable loss can result. A set of furniture that was sold in 1923 still covered with its original silk, granted in bad condition, is today in the Metropolitan Museum, after having passed through the Blumenthal collection. It is now covered in an uninteresting modern silk. No one knew that the old tattered silk was embroidered by Marie-Antoinette herself. The logical conclusion is that furniture with original fabric should be treated like museum pieces, respected and removed from use. Why not, since such pieces are becoming more and more scarce? The use of dust sheets is also recommendable for the best protection against light. The Haarlem furniture in the Rijksmuseum in Amsterdam offers a delightful example of a well-preserved set of furniture where both paint and upholstery are still fresh.

When the original silk, tapestry, petit point, or leather coverings are still present, they are usually worn, dirty, and torn. They must be cleaned and consolidated with care. When one is lucky enough to find furniture with its original upholstery, one should treat it with respect, even keeping the original webbing (figs. 53, 168), after replacing the horsehair if necessary.

Usually it is necessary to restore the piece and try to give it the appearance of eighteenth-century upholstery. To this end, nineteenth-century work must be undone, springs must be removed, and the piece recovered in eighteenth-century fashion, i.e., without too much thickness, and with cushions if the seat seems to have had them. The upholsterer should avoid overstuffing and making the upholstery too heavy, or putting on modern fabrics like solid-color satin even if they are fashionable. Effort should be made to

156. Dining room chairs. Carved natural wood. Having much in common with the Régence armchair at Châalis (fig. 138), including the shell carved on the seat-rail, but with a seat of normal height, upholstered back, and the arm support set back from the front legs. Part of a set of armchairs that are said to have belonged to the fermier général Perinet de Jars (1670–1762) and preserved along with other furniture belonging to this wealthy personage in a French château. Unsigned. Circa 1730. (Private collection)

157. Dining room chair. Carved and gilded wood. Similar in decoration but with more graceful and sophisticated lines than the preceding armchairs. Part of a set of chairs in the de Luynes family since the eighteenth century. Charles-Philippe d'Albert, duc de Luynes (1695–1758), author of the celebrated *Mémoires,* and his wife, lady-in-waiting to Marie Leczinska, were part of the inner circle at Versailles; therefore it is not surprising to find in their home works by suppliers to court. Stamped by N.-Q. Foliot. Circa 1745. (Château de Dampierre, Yvelines)

158. Armchair with an exceptionally wide, low back. Carved and gilded wood. Transitional in style, retaining supple Louis XV lines combined with Louis XVI carved ornament. Similar to six armchairs of normal proportions in the Wallace Collection (cat. F.179–84, which in the nineteenth century were in Château d'Eu). The unusual dimensions of this chair back are 0.42m, 16½ in. high by 0.55m, 21⅝ in. wide. Belonged to the great collectors of French eighteenth-century art, Baron and Baroness Teil Chaix d'Est-Ange. Stamped by M. Gourdin. (Collection Chaix d'Est-Ange, Musée Sandelin, Saint-Omer)

159. Dressing table chair. Carved and gilded wood with caning and a mechanism that allows the seat to swivel. The design of the legs is particular to the Transition period. Probably made for Mme Du Barry at the Petit-Trianon, then incorporated into the Garde-Meuble of Marie-Antoinette at the same château. It was in the museum at Varzy (Nièvre) during the nineteenth century but it was deaccessioned. It subsequently belonged to two famous collectors in turn, Baron Double, and Isaac de Camondo. Stamped by G. Jacob. Circa 1770. (Camondo bequest, Musée du Louvre)

160. Armchair *à la reine,* termed *meublant,* to remain in place by the wall. Carved wood painted white. A beautiful Louis XV model. A fake stamp of M. Cresson is mentioned in text, but the stamp on this chair is perfectly authentic. The armchair, which is one of four, decorated the château of Balleroy (Calvados) from the eighteenth century until quite recently. Stamped by René Cresson. Circa 1750. (Private collection)

161. Armchair, termed *meublant.* Carved and gilded wood with Beauvais tapestry. Part of a superb set of furniture whose peripatetic history has been traced by James Parker. Ordered by Baron Bernstorff, the Danish ambassador to Versailles from 1744 to 1751 to decorate his palace in Copenhagen. This furniture subsequently belonged to the king of Greece, the dealer Wertheimer, J. Pierpont Morgan, and the Rockefeller family. Divided up, and tapestries put on modern frames, the set was eventually in large part reassembled. Stamped by N.-Q. Foliot. Circa 1757. (Metropolitan Museum of Art, New York)

162. Armchair, termed *meublant*. Carved and gilded wood. From the bedroom of Marie-Antoinette at Saint-Cloud. Both the model and the carving are so magnificent that they were attributed to Jacob. The armchair was part of the furnishings of the bedroom of Madame Laetitia in the hôtel de Brienne on rue Saint-Dominique, where it was noticed by Molinier who obtained the two armchairs for the Louvre. The matching bed was probably destroyed around 1900 on orders from the Defense Ministry, which took over the building. The rest of the set (two *bergères,* four armchairs, a folding screen, and a fire screen) were deposited with the Musée des Arts Décoratifs at the instruction of Clemenceau. Having lost their original upholstery, the armchairs in the Louvre were covered in orientalizing painted silk to recall their original upholstery. Unsigned. Identified on the basis of the royal furniture archives: *menuiserie* by J. B. Sené; carvings by Régnier after models by Hauré and Martin; gilding by Chatard. 1787. (Musée du Louvre)

163. Folding screen covered in Gobelins tapestry leaving nothing of the wood frame showing. Woven in the workshop of Neilson after a model by Maurice Jacques. An elegant design on a white ground with various framing elements emphasizing the compartmentalization of this fine piece of furniture. Probably made for Mme de Pompadour in 1760. (Camondo bequest, Musée du Louvre)

164a. Armchair, termed *meublant*. Carved and gilded wood with the original gold embroidered upholstery. The research of James Parker has disclosed the origin of this set of furniture: it belonged to Madame Infante, daughter of Louis XV, at Parma or Colorno. The frames and carving are probably the work of the Foliots. Circa 1750. (The Hermitage, Leningrad)

b. Detail of an armchair that was part of the same set. Note the correspondence between the carving and the embroideries, a splendor rarely seen today. The chairs were probably sent from Paris dismantled and reassembled in Parma. (Private collection)

165. *Cartonnier,* veneered with tulip- and purple wood with end-cut floral marquetry. Gilt bronze mounts with a Crowned C mark. Formerly in Oranienbaum Palace. Before even looking for a signature, it was easy to see the influence of a great Paris dealer and to guess that the *ébénisterie* was by B.V.R.B. (base) and Joseph (upper section). The clock is not original to the *cartonnier,* which has become separated from its writing table (see caption fig. 102). Possibly bought by Czarina Elisabeth. Label of Darnault and B.V.R.B. and Joseph stamps. Circa 1745. (The Hermitage, Leningrad)

166. Low table (about 0.40m). Discovered in the old pavilion of the sultan's doctor at Topkapi, Istanbul. Stamped B.V.R.B. Circa 1750.

167. Drawing in the Royal Institute of British Architects signed Vardy, architect of Richard Arundale, who owned the desk around 1746. The desk (now missing its slanted writing box and *cartonnier*) was identified by Peter Thornton and Christopher Gilbert thanks to this drawing. Passed down through the Arundale family and sold in 1972 (Vicountess Galway sale, Christie's, London, Mar. 23, no. 97), acquired by the museum of Temple Newsam House, Leeds. Stamped B.V.R.B. and F.L.

168. Underside of chair in fig. 53. Original upholstery and webbing preserved. Stamped Othon under front rail. Inside back rail upholsterer's or *menuisier's* number relating this piece to a set.

169. Assembly mark on one of 16 armchairs by Georges Jacob for the king's Salon des Jeux, Saint-Cloud, 1788. (Musée du Louvre)

170a. The stamp of Georges Jacob struck on the chinoiserie armchair illustrated in fig. 37.

b. Paper label (on the same armchair) of the type Georges Jacob often glued to the inside seat-rail of chairs indicating the exact location for which they had been ordered.

171a. Stamp of Teuné and the mark of the Paris guild wardens (enlarged) struck inside a drawer of the traveling desk illustrated in fig. 28.

b. Teuné's paper label glued inside the compartment (which was probably once lined with taffeta or watered silk) housing the mirror in the same desk.

find silks of a pattern appropriate to the period, and the expense of trimmings of the sort that would have been used on all fine furniture of the period should not be shied away from.

To return to the example of the Jacob armchairs cited earlier: I was lucky enough to find the model for the original silk coverings in Lyons. Its pattern restored the chairs to their original presence. The recreation was carried out almost to perfection. I say *almost* because the Louis XVI edging strips were made up of rose branches cut out from the silk and appliquéd on grosgrain, since the pattern had no woven borders. With the exception of this detail I believe the chairs are covered today just as they were in the time of Louis XVI.

To summarize the attentions that must be lavished on eighteenth-century furniture: effort must be made to retain the maximum possible of original elements even if they show wear; failing that, every attempt must be made to approximate the original look without giving way to passing notions of fashion.

EBENISTERIE FURNITURE

Wood

If ideal conservation conditions for *ébénisterie* furniture of a stable climate with steady moderate humidity can be maintained, no more than a feather duster or a dust cloth is needed for upkeep. Unfortunately, atmospheric changes, or jolts that occur when pieces are in daily use, pose certain problems for wood that should be studied and should not be underestimated for bronze mounts or marble tops.

The carcass of an *ébénisterie* piece should be considered by itself as a piece of *menuiserie*. One should keep an eye on the solidity of the joins and the legs, be sure the wood remains sound, and avoid excessive weight being placed on the piece as it will make the cross-members sag: this is how commodes and large writing tables get "broken backs." A leg can be broken off in moving if the marble top has not been removed first or if all four legs are not lifted at the same time. Dampness and worms are to be feared just as with *menuiserie* furniture.

Here the problem is complicated by the decorative sheathing of the piece with veneer. Marquetry and veneers are composed of different woods from the carcass and so have different rates of play. If they pull too much for the glue, or if the glue simply dries out, the veneer woods will lift. Eighteenth-century veneers were thick, not like the thin, cross-grained layers of modern plywood. They resist changes in temperature for some time, especially if the change is gradual. Both wood and glue have certain elasticity: if the physical conditions evolve in such a way that the elements can remain together and one does not rupture, the piece of furniture will hold. A sudden cold snap or draft will do more damage than steady cold. This was proved during World War II, when the Louvre's furniture was kept in sealed-off rooms where the temperature went down as far as 32° F. in the dead of winter, then, without any movement of air, rose almost so gradually as to be imperceptible over weeks until summer, and the furniture suffered no damage at all. An open window, a nearby source of heat, and especially a ventilator blowing warm air, are infinitely more dangerous. The ideal balance of constant 63° F. temperature and 50 percent humidity can be achieved even without an expensive climate-control system by several heaters and humidifiers. Damages incurred by abrupt changes of temperature, such as are common on the East Coast of the United States, and overheating and excessive dryness, which make the glue lose its bonding power, as well as damages resulting from impact to the piece of furniture should be carefully examined as to their nature and extent before remedies are planned.

A veneer can be, to all appearances, sound, but tapping can reveal a problem that would be more easily prevented than cured. When tapping lightly across the surface of the piece, a hollow sound in some areas is a sign that the glue is no longer holding and the veneer is coming away from the carcass. The causes listed above—heating, dryness, and drafts—must be investigated and another location for the piece must be found. If the problem worsens due to heedlessness or negligence, the effect becomes visible in different guises: the veneer cracks; a granulated network unsightly and unpleasant to the touch covers the surface; then the surface becomes uneven, breaking into segments that curl up. The reason may be that the wood used in the construction of the piece was not sufficiently dried, but more often the piece has been exposed to prolonged humidity followed abruptly by heat, causing the epidermis of the wood to contract. Often the problem is more than superficial, with the veneer lifting from areas of varying size and even becoming detached and lost. In a still more serious condition a piece can retain all its veneer but, just like a human being, be eaten away from the inside—that is, the carcass—by a serious malady whose symptoms are discernible only to a few. The outline of cracks, thin and barely perceptible, but running the length of a panel will be suggested if not seen. They do not necessarily come through as cracks in the veneer or marquetry but can remain undulations discernible to the eye or hand. Underneath the veneer the panel of the carcass has cracked and split, either because of poor construction in the first place or because of the factors cited above, excessive weight, heat, or humidity.

It goes without saying that remedies that will restore the piece not only to its original appearance but to its solidity vary in expense according to the severity of the condition. Rubbing down with pumice and a coat of varnish will eliminate superficial cracks. If the veneer has lifted but there is no damage to the carcass, the treatment prescribed by Roubo is still valid: "One reactivates the glue by heating it with an iron, and if it is too rolled to flatten with a marquetry hammer one holds it down with pins when possible or with clamps." Almost invariably the repair of *ébénisterie* entails the replacement of lost pieces of veneer. Then an experienced *ébéniste* with taste and a feeling for eighteenth-century furniture is needed to find a match for the woods so that the repair will not be obvious. If possible, antique or semiantique wood should be used because it will have been cut by hand and so be of the same thickness as the original elements, and it will also have faded naturally through exposure to light over time. For this purpose the best furniture restorers use parts from eighteenth- or more often nineteenth-century furniture, mainly pieces veneered in mahogany or violet wood. More often, however, wood that has been chemically bleached is used because it is cheaper and easier. The veins of the wood are affected by the process and that is why you find areas of repair in the middle of a tulipwood or violet-wood marquetry which, although carefully made of matching wood, remain weeping and alive in the depth of their fiber. When the carcass of the piece is affected, the problem is more difficult. The joins of the veneer and the design of the marquetry do not coincide with the pieces of the carcass, and so when the carcass splits it tears the marquetry apart. A superficial repair limited to just the marquetry can give the illusion of restoration, but it is only camouflage for the underlying problem and the marquetry will break again. A piece that has been repaired in this way waits on the proper repair, which really must be done, because the marquetry over the carcass cracks will soon split. The condition can be felt when running a hand over the piece. Different levels and undulations should give the warning and signal that there is a profound disorder, badly repaired. Certainly the needed work is costly, but it is necessary. An *ébéniste* must repair the carcass with wood fillers or keys, and when the carcass is sound and solid he must glue on the veneer again after repairing its splits and losses, which will naturally be numerous.

Each time an area of veneer is to be restored, the *ébéniste* must remove the varnish, pumice the surrounding area, and then revarnish after the repair. Since the old veneer is thick, this task can, in principle, be repeated a number of times over the life of the piece. However, in practice the sheets of veneer and marquetry thin down little by little to a dangerous point, and if the marquetry has been decorated, the engraving will gradually disappear with the pumicing, and details will have to be reengraved. Therefore restraint must be exercised. Varnish protects the wood from the air, and its oil feeds the wood and prevents it from drying out. Moreover, it gives furniture the shine that was so appreciated in the eighteenth century. Too many revarnishings cause premature wear on a piece, but this did not slow down the practice in the eighteenth century: a note in the daybook of Lazare Duvaux informs us that in 1755 the great dealer, for the sum of 48 livres, "restored and rescraped a commode, revarnish the bronze mounts to resemble the color of gilding" for the Count Moras de Saint-Priest. Over the twenty years following the delivery of the king's cylinder desk at Versailles, Riesener restored, "scraped, and repolished" it at least twice. Today, however, it is impossible, not to say dangerous, to try to keep a piece looking absolutely new. Restoring it is necessary, however, as is revarnishing when it gets too dark or dry, so it is a question of undertaking the restoration in a sensitive, prudent way.

The problem is also delicate in regard to furniture covered with lacquer or polychrome varnish. Such pieces crack, split, and lift for the same reasons and in the same conditions as veneer and marquetry. In addition they become hazy and moldy, rather like paintings, when the humidity is too high. Repair can be done with shellac if the carcass has not been affected. Repainting should be avoided as much as possible because it will change and yellow. Sometimes all the protective varnish has changed color. In the eighteenth century they did not hesitate to clean and renew the varnished blue and white corner cabinet given by Louis XV to Mme de Mailly (donated to the Louvre by R. Penard in 1950). Today we are more respectful of what is called the "patina of age," which recovers old, unrestored panels with a kind of light veil. When the carcass of such a piece is split, restoration is an extremely tricky job.

Bronze Mounts

Ideal conservation conditions for bronze are different from those for wood. While bronze darkens and gets verdigris in humidity, it suffers no ill effects from dryness: dry air rather preserves the brilliance of bronze mounts, and the dust that may accumulate can be removed with a cloth or brush. A balance must be established between the opposing components of a piece of *ébénisterie*. This takes on greater weight in questions of cleaning and repair. The solutions for difficult problems differ but in absolutely no event can commercial cleaning products for bronze and copper be used on furniture mounts.

When bronze furniture mounts are blackened, they have to be cleaned. This process should not be undertaken too often as it wears off the gilding, and at the same time it fatigues the wood through the removal and reaffixing of the mounts. It is impossible to establish rules on this subject. Just as for bronzes used in furnishing in general, it is recommendable after cleaning to reduce the brilliance a little with smoke. I disagree on this point with others who favor restoring bronze mounts of fine eighteenth-century furniture to their maximum brilliance. The woodwork of a piece, even when restored, repumiced, and revarnished, is far from having the strength of color of the original. Mahogany, violet wood, and tulipwood cannot retain the original character that made a piece so striking when new. Since one cannot retrieve the original effect, which was certainly quite vivid, one must, in order to avoid shocking contrast, try to create a balance between the shine of the bronze and the current state of the wood.

Whether the bronzes have been mercury gilded or simply varnished, there is a harmony to be maintained, not only between the bronze and the wood but also between bronze and copper. In both the Louis XV and XVI periods copper moldings often accompanied bronze mounts, emphasizing the lines of a piece. These copper moldings, which react differently from the bronzes to wear and cleaning, must equate in color and brilliance in order to harmonize with the bronzes.

In taking off and reaffixing the bronze mounts, the original fixtures should be respected as much as possible. It is unpleasant to see a piece of furniture in good condition with fine bronze mounts denatured by modern screws, whose new, mechanical heads look quite awkward. When the old screws cannot be reused or when they have already been replaced, a minor reworking of the screwheads seems to me not to be dishonest in itself, especially if it is admitted to. The overall effect of the piece will be more pleasing.

Finally, one must not allow oneself to take lightly the issue of bronze mounts on old furniture. One goes to a specialist for the repair of the *ébénisterie,* and yet one believes one can clean and reaffix bronze mounts oneself. The bronzes need just as skillful handling as the woodwork and the mounts must have an accord that only experienced restorers know how to obtain.

Marbles

It is necessary to preserve a marble top whenever possible. The upkeep of marble does not pose any problem in principle. If it is too dirty it can be washed. It can be lightly waxed to give it shine. But moving marble tops, which are often large and rather heavy, can cause breakage if the marble is handled incorrectly and not carried on its side. Even a broken marble can be repaired, repolished, and the breaks camouflaged. Certainly it will be more fragile, but, if it is the original marble for the piece, the decorative effect is still retained.

There is no such thing as a perfect state of preservation. One cannot retain mint condition or exactly recreate the past, but one can, with care, respect, and taste, approximate the original state and maintain the harmony accrued over time despite cleaning. All the slavish attentions, the understanding of the natural ways in which old things evolve, and the scrupulous preservation of the past that is required may seem impractical and even paradoxical in our century. It is the hard lesson of love imposed by antique furniture on those who want to live with it.

Chapter 19

THE MOST IMPORTANT PUBLIC

COLLECTIONS

THE EYE is trained by direct observation of works of art, and museums are there to assist. We shall trace a sort of memorandum to help the pilgrim.

To present an overview of the most important collections accessible to the general public, it seems practical to divide the subject of French furniture into three categories, the largest being Parisian, then provincial, and finally colonial.

It should be noted by a traveler wishing to add such an objective to his journey that what follows are only summary notes, provisional and incomplete: summary in order to avoid going into details and lists (which belong in a guidebook or dictionary and should be accompanied by a bibliography); provisional, given the constant acquiring of many museums (which obliged me to modify many of my observations made in 1955); and incomplete because of the omissions, either by neglect or for lack of information that I should gladly include.

PARIS FURNITURE

The Louvre and its neighbor, the Musée des Arts Décoratifs, have the two greatest collections of Paris furniture, which is only to be expected. The two collections can be taken together; the more exceptional pieces belonging to the Louvre, with the less-exalted pieces, in the Musée des Arts Décoratifs, providing an intelligent complement. Why observe the nicety of not bringing up the past? Why not make a point of the treasures included in the inventories of these two museums and the reasons for continued hope.

Some of the most beautiful pieces of furniture known belong to the Louvre, and they are all Parisian, from Delanois to Jacob, from Boulle to Riesener and Benneman; the mobilier des dieux (by N.-Q. Foliot, and part of the Camondo bequest); the desk of the elector of Bavaria (acquired in 1953); the *bureau du Roi* (the cylinder desk of Louis XV now at Versailles); the Bercy table and the chairs, some sumptuous, others simple, executed for Marie-Antoinette (fig. 162) and Madame Elisabeth, etc. Pieces with royal provenance are dominant. There are others of almost equal quality, and scholars will little by little uncover their histories, finding them to have been commissioned by important figures of the time. It must be said that recent years have hardly been favorable. Government ministers who have been ill-advised or simply too sure of themselves and wrongheaded, have believed they could refurnish the château of Versailles drawing on the collections of the Louvre. The goal was good, but the source and the method disastrous. In spite of the best intentions in the world, they weakened the Louvre and brought only disorder to Versailles. Acquisitions, however, purchases, bequests (figs. 136, 145, 154), the superb donation made with life interest by M. and Mme Grog-Carven (who well understood that the Louvre is the most important museum in the world for French furniture of the highest quality) (fig. 135), a few fortunate moves by high officials, and one or two curators who have worked in the cause, all are indications that allow the prediction of a healthier future. But in order for the Louvre to regain its former prestige it will also be necessary to continue to acquire what is still lacking.

The Louvre is stronger in *ébénisterie* furniture than in *menuiserie,* and stronger in Louis XVI furniture than in Louis XV. But what incomparable examples! Some of the illustrious artisans have just been cited: one could add on the same level Heurtaut, Gourdin, Boulard and Lelarge, Migeon, B.V.R.B. (the Guérault table and the Choiseul-Patiño armoire), Dubois, Oeben, Leleu, Garnier, Stockel, and Carlin. Further, it must be recalled that there is state aid in addition to private benefactions, and the Société des Amis du Louvre have on many occasions helped to enrich the museum in remarkable ways: in particular, the writing tables justly or wrongly associated with famous names, which were being ruined in ministerial offices, were copied so that the originals would go to the Louvre giving it a magnificent collection of eighteenth-century desks. Sheltering a treasury of French furniture, presenting it for the admiration of the crowds and the joy of connoisseurs—this is one of the missions of the Louvre.

In Paris the Musée des Arts Décoratifs offers the ideal collection for the lover of eighteenth-century furniture who wants enlightenment, as well as the student and scholar who want to know more and can benefit from an extraordinary range of examples. There also are certain regrettable things which one can hope will be soon redressed. This museum is the product of private initiative. It was headed by great connoisseurs rather than scholars. It has received inestimable gifts, almost exclusively from private collectors and dealers. It has been the inspiration of many a connoisseur, since the furniture is presented at close range, within reach, so to speak, of the visitor. What a privilege it was for many of us to work in this peaceful and inviting place. Changes have occurred that have not always been for the better. Fashionable installations that have forced too many interesting pieces into storage, abusive restorations, the disappearance of the discreet educational program that combined labeling with a useful guidebook, an exaggerated penchant for contemporary furniture (which must be recognized as an obligation of the Union Centrale des Arts Décoratifs, but nonetheless a negation of the traditional arts of *menuiserie* and *ébénisterie* in favor of a mechanical industrialism better suited to Beaubourg), but these are passing misdemeanors. What riches are offered to the student and collector!

The Musée des Arts Décoratifs has a great variety of furniture, isolated specimens, individual pieces rather than whole sets, very little Louis XIV, but a great deal of Régence, which is rare, and the eighteenth century in all its diversity right up to its close represented by both its simplest and most refined products. Add to this a large number of ornament drawings, not too much money (which has its good side as it helps avoid making mistakes, but some is necessary to fill in the gaps in the collection and not have to pass up a vital or particularly intriguing piece), considerable resources in objects, which is essential and results in a kind of balance. An abundance of chairs of a wide variety of models stamped by the best Paris *menuisiers,* and the presence of daybeds, armoires, cupboards, consoles, and tables are complemented by an appreciable number of pieces of *ébénisterie* furniture of different types, mainly small pieces, and a series of bronze furniture mounts (notably the Larcade donation). This is the study museum par excellence (fig. 10).

We cannot leave the subject of the means and documents put at the disposition of the student and collector by the museums of Paris without mentioning these: the Musée Carnavalet, which has added to its fine holdings the collection of the well-known dealer Mme Bouvier (fig. 152) and whose paneled rooms make a delightful setting for the display of furniture; the Musée Jacquemart-André, whose collections include some very good pieces of furniture, mainly of the Louis XV period; the Musée Cognacq-Jay, where there are some Louis XVI pieces; the Musée du Petit Palais, which has many very interesting pieces; the Musée Marmottan, where one might well linger to study the end of the century; and especially the Musée Nissim de Camondo (bequeathed to the Union Centrale des Arts Décoratifs in 1936), of unequaled sumptuousness, the residence of a banker who was a fine collector enamored of the Louis XVI style and assembled remarkable examples, in the main from the great sales of the first third of the twentieth century (fig. 144).

Further in Paris the Archives Nationales, the Bibliothèque Nationale, the Bibliothèque Mazarine, the Bibliothèque de l'Arsenal, the Musée de l'Assistance Publique, a hospital like the Salpêtrière, the Conservatoire des Arts et Métiers, and also some churches retain a certain number of pieces of furniture of iron-clad authenticity that have been assembled over the course of a long history. In public collections, but more difficult of access, is the furniture that belongs to the Mobilier National which is used to furnish official palaces (the Elysée, Présidence de l'Assemblée Nationale, and the Senate) and the ministries (especially Foreign Affairs, Navy, and Finance). In sum, prodigious riches of Paris furniture of the first rank are contained in the capital, and that is only addressing public collections!

The former royal châteaus of Versailles, Trianon, Fontainebleau, and Compiègne exhibit furniture in conditions that may give the connoisseur pause for thought. Some of the most beautiful eighteenth-century furniture is mixed in with nineteenth-century pieces, copies have been added at different periods, gifts and purchases leave much to be desired, chair frames have been repainted or regilded and the bronzes have been restored to a greater or lesser degree over the course of time. This mixed presentation, whether intentional or not, can serve as an education for the eye. There are some very fine works, and one can take pleasure in picking out those by the great *ébénistes* and *menuisiers* of Paris—Gaudreaux, Leleu, Joseph, Riesener, Schwerdfeger, Levasseur, Delanois, Tilliard, Séné, Jacob, and Lelarge. The harmony established when the two pieces of furniture of mother-of-pearl, gilt and silvered bronze, and green sycamore created by Riesener for Marie-Antoinette were returned to the boudoir of the queen at Fontainebleau can be admired without reservation. An undeniable richness exists, which, though it has not been well exploited, remains glorious. Like other illustrious buildings these châteaus merit the development of a well-thought-out program (fig. 2).

All of France offers surprising reserves of simpler furniture of extremely pure lines that collectors and curators are discovering little by little. The Service des Monuments Historiques has made enormous efforts to list and categorize much of it, especially in churches where fine chairs and richly carved console tables are often found. It has documented the contents of entire châteaus furnished with pieces worthy of serious attention: Aulteribe (in Puy-le-Dôme), Bouges (Indre) (fig. 51), Jossigny (Seine-et-Marne), La Motte–Tilly (Aube), and Talcy (Loir-et-Cher). The château of Azay-le-Ferron (Indre) belongs in the same context.

The devotee will find scattered examples in almost all the provincial museums, such as those listed alphabetically here: Amiens (hôtel de Berny) Autun, Auxerre, Avignon, Bayeux, Bourges (hôtel Lallemand), Caen, Chartres, Châteauroux, Clermont-Ferrand (Musée Du Ranquet) (fig. 150), Creil, Dijon (Musée des Beaux-Arts and Musée Magnin), Grasse, Langres, Le Mans, Lyon (Musée des Beaux Arts), Mâcon, Marseille, (Musée Grobet-Labadié), Meaux, Nancy (Musée Lorrain), Poitiers, Pontoise, Reims, Rouen, Saint-Omer (fig. 158), Saumur, Strasbourg, Tours, Versailles (Musée Lambinet), Vesoul, and I could go on! The list grows longer with every trip one takes and with the activities of local curators. The Musée des Arts Décoratifs of Lyon should be set apart because there a man of great taste has succeeded, through donations and purchases, with the support of the Chamber of Commerce of the city, in assembling and exhibiting with real elegance a collection of Paris furniture more important than that of any other provincial museum (fig. 114).

I hesitate to categorize, with the other residences and museums, Rambouillet (Yvelines) and Champs (Seine-et-Marne), châteaus that belong to the presidency of the republic, and three residences that belong to the Institut de France: the Villa Ephrussi-Rothschild, or Musée Ile-de-France, at Saint-Jean-

Cap-Ferrat (Alpes-Maritimes), the Musée Jacquemart-André in the former abbey of Châalis (Oise) (fig. 138), and especially the superb château of Chantilly where the duc d'Aumale assembled works by Jacob and Sené, Riesener, and Leleu, which equal in quality the finest furniture in the Louvre and the Wallace Collection.

Not mentioning furniture owned privately (either purchases made by collectors or furniture transmitted by inheritance sometimes going directly back to the eighteenth century) (figs. 156, 160), or what can be seen in the many châteaus that are open to the public (figs. 155, 157), it is astonishing what remains in France and the resources that this country offers devotees and students.

We have noted the almost universal homage accorded the furniture makers of Paris in the eighteenth century beginning with the reign of Louis XIV. The devotee of French furniture eager to learn and extend his horizons will find frequent rewards. A quick survey indicates the avenues open to him.

In Europe, England follows France as an immediate second in the importance of its holdings of French furniture. The Wallace Collection in London has fine seat furniture by Paris *menuisiers,* notably Gourdin, Jacob and Sené, but of still greater interest are its incomparable *ébénisterie* pieces of which a good handful are among the most important pieces of royal furniture: Cressent and Gaudreaux represent the Louis XV period, and Joubert, Dubois, Garnier, Leleu, and most importantly Riesener illustrate the Louis XVI style. It is no exaggeration to compare the ensemble at Hertford House to the holdings of the Louvre and the Metropolitan Museum, with two reservations: one is that the Wallace Collection does not make acquisitions; another is the London climate, together with repeated cleanings, has ruined some of the bronzes producing much the same effect as the abuses of use in the ministerial offices has had on pieces in the Louvre (fig. 15).

The Victoria and Albert Museum in London exhibits a remarkable group of works by Tilliard, Jacob, Joseph, and Carlin among others, commodes, desks, and smaller pieces ranging from Louis XIV to Louis XVI. The nucleus of the collection is the Jones bequest of 1882 (fig. 52).

Other museums in Great Britain have holdings of French furniture worth knowing about, such as Temple Newsam House near Leeds, which acquired a superb writing table by B.V.R.B. (fig. 167), and the Bowes Museum at Barnard Castle in Yorkshire. As in France, the castles of England and Scotland can be visited by the public and they still contain a good deal of French furniture. Long regarded as of secondary importance compared to their English furniture, the French pieces are now being featured more and more in these houses. Among many others, Goodwood House in Sussex, Longleat House in Wiltshire, and the castles of the dukes of Buccleuch in Northampton and in Scotland can be mentioned.

In Berlin the major collections assembled by the Hohenzollerns and augmented by the intelligent efforts of several curators of the Kaiser-Friedrich-Museum in the early twentieth century survive only in part. What is exhibited in Charlottenburg in West Berlin and especially at Kopenich in East Berlin is far from negligible. Other pieces may yet reappear, and one especially hopes to see the extraordinary chairs that Marie-Antoinette commissioned from Jacob just before the Revolution, which had retained their original silk coverings.

An attentive tourist in Germany visiting all the former princely residences would discover almost everywhere French furniture mixed in with a great many local imitations. Citing what can be seen at Berchtesgaden, Darmstadt, Ludwigsburg, and Wilhemshohe is to invoke the elector of Bavaria, the landgrave of Hesse-Darmstadt, the elector of the Palatinate, and the landgrave of Hesse-Cassel. Dresden especially offers a unique group of furniture by B.V.R.B. and Latz: the pieces from the former royal house of Saxony are kept today, in the main, along with some lesser pieces, in the castles of Moritzburg and Pillnitz.

In Austria the Oesterreichisches Museum für Angewandte Kunst in Vienna offers French *ébénisterie* on the highest level from the old collections and various acquisitions, especially the impressive donation of Adolphe de Rothschild (fig. 127).

Switzerland has at least two collections worth studying: in the Musée Ariana in Geneva is the *ébénisterie* furniture lent by Lord Michelham (which is in need of restoration); and in the Historisches Museum of Basel, where the recent Emile Dreyfus donation has been added to the museum's collection (fig. 13).

Belgium, which is rich in French furniture in its royal palaces and private collections, has little to show in its museums. Nonetheless, the Solvay-Tournay bequest has made it possible for the Cinquantenaire Museum to have some representation.

In Amsterdam the Rijksmuseum has acquired, primarily thanks to the Mannheimer collection, some very beautiful eighteenth-century French furniture (fig. 107). Copenhagen with its Decorative Arts Museum, the D. L. David collection, and the castle of Frederiksborg offers exceptional examples. Oslo, in its Kunstindustrimuseet, also has some outstanding pieces that did not escape the attention of Comte François de Salverte. Helsinki displays examples in its Museum of Fine Arts. Budapest has gathered French furniture of the first rank that belonged to the old families of Hungary in its Decorative Arts Museum (fig. 83). These are stopovers that should not be missed on the way through the east and north of Europe toward the three great domains of eighteenth-century French furniture that are Poland, Sweden, and the U.S.S.R.

Poland has succeeded in preserving a number of beautiful pieces of Paris furniture. To identify a precious table with Sèvres porcelain plaques as that sent by the comte d'Artois in 1783, in the royal castle of Warsaw during its reconstruction, seems almost paradoxical. In the National Museum in Warsaw and the castles administered by it, Lazienki, Wilanow, and Nieborow, evidence is still more plentiful. The Polish curators study the furniture and copy the marks with fervid conscientiousness. In the south, Lanshut, one of the residences of the Potocki family, once contained a quantity of French furniture but it now has only unimportant remains, while one knows of great pieces coming from this castle which are now in the United States and even in Paris. On the other hand, in Cracow and Wavel one can still find pieces with Paris signatures.

Sweden occupies a privileged place in the eighteenth-century art of furniture: it imported, imitated, and invented, and, since it was spared war and revolutions, it preserved a great deal. There is nothing surprising in finding Parisian objects as numerous as they are varied in the Royal Palace, the National Museum of Stockholm, in the castles of Gripsholm and Haga, and in the Röhsska Museum at Göteborg (fig. 97).

The court of Russia was one of great luxury. Many of the pieces of furniture imported from France in the eighteenth century are still preserved, and almost all of them are remarkable (figs. 164, 165). One sees a few in the castles around Moscow, but much more in Leningrad and around this former capital. The Hermitage, the imperial palace, a museum that has accrued works for a hundred years, exhibits some especially beautiful examples. More than any of the other residences of the czars, it is the palace of Pavlovsk where one feels the ardent admiration for French furniture of the Louis XVI period: Jacob, Carlin, Gouthière, and their followers, French furniture and bronzes, or Russian imitations so perfect that they cause confusion. A lesson in modesty and a real pleasure to the eye.

Southern Europe should have an important place in this tour, but such is not the case. A curious phenomenon can be observed: a powerful French influence comes into conflict with the vigor of local production, itself anxious to imitate the art of Paris. Spain seems to possess very little French furniture even though the royal palace in Madrid has several Louis XVI pieces of the first order signed Carlin and Weisweiler. Italy is in a slightly more favorable position. The furniture collected in Parma by the daughter and son-in-law of Louis XV was dispersed (fig. 164), but much was used to decorate the royal castles of the house of Savoy. Thus fine French furniture, *menuiserie* and especially *ébénisterie,* of the time of Louis XV can be seen today in Stupinigi near Turin. The royal palace in Genoa, the Pitti Palace in Florence, in the Quirinal, and in the royal palace in Naples. As for Portugal, a certain number of pieces are shown in the Museu Nacional de Arte Antiga coming from several donations as well as the episcopal palaces of Portugal and the royal castles. There are Louis XVI chairs by Chevigny and Lelarge in the palace of Ajuda. Portugal especially benefited from the amazing Gulbenkian Foundation, which has endowed Lisbon with one of the world's great museums of French furniture (fig. 148) with preeminent works by Sené, Jacob, Cressent, Riesener, and Carlin.

Turkey can hold surprises. Discovering one of the best writing tables by B.V.R.B. (fig. 166) or a lacquer commode by Delorme in the pavilions tucked away in the gardens of Topkapi Sarayi in Istanbul leaves one perplexed. In spite of the overdone Napoleon III ensembles furnishing the palaces of the Bosporus that are so discouraging, the warehouses of the sultans probably still exist, and they could hold other interesting pieces.

The United States, developing its museums, cultivating patrons of the arts, and overflowing with money has advanced its situation in the domain that is our subject. It has reached a disquieting level for Europe. Taste has been refined; fakes and hybrid furniture have been generally cast aside. What astonishing progress I have seen since 1955!

The museums of Washington, Philadelphia, and Baltimore, enriched respectively by the collections of Widener, Hamilton Rice and Walters, remain interesting, but they have evolved very little in our area in recent years. On the contrary, the holdings of the Metropolitan Museum of Art in New York, which were already remarkable (fig. 161), have become enormous; one can even wonder if they will not soon become the most important in the world. In the face of the momentary weakness of the Louvre and the obligatory stabilization of the Wallace Collection, the progress of the Metropolitan appears all the more prodigious. To the superb furniture in the Morgan, Vanderbilt, Blumenthal, Bliss, and Bache collections given between 1906 and 1949 are added the equally valuable Kress donation of 1958, Wrightsman donations from 1971 to 1976, the Sheafer bequest of 1973, and the Linsky gift of 1982, to touch on only the high points. What masterpieces are gathered in the French furniture galleries now called the Wrightsman Galleries! (fig. 100). Generous donors, dedicated curators, and elegant installations have led to justly deserved success. Royal pieces and pieces of royal quality, *ébénisterie* as well as *menuiserie,* Joubert and Riesener, Foliot and Jacob, all are there in their most sumptuous production. Given that New York has, in addition to the Metropolitan Museum, the Frick Collection (fig. 153), which also shows furniture of the first quality (B.V.R.B., Riesener, Carlin, etc.) and that the city abounds in great private collections, one understands that it has become one of the centers where one must go to see French furniture just like Paris and London.

The Boston Museum of Fine Arts has added to the fine Louis XVI furniture brought back to the United States by James Swan during the French Revolution the collection of Forsyth Wickes (fig. 151) and several good purchases. The Detroit Institute of Arts owes a great deal to the generosity of Mrs. Dodge (pieces by Carlin, Levasseur, and Riesener). Pittsburgh has two museums, the recently founded Frick Art Museum and the Art Museum of the Carnegie Institute, which received the important collection of Ailsa Mellon Bruce in 1971. In these museums as well as those of Toledo, Chicago, and Saint Louis interesting models are to be found.

In all the United States the museum that seems to me to have the most balanced collection, somewhat analogous to what one would find in certain French châteaus, remains that of Cleveland, where a director [Sherman Lee] of the highest caliber has known how to orchestrate judicious purchases and great donations.

The development of the West Coast has favored the growth of museums and furniture collections. Four museums stand out: in San Francisco the Palace of the Legion of Honor and the De Young Museum, which have some good pieces of French furniture; and still more in Los Angeles the Huntington Library and San Marino Art Gallery, which has furniture by Joseph, Leleu, Carlin, etc., and the J. Paul Getty Museum in Malibu (fig. 3). This last institution, where an enthusiastic wealthy collector was able in a short time to assemble an exceptional group of pieces by B.V.R.B., Cressent, Joseph, Joubert, Riesener, Molitor, and others, has been endowed with a fabulous fortune that allows it to give dangerous competition to the museums of Europe and New York by attracting the finest examples offered on the international market.

South America occupies an excellent position thanks to Argentina, a country where wealthy families like to surround themselves with furniture reminiscent of the styles of eighteenth-century France. Copies and old pieces are mixed together, but growing awareness is bringing about the necessary sorting out. Through a 1968 exhibition, the Museum of Decorative Arts in Buenos Aires succeeded in presenting a sizable ensemble of the best of these pieces and keeping several for the permanent collection.

PROVINCIAL FURNITURE

Without losing sight of the distinction between the furniture of the aristocracy, on the one hand, and the bourgeoisie and peasant furniture, on the other, a number of French museums can be listed where furniture made in the provinces is to be seen.

In the category of furniture made in the city, for a well-organized collection of pieces made by local *ébénistes* and *menuisiers* one can look to the museums of Strasbourg, Montbéliard, Dijon, Lyon (Musée de Vieux-Lyon), Grenoble, Avignon, Carpentras, Marseilles (château Borely), Grasse, Toulouse (Musée Paul-Dupuy), Bordeaux (Musée Lalande), Nantes (Musée Dobrée), and Lille.

For the second category of village and country furniture where the makers are almost totally anonymous, an incomplete list follows of museums devoted all or in part to the furniture of the region (to which must be added the museums cited above): Arles (Musée Réattu and Museon Arlaten), Bayonne (Musée Basque), Bourg-en-Bresse, Clermont-Ferrand (Musée Du Ranquet), Epinal, Hennebont, Honfleur, Lourdes, Marseilles (Musée du Vieux-Marseille), Nancy (Musée Lorrain), Obernai, Pau (Musée Béarnais), Quimper, and Riom. Each of these museums is devoted to the art of its region. Only the Musée des Arts et Traditions Populaires in Paris has a collection of furniture from many different parts of France and relevant pieces are shown in the exhibitions it presents.

COLONIAL FURNITURE

Canada has assembled French-Canadian furniture in the museums of Montreal and Quebec. There are also a few examples in the United States in the Detroit Institute of Arts since, with Fort Pontchartrain, there was a French presence in the region of the Great Lakes for a long time.

In Louisiana the New Orleans museums (New Orleans State Museums, and the Cabildo and Madame John's Legacy) have begun to collect furniture and documents of the French colonial era. Visiting private collections, fledgling museums, and homes and plantations allows one to see some pieces made before the nineteenth century in the bayous and the Acadian region, but they are usually very simple.

Martinique has, in the departmental museum of Fort-de-France, a number of pieces of furniture of which several may well date back to the eighteenth century. Most of the eighteenth-century furniture in Guadeloupe as well as Martinique remains with the old families and sometimes in the sacristies of churches. More and more frequently, however, one finds it sought by well-informed collectors. One relevant observation—many such pieces were abandoned to the slaves by masters who preferred "the beautiful nineteenth century" and major repair may have ensued. There were also mixtures, and when the demand is too great, furniture is supplied from other islands, like the English Antilles, according to wherever antique dealers are able to find it.

To this embryonic list, the furniture of Ile Bourbon (today Réunion) and Ile de France (Maurice) and the French settlements in India must be added, and their museums and private collections should be studied.

BIBLIOGRAPHY

INDEX

Bibliography

A LIBRARY dedicated to French furniture of the eighteenth century could be divided in two unequal categories: a few works that enable initial identification of objects, e.g., compendia, dictionaries, and manuals, and all the rest of the publications that allow one to pursue the subject in depth.

I. TO BE KEPT WITHIN IMMEDIATE REACH

Here I list books that can furnish a quick identification, supply or confirm a first name, a mark, the usual style of a *menuisier* or *ébéniste,* the typical characteristics of a type of furniture, the characteristics of a style and its evolution—in short anything that cuts through the labor involved and facilitates moving on to the next step.

First, two reference books:

Viaux, Jacqueline. *Bibliographie du Meuble (Mobilier civil français).* Paris, Société des Amis de la Bibliothèque Forney, 1966. A compendium of considerable size that has not yet been sufficiently appreciated: 5,008 listings (covering also the nineteenth and twentieth centuries). Offset printed. A new printed edition is to be hoped for with corrections of minor errors (typographical errors, especially in the otherwise excellent index; a few omissions, particularly in respect to American museums). It covers only works published through January 1, 1965; updates at regular intervals would be desirable. [A supplement covering 1965–85 was published by the Agence Culturelle de Paris in 1988.] We will refer here to "Viaux" numbers for bibliographic details of works published before 1965.

The Journal of the Furniture History Society. Founded in London in 1964–65, the Furniture History Society is closely connected with the furniture department of the Victoria and Albert Museum, whose recently retired curator, Peter Thornton, is an eminent furniture historian. This society, whose title is self-explanatory, publishes a *Journal.* The *Journal* presents hitherto unpublished research accompanied by illustrations, reviews, and listings of books and articles. In addition to English furniture, French furniture is also treated (vol. 8 is entirely devoted to it). One wish: the bibliography might be more systematic or exhaustive, particularly on eighteenth-century French furniture.

Three essential dictionaries must also be given preeminent rank:

Salverte, comte François de. *Les ébénistes du XVIIIe siècle, leurs oeuvres et leurs marques.* Paris: Les Editions d'art et d'Histoire, 1922, 7th ed., F. de Nobele, 1985. *Viaux, no. 1974*

BIBLIOGRAPHY

Vial, Henri, Adrien Marcel, André Girodie. *Les artistes décorateurs du bois*. Paris: Bibliothèque d'art et d'Archéologie, 1912 (vol. 1, A to L) and Schmitt, 1922 (vol. 2, M to
Z, and supplement to vol. 1). *Viaux, no. 1973*

Havard, Henry. *Dictionnaire de l'ameublement et de la décoration depuis le XVIIIe siècle jusqu'à
nos jours*. 4 vols. Paris, [1887–89]. *Viaux, no. 4*

Salverte is the most important of these three works. The author died in 1929.
Notable changes have been made in the most recent editions, but the second and
third editions (1927 and 1934) remain, in my opinion, the best. In spite of the enormous amount all furniture historians and collectors owe this remarkable and conscientious work, it must be admitted that this classic and essential tome would benefit
from updating.

Vial, which is also quite old, contains an enormous amount of information (especially about French auctions) as well as the names of *menuisiers* and *ébénistes,* particularly in the provinces, that were unknown to Salverte. The two references amplify
each other and should be used together (without forgetting the supplement to vol. 1
at the end of vol. 2 of Vial).

Havard represents quite another type but is just as indispensable; a work which is
not at all dated in spite of an old-fashioned layout and an overextended subject (it
covers the Middle Ages as well as the nineteenth century, for which it is particularly
valuable); innumerable extracts and documents defining words and terms like an
encyclopedia devoted exclusively to French furniture. Artists' names are only included in the context of discussions of words like *menuiserie* and marquetry.

I don't believe it immodest to add to these great names the present volume containing the names and marks of *menuisiers* and *ébénistes,* including some that are not
in Salverte, but also lacking some Salverte knew. In sum, nothing exists which is
definitive and comprehensive.

Three recent publications are useful to keep at hand because even though their listings of
menuisiers and *ébénistes* are selective, they reproduce so many examples that it is frequently
necessary to consult them.

Nicolay, Jean. *L'art et la manière des maîtres ébénistes français au XVIIIe siècle*. Paris: Guy Le
Prat, 1956–59. Reprint, 2 vols. in 1, Paris: Pygmalion, 1976. *Viaux, no. 1979*

Meuvret, Jean, Claude Fregnac, Francis Spar. *Les ébénistes du XVIIIe siècle français*. Paris:
Connaissance des Arts-Réalités-Hachette, 1963. *Viaux, no. 1979 bis.*

Kjellberg, Pierre. *Le mobilier français*. 2 vols. Paris: Guy Le Prat, 1979–80.

Nicolay draws on Salverte and the catalogs of auctions at the Hôtel Druout. It is
copious, often labored, gives many names and summary reproductions of many
marks: the illustrations are numerous, varied, and useful for further study. It contains
a great deal of information that requires critical evaluation.

The two other works are more limited and more reliable. They incorporate the
progress made since Salverte. Historical introductions preface their well-illustrated
entries on the principal *ébénistes* and *menuisiers,* a discussion of the eighteenth century,
and an overview of French furniture, respectively. They are serious and useful works.

Two volumes of constant practical interest have still to be mentioned. By virtue of their
text and well-chosen illustrations they give quick information on a conservation problem
or a restoration technique, in one case, and on a species of wood in the other.

Fonvieille. *La dynastie des Hache*. Grenoble: Dardelet, 1974.

Quarré, Pierre. "Deux notices sur les *ébénistes* Julien à Beaune et Courte à Dijon, *Mémoires de la Comm. des Antiq. de la Côte-d'Or* 30 (1976–77): 92–114.

Deloche, Bernard. *Le mobilier bourgeois à Lyon (XVIe-XVIIe siècle)*. Lyon: L'Hermès, 1980.

For regional furniture, i.e., country furniture in eighteenth-century style but usually made in the nineteenth century, there are many publications, but the quality is uneven. Viaux, chap. 2, pp. 138–68, nos. 1545–1822, classifies them by region and province. There are several series, notably Massin and the Hachette *La Vie à la campagne*, and most recently Fréal, with excellent volumes by Hans Haug, Jacques Choux, and Guillaume Janneau. Finally, there are four books on the general subject:

Tardieu, Suzanne. *Meubles régionaux*. Paris, 1950. *Viaux, no. 1552*.

Gauthier, J. Stany. *Le mobilier des vieilles provinces françaises*. Paris, 1960. *Viaux, no. 1551*.

Claude-Salvy. *Les meubles régionaux en France*. Paris: Gründ, 1967.

Boulanger, Gisèle. *L'art de reconnaître les meubles régionaux*. Paris: Hachette, 1974.

On the subject of colonial furniture, French Canadian furniture is distinguished by the result of the research published in Gérard Morisset's Champlain series on the arts of Nouvelle-France, which is the object of a solid and extensive publication:

Palardy, Jean. *Les meubles anciens du Canada français*. Paris: Arts et Métiers graphiques, 1963.

In Louisiana archival research has begun at the Cabildo museum in New Orleans under the direction of Mrs. Pleasonton. So far we have only the catalog of the 1972 exhibition at the museum, which reproduces the furniture of the Ursuline convent in New Orleans.

8. Supplementary Illustrations and Information

Champeaux, A. de. *Portefeuille des Arts décoratifs*. Paris: Calvas, 1888–98.

Williamson, E. *Le Meubles d'art du mobilier national* 1888. *Viaux, no. 3747*.

Dumonthier, E. *Mobilier national* . . . 1913–24. *Viaux, nos. 3753–59*.

Dilke, Lady. London, 1901. *Viaux, no. 303*.

Graul, Richard. Berlin, 1905. *Viaux, no. 304*.

Ricci, Seymour de. 1913 and 1929. *Viaux, nos. 310 and 318*.

Felice, Roger de. 1922–29. *Viaux, no. 52*.

Theunissen, André. 1934. *Viaux, no. 1976*.

Devinoy, Pierre. *Le siège*. 1948. *Viaux, no. 82*.

———, and G. Janneau. *Le meuble léger*. 1952. *Viaux, no. 84*.

The French periodical *L'estampille*, the English periodicals *Country Life, Apollo*, and *Connoisseur*, and the German periodical *Pantheon* should be added to those listed in Viaux and those already mentioned, *Connaissance des Arts* and the *Gazette de l'Hôtel Drouot*.

Finally the iconographic and documentary resources consisting mainly of illustrations cut out of periodicals and sales catalogs that have been gathered in various places should not be overlooked: in Paris the two principal resources are at the Bibliothèque des Arts Décoratifs (Maciet albums) and the Bibliothèque Forney (excellent on the subject of

Alcouffe, Daniel. *Restauration du mobilier*. Fribourg: Office du Livre, 1977.

Schafflutzel, Hanz. *Die Nutzhölzer in Wort und Bild*. Zürich: Verband Schweizer, Schreinermeister und Möbelfabrikanten, 1946. With listing of woods in French, German, and sometimes English, Latin botanical terms, and sources and characteristics of the woods, with 107 color reproductions.

II. FOR FURTHER RESEARCH

One must have recourse to references that can be arranged under the twelve headings that follow:

1. Technique (Eighteenth-Century Publications)

Encyclopédie ou Dictionnaire raisonné des sciences, des arts, et des métiers par une société de gens de lettres [under the direction of Diderot and d'Alembert]. Paris, etc., 1751–77. 33 vols. with supplements, including 12 volumes of plates. Vol. 5 (p. 214, article on *Ebénisterie*) and vol. 10 (pp. 137–43, article on *Marqueterie*, and pp. 346–57, article on *Menuiserie*) of the text, and vol. 4 (*Ebénisterie-marqueterie*) and vol. 7 (*Menuiserie en meubles*) of the plates are of particular relevance.

Dictionnaire raisonné universel des Arts et métiers . . . New ed. Revised by M. l'abbé Jaubert of the Académie Royale des Sciences de Bordeaux, Paris, Didot, 1773. 5 vols.

Roubo. *L'art du menuisier*. Paris, 1769–74. 5 vols. *Viaux, nos. 4465–68*. Vol. 3, part 2, is devoted to *menuiserie;* vol. 3, part 2, to *ébénisterie*. Reprint, Paris: Laget, 1976.

Watin. *L'art du peintre, doreur, vernisseur* . . . 2d ed. Paris, 1773. Reprint, Paris: Laget, 1977. *Viaux no. 4483*

Bimont. *Principes de l'art du tapissier*. Paris, 1770. New ed., Paris, 1774. *Viaux, no. 4464*

Valmont de Bomare. *Dictionnaire raisonné universel d'histoire naturelle*. New ed. after the fourth, rev. and augmented by the author. 15 vols. Lyon: Bruyset, Revolutionary year VIII (1800). Valuable for the sources and quality of woods used at the end of the eighteenth century, but without illustrations.

2. General History of French Furniture

From an abundance of literature (see Viaux, summary and author index), the following volumes can be selected:

Champeaux, Alfred de. *Le meuble*. 2 vols. Paris, 1885, and subsequent eds. *Viaux, no. 14*

Feulner, Adolf. *Kunstgeschichte des Möbels*. Collection Propylées. The 3d ed. [c. 1930] is preferable, being twice as large as the first; covering classical antiquity to Empire and Biedermeier, it comprises 827 pp. and 664 ills. *Viaux, no. 56*

Molinier, Emile. *Le mobilier au XVIIe et au XVIIIe siècle*. Vol. 3 of *Histoire générale des arts appliqués à l'industrie*. Paris. [c. 1900]. *Viaux, no. 21*

Janneau, Guillaume. *Les sièges*. 2 vols. Paris, 1928. *Viaux, no. 58*

———. *Les meubles*. 3 vols. Paris, 1929. *Viaux, no. 61*

———. *Les beaux meubles français anciens*. 5 vols. Paris, 1930. *Viaux, no. 65*

Verlet, Pierre. *La maison du XVIIIe siècle en France: Société, Décoration, Mobilier*. Fribourg-Paris, 1966. With three inventories in appendixes.

3. Great Styles in French Eighteenth-Century Furniture

Alcouffe, Daniel. Two theses, one at the Ecole des Chartes on the *ébénistes* of the faubourg Saint-Antoine at the time of Louis XIV (*Viaux, no. 5004*), the other at the Ecole du Louvre on the *ébénistes* of the Régence and the early years of Louis XV, for which the author gathered a considerable amount of documentation which he is very generous in sharing. It is to be hoped that these theses will be published.

Verlet, Pierre. *Le style Louis XV.* Paris: Larousse, 1942. Furniture covered in pp. 45–63. *Viaux, no. 323*

Eriksen, Svend. *Early Neo-classicism in France . . .* London: Faber & Faber, 1974.

Watson, Francis. *Louis XVI Furniture.* London: Tiranti, 1960. French trans. *Le meuble Louis XVI.* Paris: Les Beaux-Arts, 1963. *Viaux, no. 332*

Ledoux-Lebard, Denise. *Les ébénistes parisiens du XIXe siècle (1795–1870).* Paris: De Nobele, 1965.

4. The Paris Guild, the Ornamental Designers, and the Dealers

Verlet, Pierre. *L'art du meuble à Paris au XVIIIe siècle.* 2d ed. Paris: Presses Universitaires de France, 1968. *Viaux, no. 4856*

Salverte, comte François de. *Le meuble français d'après les ornemanistes . . .* Paris, 1930. *Viaux, no. 1829*

Guilmard, D. *Les maîtres ornemanistes . . .* 2 vols. Paris, 1880. *Viaux, no. 1825*

Bellaigue, Geoffrey de. "18th Century French Furniture and Its Debt to the Engraver." *Apollo,* Jan. 1963, pp. 16–23. *Viaux, no. 1834*

————. "Engravings and the French Eighteenth-century Marqueteur." *Burlington Magazine,* May 1965, pp. 240–50, and July 1965, pp. 357–62.

Livre-journal de Lazare Duvaux, marchand-bijoutier ordinaire du Roy 1748–1758. 2 vols. Published by Louis Courajod, Paris, 1873. The first volume is a study of the market in works of art in the eighteenth century, the collectors and the dealers. Reprint. Paris: De Nobele, 1965. *Viaux, no. 300*

Verlet, Pierre. "Le commerce des objets d'art et les marchands-merciers à Paris au XVIIIe siècle." *Annales,* Jan.-Mar. 1958, pp. 10–29. *Viaux, no. 4998.* The article, although somewhat summary and written a long time ago, seems still to be the only overall study of the subject; to this must be added the informative notes by Eriksen (above, section 3) and Bellaigue (below, section 11) on the dealers Daguerre, Duvaux, Granchez, and Poirier.

Lespinasse, René de. *Les métiers et corporations de la ville de Paris.* Vol. 2, Paris, 1892, especially pp. 645–60 (*menuisiers* and *ébénistes*). See also the chapters dealing with painters and sculptors, dealers, founders, *tabletiers,* and upholsterers. *Viaux, no. 4797*

Stürmer, Michaël. *Herbst des Alten Handwerks.* Munich: Deutscher Taschenbuch Verlag GmbH, 1979. Publication with commentary of interesting documents pertaining to the guilds, economy, and social history of the end of the seventeenth and the eighteenth centuries, focusing on German-speaking countries but also touching on France and England.

5. Monographs on *Menuisers* and *Ebénistes*

B.V.R.B. [Bernard Van Risen Burgh]: Baroli, 1957. *Viaux, no. 2194*

Cressent: Ballot, 1919. *Viaux, no. 2054*

Delanois: Eriksen, Svend. *Louis Delanois menuisier en sièges . . .* Paris: De Nol

G. Jacob: Lefuel, 1923. *Viaux, no. 2084*

Latz: Hawley, Henry H. "Jean-Pierre Latz, Cabinetmaker." *Bulletin of the [...] seum of Art,* Sept.-Oct. 1970, pp. 203–59.

J.-F. Oeben: Stratmann, Rosemarie. *Der Ebenist Jean-François Oeben.* Doc. t[...] sity of Heidelberg, 1971. Offset, 426 pp. without illus.

Riesener: Verlet, 1955 (in German). *Viaux, no. 2135*

    See also the works by Nicolay, Meuvret-Frégnac-Spar, and Kjellbe[...] and numerous articles, often well illustrated and documented in *Conna*[...] especially *Viaux,* under the heading "Artistes," *nos. 1997–2202.* The [...] mature but interesting work by Boutemy can also be added:

Boutemy, André. *Meubles français anonymes du XVIIIe siècle: Analyses sty*[...] *d'attribution.* Brussels, Editions de l'Université de Bruxelles, 1973.

6. French Royal Furniture

Verlet, Pierre. *Le mobilier royal français.* 4 vols. Vols. 1 and 2, Paris, 19[...] *French Royal Furniture . . . ,* London, 1963. *Viaux, nos. 3760 and 40*[...] 1990.

7. French Provincial and Colonial Furniture

Dictionaries of artisans have been compiled for only two provinces; and [...] part of the same series as Vial they give little information on furniture:

Audin, Marius, and Eugène Vial. *Lyonnais (Dictionnaire des artistes et [...] France).* 2 vols. Paris: Bibliothèque d' Art et d'Archéologie, 1918–

Brune, abbé Paul. *Franche-Comté.* Paris, 1912. *Viaux, no. 1972*

    The publication of inventories brings information to light. See es[...]

Mély, F. de, and E. Bishop. *Bibliographie générale des inventaires imp*[...] 1892–95. *Viaux, no. 4332*

Viaux, nos. 4402–51, covers the inventories concerning the eighteenth [...] all deal with the provinces, châteaus as well as peasant homes, [...] date of the previous entry.

Arnaud d'Agnel. *Ameublement provençal et comtadin . . .* 2 vols. Paris [...] *Viaux, no. 1784.* Vol. 2 is almost exclusively devoted to the eig[...] has many references to the texts of inventories.

Lerch, Charles-Henri. "Le goût artistique en Franche-Comté au X[...] registre de comptes du chevalier du Ban." *Mém. Soc. émul. Do*[...]

    There are very few monographs on provincial *ébénistes.* The [...] noted:

Couleru, Edmond. *Un vieux maître montbéliardais: l'ébéniste Abrahan*[...] 1812. Lausanne, 1908. *Viaux, no. 2050.*

Fyot, Eugène. *Les artistes bourguignons. Une famille d'ébénistes: les*[...] *Viaux, no. 2060.*

Marot, Pierre. "Recherches sur les 'sculpteurs en bois de Sainte-[...] pays lorrain,* 49th year, no. 1, Nancy, 1968, pp. 1–46.

furniture). The most important collection of this sort so far seems to be that of Mr. Theodore Dell in New York, and the Photo Archive of the J. Paul Getty Center for the History of Art and the Humanities in Santa Monica.

9. Fakes

There is no comprehensive treatment, but scattered accounts, which are often interesting and spicy.

Mailfert, André. *Au pays des antiquaires: Confidences d'un maquilleur professionnel.* Many printings since 1935. *Viaux, no. 4853.*

Huth, Hans. *Ueber gefälschte Möbel.* 1929. *Viaux, no. 4940.*

————. *The Gentle art of Faking.* 1936. *Viaux, no. 4944.*

Bellaigue, Geoffrey de. "Edward Holmes Baldock." *Connoisseur,* August 1975, pp. 290–99, and September 1975, pp. 18–25.

10. Comparisons with Furniture Other than French

The subject is useful but too broad to be encompassed here. Suffice it to mention certain recent works that cover a large area:

Edwards, Ralph. *The Dictionary of English Furniture.* 3 vols. Antique Collectors' Club, 1954; rev. ed. 1983.

————. *The Shorter Dictionary of English Furniture.* London: Country Life, 1977.

Beard, Geoffrey, and Christopher Gilbert. *Dictionary of English Furnituremakers, 1660–1840.* Leeds, Maney, and Furniture History Society, 1986.

Kreisel, Heinrich, and Georg Himmelheber. *Die Kunst des deutschen Möbels.* 3 vols. Munich: Beck, 1968–73. Vol. 2, *Spätbarock und Rokoko;* vol. 3, *Klassizismus . . .*

Philippe, Joseph. *Meubles, styles et décor entre Meuse et Rhin.* Liège: E. Wahle, 1977.

Hayward, Helena, et al. *World Furniture.* London: Hamlyn, 1965.

Verlet, Pierre, et al. 2 vols. *Styles, meubles, décors du Moyen Age à nos jours.* Paris: Larousse, 1972.

Praz, Mario. *An Illustrated History of Furnishing . . .* New York: Thames and Hudson, 1964, 1982. French ed. *L'Ameublement.* Paris: Tisné, 1964. *Viaux, no. 99.*

Honour, Hugh. *Cabinet Makers and Furniture Designers.* London: Weidenfeld & Nicolson, 1969. French ed., *Chefs d'oeuvre du mobilier de la Renaissance à nos jours: Des ébénistes aux designers.* Paris: Bibliothèque des Arts, 1971.

Thornton, Peter. *Authentic Decor: The Domestic Interior 1620–1920.* London: Weidenfeld & Nicolson, 1984. French ed. *L'époque et son style: La décoration intérieure 1620–1920.* Paris: Flammarion, 1986.

11. Catalogs of Public Collections

A continuously growing category that requires a long bibliography. In presenting a summary list of titles, I repeat some of the museums enumerated in the previous chapter. The first listed, by Sir Geoffrey de Bellaigue, can be considered a model of the genre for its perfect text and numerous illustrations.

Bellaigue, Geoffrey de. 2 vols. *The James A. de Rothschild Collection at Waddesdon Manor: Furniture, Clocks and Gilt Bronzes.* London: The National Trust; Fribourg: Office du Livre, 1974.

BIBLIOGRAPHY

For the Louvre museum the last catalog to have been published is that of Carle Dreyfus (2d ed., 1922, *Viaux, no. 3792*). Considerable changes have taken place since, both in scholarship and the museums holdings. In the furniture galleries, where the entire collection of the Louvre is exhibited, including many donations and purchases, I installed labels identifying each piece with a resumé of all I could learn about it. A new catalog should be undertaken using this as a basis.

For the museums of Paris, little has been published recently.—Musée des Arts Decoratifs: *Guide*, 1934, *Viaux, no. 3950*.—Musée Carnavalet: *Catalogue de la collection Bouvier*, Paris, 1968.—Musée Jacquemart-André: *Catalogue*, 7th ed., 1933, *Viaux, no. 3977*; a new catalog is in preparation.—Musée Cognacq-Jay: *Catalogue*, 1929. *Viaux nos. 3934–35*.—Musée du Petit Palais, coll. Duthuit: *Catalogue*, 1925. *Viaux, no. 3938*.— Musée Marmotan: *Catalogue*, by Hector Lefuel, 1934. *Viaux, no. 3981*.—Musée Nissim de Camondo: *Catalogue*, by Jean Messelet, 4th ed. 1960. *Viaux, no. 3970*.

The châteaus administered by the Musées Nationaux and the Monuments Historiques have small guidebooks that mention the furniture. A catalog of the furniture in the château of Chantilly has been written by Raoul de Broglie but is not yet published. For the Musée Jacquemart-André de Châalis there is the *Guide sommaire* by Louis Gillet, 1913 (*Viaux, no. 3974*), and a furniture catalog is in preparation.

Penury rules in provincial museums. When scholarly catalogs are undertaken for the furniture in the Musées Nationaux, one can hope for a catalog of the furniture covering all French museums. One can cite a few guidebooks and articles as well as a few volumes of *Memoranda* Laurens (*Viaux, nos. 3983–4057*) in addition to what has already been noted above in the plentiful literature on regional furniture.

For England we have the benefit of the remarkable catalog of the Wallace Collection by Francis Watson, 1956 (*Viaux, no. 4096*), the older catalog of the furniture in the Jones Collection at the Victoria and Albert Museum (*Viaux, no. 4074*) and the publications of Francis Laking and Clifford Smith on the furniture in the royal collection (*Viaux, nos. 4115–16*), and finally, in addition to the Waddesdon catalog cited above, the recent publication of Christopher Gilbert, *Furniture at Temple Newsam House and Lotherton Hall*, 2 vols., 1978. French eighteenth-century furniture under nos. 559, 561, and 563.

In Germany the articles by Adolf Feulner and Hans Huth, "Französische Möbel in Deutschland," *Pantheon*, 1929–32, are going to be continued in the same periodical by Rosemarie Stratmann, *Pantheon* 2 (1979): 164–68.—In Austria, Franz de Windisch-Graetz has done excellent work, notably "Französische Möbel aus des 18. Jahrhundert in Wiener Privatbesitz," *Alte und moderne Kunst*, January-February 1965, pp. 26–31.—In Switzerland, *Die Stiftung Dr. H. C. Emile Dreyfus*, by Hans Lanz and Hans Christoph Ackermann, Basel, Historisches Museum, 1969.—In Holland the *Catalogus van Meubelen* by Th. H. Lunsingh Scheurleer in 1952 (*Viaux, no. 4126*).— In Denmark, the catalog of the *C. L. Davids Samling*, published in Copenhagen in 1953, which has a chapter on furniture written by Erik Zahle including French furniture and pieces by Roentgen (pp. 200–217 and 228–29).

In Hungary, Poland, and Russia books devoted primarily to furniture have been published by Hedvig Szabolcsi, *Francia Butorok*, Budapest, 1963, with a French summary; and especially *Meubles français en Hongrie*, Budapest, Corvina, 1964; Bozenna Maszkowska, *Z Dziejow Polskiego Meblarstwa*, Warsaw, 1956, with a list of illustrations in

234

French and English; Tatiana Sokolova, a specialist in Russian furniture who published a small, well-illustrated book on decorative arts in 1972 including many fine pieces of French furniture in the Hermitage, had previously published a book on Western European furniture of the fifteenth through the nineteenth century, Leningrad, 1966, written in Russian but profusely illustrated. The catalog of the 1973 exhibition of French art at the Poznan museum can also be referred to for illustrations of some good French furniture in Poland. *Pavlovsk: Le palais et le parc,* by A. Koutchoumov, Leningrad, French ed., Editions d'Art Aurore, 1976, should be added. Last, refer to *Viaux, nos. 4120–24* and *4128–30.*

In Spain, French furniture has been studied by Paulina Junquera, in her *Guide du Palais royal de Madrid,* 1950, and in several articles in the periodical *Reales Sitios.*

For Italy there is a publication that gives a great deal of information on the furniture of Madame Infante: Chiara Briganti, *Curioso itinerario delle collezioni ducale parmensi,* Parma: Cassa di Risparmio, 1969.

In Portugal, Maria Helena Mendes Pinto, *Museu nacional de Arte antiga. Artes decorativas francesas sec. XVIII. Mobiliario. Relogios,* Lisbon, 1977. By the same author, *Doaçao Antenor Patiño,* Lisbon, 1974. P. Verlet, *Objets d'art français de la collection Calouste Gulbenkian,* Lisbon, 1969.

In the United States every major museum has its own review or bulletin where purchases and donations are listed. (see *Viaux nos. 4143–4234*) and I limit myself here to drawing attention to certain special publications.

Dauterman, Carl Christian, James Parker, and Edith Appleton Standen. *Decorative Art from the Samuel H. Kress Collection at the Metropolitan Museum of Art.* New York: Phaidon Press, 1964. *Viaux, no. 4169.*

Watson, F. J. B. *The Wrightsman Collection,* 3 vols. (devoted in whole or in part to furniture), New York, The Metropolitan Museum of Art, 1966–70 (most of this collection has been donated to the Metropolitan Museum).

Hackenbroch, Yvonne, and James Parker. *The Lesley and Emma Sheafer Collection: A Selective Presentation.* New York: Metropolitan Museum of Art, 1975.

Parker, James, and Clare Le Corbeiller. *A Guide to the Wrightsman Galleries . . .* New York: Metropolitan Museum of Art, 1979.

The Jack and Belle Linsky Collection in the Metropolitan Museum of Art. New York: Metropolitan Museum of Art, 1985. French furniture entries by William Rieder.

The Frick Collection: An Illustrated Catalogue of the Works of Art in the Collection of Henry Clay Frick. Vols. 9 and 10. Gaston Briere, *French Furniture and Ormolu.* 2 vols. in folio. New York: The Frick Art Reference Library, 1955.

Rice, Howard C. "Notes on the 'Swan Furniture.'" *Bulletin of the Museum of Fine Arts,* Boston, June 1940, pp. 43–48. *Viaux, no. 4155.*

Catalogue of the John L. Severance Collection. Cleveland Museum of Art, 1942.

Catalogue of the Elisabeth Severance Prentiss Collection, Cleveland Museum of Art, 1944. *Viaux, no. 4217.*

Wark, Robert R. *French Decorative Arts in the Huntington Collection.* San Marino, Cal.: The Huntington Library, 1961.

Wilson, Gillian. *Decorative Art in the J. Paul Getty Museum,* 1977; idem, *Selections from the Decorative Art in the J. Paul Getty Museum,* 1983; and with Adrian Sassoon, *Decorative Arts: A Handbook of the Collection of the J. Paul Getty Museum,* 1986, Malibu, Cal., and

"Acquisitions made by the Department of Decorative Arts," *The J. Paul Getty Museum Journal,* from vol. 6–7, 1978–1979 to the present.

12. Auction Sales and Prices

A firm base of documentation on auctions before 1900 has been assured by the monumental publication by Frits Lugt, *Répertoire des catalogues de ventes publiques . . . ,* 3 vols., The Hague, 1938–64. vol. 1, 1600–1825; 2, 1826–60; 3, 1861–1900. *Viaux, no. 4235.*

Some information on the auctions, prices, and great collections of the second half of the nineteenth century is given by Alph. Maze-Sencier, *Le livre des collectionneurs.* Paris, 1885. *Viaux, no. 1967.*

For the period after 1900 the specialized periodicals mentioned in section 8 supply a great deal of information. The principal auctioneers publish yearbooks with outstanding sales which include French eighteenth-century furniture. The same is true of publications that specialize in sales results in France, Germany, England, and the United States.

Last, for still more extended research, the catalog collections and the archives of the auctioneers in Paris and those of the auction houses in London, New York, Brussels, Zurich-Berne, Stockholm, and elsewhere furnish first-hand documents.

Index

INDEX